C000068106

'This book reminds us that to embrace life we must also prepare to embrace death when it comes. The time, the moment, often cannot be chosen or predicted, but we can prepare. However, if through illness or accident life has become intolerable and there is no hope of recovery, then we should embrace the dignity of choosing, within the law and with the help of a supportive medical professional, the moment when the light goes out and the longed-for night takes us.'

Sir Patrick Stewart, OBE
Patron of Dignity in Dying

'Society trains millions to kill others with skill and precision. Yet it denies the freedom to individuals to take well considered and dignified steps to end their own lives in order to avoid overwhelming misery and suffering. This book, much of which is an account of deep love and understanding, will help to redress this monstrous injustice.'

Professor Heinz Wolff
Brunel University

'This book is aligned with the deepest human values of love, compassion and respect. Issues which any civilized community needs to explore are discussed with clarity and integrity. Christians with the courage to think beyond the traditional position will find this a very challenging read.'

Reverend Canon Rosie Harper
Member of Inter-Faith Leaders for Dignity in Dying

ASSISTED DYING

ASSISTED DYING

Who Makes the Final Decision?

Edited by

LESLEY CLOSE
JO CARTWRIGHT

PETER OWEN
LONDON AND CHICAGO

PETER OWEN PUBLISHERS
81 Ridge Road, London N8 9NP

Peter Owen books are distributed in the USA and Canada by
Independent Publishers Group /Trafalgar Square
814 North Franklin Street, Chicago, IL 60610, USA

First published in Great Britain by Peter Owen Publishers 2014

ISBN 978-0-7206-1014-7

A catalogue record for this book is available from the British Library

Typeset by Octavo-Smith Ltd in StonePrint (text) and Adobe Garamond Pro (display)

Printed and bound in the UK by
CPI Group (UK) Ltd, Croydon, CR0 4YY

Acknowledgement: Ray Tallis's chapter is a slightly modified version of an
essay that first appeared in his book *Reflections of a Metaphysical Flâneur and Other Essays*
(Acumen, Durham, 2013). The editors and publishers of the current volume are very
grateful to the publisher Steven Gerrard for permission to reprint the essay as the
concluding chapter of this book.

Half of the royalties earned on sales of this book go to fund the work of
Dignity in Dying.

This book is dedicated to all those who have travelled to Dignitas to be given help to die. It is also dedicated to the countless other people who have suffered intolerably because they could not have that same compassionate help to die in the UK. Above all, it is dedicated to my late brother, John Close, for the action he took which started my journey into an understanding of the issues surrounding assisted dying and the need to change the law in the UK.

Lesley Close

I would like to dedicate the book to the people who make the campaign important – all those who have suffered and are suffering because there is insufficient choice at the end of life – and specifically to Clare Forder, my inspiration to be part of the fight.

Jo Cartwright

Acknowledgements

This is the book I have wanted to help bring into existence since John's death. I cannot thank Jo Cartwright enough for suggesting that we could make it happen by working on it together. I would not have been able to write the life stories of those facing death without the help and support of my partner Michael. Above all, I am deeply indebted to the families who agreed to share their stories with me. Julie and Kay Clinch, Lizzie Love, Kelley Marriage, Heather Pratten, Liz Smith and Pamela Tuson all gave freely of their time, and their words moved me to tears on more than one occasion. Thank you for teaching me so much, for your deeply touching honesty and for setting me off on an emotional rollercoaster when you agreed to let me write about your beloved relatives.

Lesley Close

I would like to thank my father for encouraging me to think, Mamma C. for teaching me to care, my brothers for giving me no option but to learn to fight, Elliott and Jack for forcing me to stop and play, Andy for his unwavering support and Abi for reminding me that it's important to look good while you're doing it. Above all, I am incredibly grateful to Dignity in Dying for allowing me to spend my days doing what I love and to Lesley for making what initially seemed impossible possible.

Jo Cartwright

Foreword

I don't fear death, but, like many other people, I do fear dying badly.

This book explores assisted dying by looking boldly at the historical, medical, legal, philosophical and ethical aspects at the heart of the matter. It punctuates these with the stories of real people's deaths, of real suffering and the fight that has been inspired in the people living with memories of those deaths.

Some of the people in this book, much like Peter Smedley who invited me to witness his assisted death at Dignitas, died too soon to ensure that they could die well. In years to come people will look back, aghast, at a time – this time – when people were forced to choose between living on and dying well.

This book will undoubtedly move the debate forward and help us get to the stage when the choice to die as we wish is one that we can make at home, surrounded by the things and people that have made our lives what they are. That's a time to look forward to, when the fear of dying badly will have been consigned to history books.

Sir Terry Pratchett, OBE
October 2013

Contents

'We are told that suicide is the biggest act of cowardice and even, in a completely meaningless phrase, that suicide is "wrong" when it is apparent to everyone in the world that there is nothing over which a person has an indisputable right more than their own life.' – Arthur Schopenhauer

Introduction

Some of the people you will read about in this book died when a terminal illness became intolerable. Others died prematurely: they feared life would become intolerable if they did not take control while they were still physically able to do so. They did not know how long they might continue to suffer, with no control over their fate, if they waited for their illness to reach its conclusion.

That is an important point. If assisted dying, as described in this book and as campaigned for by Dignity in Dying – assistance to die for competent adults who are already dying – was legal in the UK, it would only be available to people who were in the final stages of a terminal illness. Not all of the people in this book would have been able to choose an assisted death at the time they chose to die, even if it had it been a legal option.

Two days after his wedding Colin Marriage cried when he was told that he could expect to live for a few more days, not because he wanted to live longer with cancer but because he could not bear to suffer any more. His sister Kelley, who had not seen him cry since he was a child, heard him pleading with doctors to carry out a procedure that was intended to relieve his suffering but which would have ended his life. Kelley is adamant that he would have asked for help to die if the law allowed. Even if this book contained just one story, Colin's, it would demonstrate the need to change the law. It highlights the limitations of palliative care which, despite repeated assertions to the contrary, can neither prevent all suffering nor provide a peaceful death for every patient who is terminally ill.

Efstratia Tuson's decision to stop eating and drinking to bring about her death is an option that is open to anyone regardless of physical infirmity. I wrote her story while my partner's ninety-year-old mother lay in a hospital bed, apparently suffering from the early stages of dementia and refusing to eat or drink. Because of the emotional torment of that situation I found it very difficult to write about Efstratia's mentally competent decision to bring her suffering to an end, but her story is an important one. As her daughter reminded me, no one who is mentally competent can be force-fed against his or her will, but, even with palliative support, starving oneself to death can add to one's suffering. If professional medical assistance were available to someone like Efstratia – who, of her own volition, had made the mentally competent decision to end her life to put a stop to intolerable suffering – such extreme measures would not be necessary.

Liz Smith's mother Barbara was terminally ill with dementia when she decided to end her life with her husband Don's support. Don later committed suicide when his suffering with cancer became intolerable just a week after a hospice nurse told Liz that her father had weeks to live. Don took an overdose of medication to end his life, but if he had been able to call on professional help he would not have been obliged to guess – wrongly – how many tablets he needed to take to end his life quickly. It took two days for Don to die, and Liz is still haunted by the terrified expression on her father's face every time he regained consciousness during that period. If Don had known that he would be able to talk to his doctor when he was ready to die he might have lived a little longer. What is certain is that his daughter would have found his assisted death less difficult to witness than his suicide. The law in its current guise meant that the deaths of Barbara and Don were made even more difficult for them and for their family by the lack of choice.

Heather Pratten pleaded guilty to aiding and abetting the suicide of her son Nigel who had Huntington's disease. Family experience of the condition meant that Nigel knew what lay ahead, and he had reached what he considered to be an acceptable life span with the disease. He took the decision to end his life while he was still capable, physically and mentally, and Heather watched him take an overdose of heroin then lose consciousness. She fell asleep beside him, and when she woke up, some hours later, she realized that his suffering was not quite over. To hasten the inevitable end of Nigel's life she held a pillow over his face. She is comforted by the memory of his peaceful expression once his intolerable suffering – and his life – had ended. In my opinion that's not aiding and abetting a suicide or 'mercy killing' – it's compassion in action.

The nature of Neil Love's illness meant that his prognosis could not be given with any accuracy. The doctor who carried out his post-mortem told his widow Lizzie that Neil was probably just a few months away from death when he committed suicide. I find it almost unbearably sad that because Neil, an ex-policeman, was aware that his wife might be implicated under the current UK law if he told her his intentions she was unable to say goodbye to the husband she adored. The guidelines issued by the Director of Public Prosecutions following Debbie Purdy's appeal would have alleviated some of that anxiety.

I am certain that my brother John Close was only a few weeks away from dying when we made the journey to Dignitas. He was almost completely helpless and would probably have died in his sleep, peacefully, but I would not have been with him to say goodbye. Because I *was* with John when he died I have no unanswered questions about his death. Without the helping hand that Dignitas was able to extend to him my memories of the end of his life could be very different.

John's decline was, I am convinced, so far advanced that any physician would have judged him to be living through the final weeks of motor neurone disease. Ron Clinch would certainly have died very soon without Dignitas's help, which he received almost nine years after my brother, but he chose to travel to Switzerland rather than suffer any longer. I had promised John that I would do whatever I could to change the law, and it was frustrating to hear the familiar details of Ron's story because they showed the lack of any real progress in the intervening time. People are still forced to travel abroad to die rather than be at home supported by their loved ones.

One significant change that has occurred is that the subject of assisted dying now appears in fiction, drama and comedy in a way that suggests it is becoming an almost acceptable part of life. This change highlights the fact that, despite public opinion polls finding overwhelming support for decades, it is only recently that people have felt able to talk about the subject openly.

The circumstances of the deaths described in this book are very different from one another, but they share a common theme, that of unnecessary suffering and anxiety at an already terribly difficult time. Jo and I have chosen to write about people from a variety of backgrounds and with a range of clinical histories to show that a law permitting assisted dying could make a positive difference to determined people across the board. That is one characteristic which came across very strongly in the interviews I conducted: everyone spoke of the dying person as being adamant in their desire to do whatever it took to achieve as peaceful and dignified a death as they could at the time of their choosing, but they wanted to avoid risking their choice having legal implications for those they loved and were leaving behind.

Whether or not they were able to achieve it, another thing these people had in common was the desire to avoid prolonged and intolerable suffering. They were all determined not to reach the stage where their lives became a burden to them

– not to their family and friends but to the person who was dying. Colin did not achieve that aim, sadly, and the deaths of Barbara and Don were both marred by efforts to reverse their actions. But it gladdens my heart to know that Efstratia, Neil, Nigel, Ron and John died before being alive became intolerable.

These deeply personal stories all revolve around death, but they are, essentially, love stories. Each of the people I have written about had the love and support of at least one close family member at the end of their life, even if, like Neil, they died alone. Each of them was, in a phrase my elderly and frail mother used in a message to her dying son, surrounded by a world of love.

I believe that one of the most loving acts you can perform for someone who is dying and suffering intolerably is to help them die with peace and dignity. If someone in that situation asks for your help to die it is easy to live with yourself afterwards because you gave that person what they asked you for.

As it says in Colin's story, nobody's life is taken in those circumstances – the dying person is giving away something they no longer want.

Lesley Close

When the publisher Peter Owen approached me to discuss the idea of writing a book on assisted dying my initial thought was: Surely it has been done before? I have spent my working life immersed in the issues surrounding assisted dying and have experienced at first hand the horrible situations created by a lack of choice and control at the end of life. As a result I was convinced that other people were just as interested in this issue as I was, and I felt certain that someone must have produced a book about the many reasons why the law should be changed.

It turned out that no one had written at length in book form on the subject – at least, not taking the comprehensive approach suggested – since Peter Owen last looked at the issue back in 1986. Recognizing that this could be a very important contribution to the debate, I decided I must find a way to make it happen.

I already had a more than full-time role as Campaign and Press Manager at Dignity in Dying, and I was aware that this was too important a task to get wrong, so I wanted to involve a trusted colleague and friend as co-editor. I approached Lesley Close, with whom I have campaigned for as long as I can remember, and she was very enthusiastic. I knew that Dignity in Dying has a wealth of experts and friends who could write eloquently on various aspects of the issue, and I knew enough people who are – or whose loved ones were – adversely affected by our current compassion-free laws to write a book rivalling *War and Peace*, at least in terms of the word count!

While Lesley worked to ensure that the families of some of those who have suffered under the current law had a voice, I drew up a list of people I could approach for contributions on different aspects of the debate. I wanted to know how professional and personal experiences had affected their view of the issue, and not one of them – colleagues, contacts and experts in the various elements of the debate – let me down.

The Reverend John Cartwright, a member of Inter-Faith Leaders for Dignity in Dying, philosophy tutor and Congregational minister, explores the doctrine of double effect and how his God fits into the assisted dying debate. Davina Hehir and Philip Satherley, Dignity in Dying's two experts on the policy surrounding assisted dying, give an insight into how practices differ around the world and what impact those countries' legislation might have in the UK in the future. Palliative care nurse Andrew Heenan looks at his own experiences in caring for the dying and explains how these have shaped his view on assisted dying. Sir Graeme Catto – Dignity in Dying's Chair, former head of the General Medical Council, member of the Commission on Assisted Dying and a doctor with more than forty years' experience – seemed best placed to look to the future. He explores what he feels is the way forward so that people no longer have to turn to Switzerland for an answer to unbearable suffering at the end of their lives, to take matters into their own hands or to ask loved ones to help them to die. Professor Ray Tallis, philosopher, writer and Chair of Healthcare Professionals for Assisted Dying, shares his views on the issue as a whole in his conclusion – and Sir Terry Pratchett offers his take on the subject in a way only he could.

With my knowledge of the history of the assisted dying debate and, having played a part in some of the more recent legal history, I was keen to tie all the research and case law into the human stories in my chapter on the history of assisted dying in the UK.

Writing and editing this book has further strengthened my view that a law to permit safeguarded assisted dying is both necessary and long overdue. I am certain that we must not rest until everyone who is terminally ill and mentally competent can exercise choice and control over the timing and manner of his or her own death.

Jo Cartwright

1

A DEATH AT DIGNITAS
John Close: 'More like a thing than a human being'

My brother John Close's penultimate conscious act was to push down on the plunger of a feeding syringe that delivered, straight to his stomach, the overdose of barbiturates that would end his life. He carried out that act with such determination there was no room for doubt: by that stage of his motor neurone disease John had only a few weeks of life left, but he wanted to die more than he wanted to live.

His last act was typical John. He smiled a warm, loving and heartfelt 'Thank you and goodbye' to the four people who were with him: me, his younger sister, our older sister Margaret, my partner Michael and John's loyal friend Peggy. We were lucky to be with John because knowing how he died has brought us comfort ever since, but he achieved the peaceful and dignified death he sought, at 4.30 in the afternoon of Monday 26 May 2003 only because he had help from Dignitas. That meant that we were forced to travel over five hundred miles from Milton Keynes to Zurich. Tragically, John could have lived a few weeks longer if he had been able to ask his GP for help to die in England. Dying at home would have relieved him of the need to be physically able to make that final journey. He could have tolerated allowing his body to deteriorate a little further before choosing to die.

John was nine when I was born, and a monochrome photo taken when I was tiny shows him cradling his baby sister with a tender smile on his face. My parents appointed him to be one of my godparents, and I believe he carried the weight of that responsibility all his life – albeit in a secular capacity. We were very close, and, in a reversal of the usual state of affairs, John often turned to me for advice which I seldom felt qualified to give. His diagnosis with motor neurone disease

(MND) did not change our relationship. In many ways it just brought us closer. Almost two years after being given the devastating news that he was dying, and before he had taken any steps towards contacting Dignitas, he asked me, via the personal organizer with which he communicated, what I thought about having help from the organization to end his life. I said that it was his life and that I would help him do whatever he wanted with it. His reply was typical of his sense of humour: he typed, 'But not tonight. I want to watch *Lord of the Rings*.'

I was ridiculously proud of my big brother, who was handsome with dark curly hair and slightly olive skin. I was thrilled to follow him to a grammar school where his name was remembered with affection and a degree of awe. Among other things John taught me to ride a bike and to play the guitar, and he cheerfully taught me the lyrics and chord sequences of songs I liked. He even explained what a honky-tonk woman was and why it was not an ideal song for a teenage girl to perform in public.

Our mother was eighty-six when John found out about Dignitas. She was frail and living in a residential home, so there was no question of her travelling with us to Zurich. His decision to seek an assisted death broke her heart, not just because he was the apple of her eye. A more important consideration was that John's decision to end his life meant that he would not be allowed into heaven. She was certain she was going there, and the thought of being deprived of her son's company in the afterlife was acutely painful. She continued to feel this way even after I reminded her that John was dying and that he was suffering intolerably in the process. I saw her almost immediately after I returned to England, when he had been dead for three days, and she asked whether he had turned to Christ as he died. She was disappointed when I told her that, apart from the four of us who supported him as he died, his comfort had come in the form of the nurse from whose hand he accepted the medication to end his life.

John was divorced at the time of his death, and the heartbreaking end of that marriage, like the end of other relationships before and after it, had inspired him to write some beautiful songs. Song-writing was what defined him for many people, although he had many different jobs, mostly in information technology after Michael and I introduced him to computers in the 1980s. From the late 1960s playing the guitar and, later, fiddle and keyboards and composing songs was what he really loved – and lived – to do. He was a self-taught musician who carried on learning his craft until he stopped writing music. That day occurred only a couple of months before he died, by which time playing a keyboard had become too difficult. Even then he spent all his time listening to music.

By the time he died John had been out of bed for almost twelve hours, and I don't think he had slept very much in the previous thirty-six hours. I got very little sleep after Michael and I said goodnight to him around midnight on Sunday 25 May 2003. Our readiness for sleep was not helped by John's suggestion that the three of us should watch the funniest bits from his favourite film, *Monty Python's Life of Brian*, one last time.

In the final week of John's life Michael and I looked after him because his social-care arrangements had descended into chaos. The three of us found that the enforced closeness made it a difficult time, but Michael and I also found it a privilege that John trusted us to look after him when he was so vulnerable. Like me, Michael derives comfort from knowing how John died: we both feared that he would die alone in his bed while asleep. This is a very common death for MND patients; it occurs because the diaphragm is weak and breathing is difficult, especially when lying down. My fear was not that John would die without waking: if he had been unaware what was happening to him death would have been peaceful. My worry was that he might have woken, alone and afraid, as he struggled for breath as his life ended.

The three of us watching a funny film the night before John died had not been part of the plan. During the week leading up to his last weekend John had decided that Sunday would be a quiet day with no visitors and that he would have an early night so he could be up with the lark on Monday. But things seldom work out as planned, and, although there were no visitors, Sunday had been a busy day.

Saturday had been even busier because John invited his friends to join him at his wake. Michael, who shared his sense of humour, knew that John would love the idea of attending his own wake and suggested it shortly after John got his date for Dignitas. John was initially concerned that the emotional lability which was part of his disease might lead to him crying and that his tears might be misinterpreted by guests who did not understand his illness.

Emotional lability had led John's GP to prescribe tranquillizers before his diagnosis. John had found himself crying in meetings at work, and he was diagnosed with stress. In fact, inappropriate emotional displays are a common symptom of MND. The sufferer may experience involuntary episodes of crying or laughing. John retained an appropriate ability to laugh right up to the day he died, but he would cry inappropriately frequently and freely.

John's informal wake was held at the pub nearest to his home in Middleton, Milton Keynes. He chose it because we could easily push him there in his wheelchair. Despite the poor acoustics of the outdoor setting next to Willen Lake we were privileged to hear many fine singers perform excellent versions of beautiful songs in his honour. We returned to the flat at around six o'clock and spent the evening at home.

On the last Sunday we made a final trip to the huge Tesco store a mile or so away. The shop's café, with its level entry and wheelchair-friendly seating, was one of its redeeming features. It was the nearest supermarket we could reach on foot. John could not get in or out of a car, and we could push him there in his wheelchair. While Peggy, Michael and I watched, John pretended to be Eric Morecambe and played the fool with some sunglasses he and Peggy had found at Willen Lake a few days earlier. Peggy, who met John when he started playing gigs in a Milton Keynes wine bar with her ex-husband in 1975, tells me she still wears those sunglasses.

After the three of us had a drink and a snack John indicated that we would take a different route home. He had lived in Milton Keynes for almost thirty years, so we had no worries about letting him navigate. As we followed his route, which was beautiful and tranquil, it started to rain. Undeterred, we wrapped John in a selection of carrier bags and recycling sacks to stop him getting too wet and cold. It was only when we were close to home that John complained of his legs feeling cold. The swift application of some Deep Heat medication to his limbs soon remedied this, and we carried on.

Later that afternoon Michael and I had something to eat, and we gave John some water. He did not want to eat – by that stage 'eating' meant that someone would give him several large syringes full of a liquid diet called Ensure through a feeding tube.

That had been John's main food source since the previous autumn. He had the operation to insert a percutaneous endoscopic gastroscopy, or PEG, in August 2002 while he was living in a nursing home. When he returned to his room after the operation he was greeted by two jolly nurses telling him that they would fix up the drip and he would remain connected to it for several hours. John was horrified by the prospect and threatened to rip out the PEG.

I had seldom seen him so angry since his diagnosis with MND eighteen months earlier, but his impatience was understandable. His enjoyment of life was already limited by the disease, and he wanted the feeding process to be over as quickly as if he was eating with a knife and fork. He clearly had not been told everything he needed to know about the PEG, and he hated the idea of being restricted in this way. The staff could see that he was furious, so they left Michael and me to calm him down and prevent him damaging his stomach by interfering with the site of his recent surgery. John had always enjoyed eating. The thought of never eating normally again was profoundly depressing. Link that to the prospect of being connected for several hours to a pump delivering gloop instead of real food and one could understand why he was so agitated.

After we had been on our own for a while and he had calmed down another nurse entered. He told us about the 'bolus' feeding method which uses a huge syringe without a needle. It was so simple I could have cried with relief. All John had to do was to empty a sachet of Ensure into a jug, put the syringe in the gloop and pull up the plunger. After connecting the syringe to the end of the PEG tube he undid the clip on the tube and squirted the mixture into his stomach. A few syringefuls sufficed. The process took minutes rather than hours, and John liked the bolus method much better than the drip.

At the time he had his PEG surgery he was still eating normally, although he took great care to avoid hard or flaky food as this made him choke. Because he always tried to anticipate the progress of the disease he was prepared for the fact that sooner or later he would have to stop eating ordinary food. He was well informed about the illness and appeared able to predict what was coming next. He was always ready for the next loss, the next development in the progression of his illness.

John's speech was one of the first symptoms that led to his diagnosis. He joked that he could no longer say 'rhinoceros', so he – and we – introduced the animal into as many conversations as possible to make us all laugh. He tried using a Lightwriter but found it slower than using an organizer or his computer: he was very tech-savvy and decided that the Lightwriter technology was designed for people who were not! He had a limp when he was diagnosed, and, within a year, it had progressed to his being unable to walk. Within eighteen months he could not support his already considerably reduced weight on his legs, so standing to transfer between his wheelchair and shower chair or from a wheelchair to his bed became impossible. John's occupational therapist provided a smooth wooden transfer board that solved the problem, as it enabled him to slide sideways. Eventually he was given a hoist, because he could no longer bear his weight during those transfers.

Once he had been hoisted into bed we would arrange his body so that he was comfortable. This was always the same position to start with, lying on his side with a pillow between his now bony knees. During the night, by making a superhuman effort, he could roll on to his back, but then he was stuck like a beetle and sometimes needed help during the night to get comfortable once more. He had a urine bottle by the bed so that he could relieve himself without disturbing his carer, but after being hoisted out of bed the following morning he would require assistance to get on to the shower chair or to use the lavatory.

MND is a horrible illness. David Niven, who died of the condition in 1983, said, 'Whatever you do, don't get this bloody awful disease.' It could almost be described as a family of illnesses, as it takes a different course in every individual who is diagnosed with it. Some people with MND can speak and swallow until the day they die. The first symptoms can be very varied and may include rapidly progressive weakness, muscle atrophy and fasciculations (twitches under the skin), muscle spasticity, difficulty speaking (*dysarthria*), difficulty swallowing (*dysphagia*) and difficulty breathing (*dyspnea*). The progression of the disease cannot be confidently predicted, and the prognosis John was given was six months to five years. To start with he lived as if he had been given six months, doing everything he considered to be important straight away. These tasks included organizing the recordings he had made of his own songs as well as their lyrics. While he was in hospital and that life-changing diagnosis wasn't even a shadow on the horizon he wrote some beautiful love songs. By the time he had the PEG inserted he had been living with a diagnosis of MND for a year and a half and had already had several simple pleasures taken away from him, including making himself understood verbally, singing, playing the guitar, walking and eating pretty much anything he fancied.

The last time John ate chips was in a Woolworths cafeteria. This was during a dreadful period from April to October 2002 after he was evicted from the room he had been living in very happily in Stony Stratford. He was offered a room in a nursing home which he accepted because it was intended as a short-term refuge while work on his newly built disabled person's flat in Milton Keynes was completed. On being made homeless he had been told that the flat would be ready in about two weeks, but every time we asked when it would be available we were told that it would be another two weeks. If we had known how long it would take to complete the work we would have made our home as John-friendly as possible and moved him in with us. But at least the nursing home was close to his friends and allowed them to visit him easily, whereas taking John from Milton Keynes to our home in south Buckinghamshire would have removed that possibility.

Every Saturday Michael and I would take him away from the ceaseless roar of televisions in the rooms of comatose patients and the constant clamour of bells ringing to summon carers who were rushed off their feet. On the day John last ate chips we had driven him from the nursing home to our house when he decided that he wanted to visit High Wycombe. Because we arrived there at lunchtime we ate at Woolworths, not for its fine dining but because there was step-free access – via a lift – to the first-floor café and a reasonable amount of room at the tables. I will never forget the look of panic on John's face as he started to choke on a chip. By then the three of us had experienced a similar situation many times, and we knew what to do. Michael and I swung into action: I administered back slaps while Michael handed John some serviettes to hold in front of his mouth. Diners around us looked horrified as John coughed and spluttered ineffectually for a couple of minutes before the problem was resolved.

I have a vivid memory of where and when I first saw John choking. About six weeks before he was diagnosed with MND our mother started a trial stay in an Oxford residential home. After two weeks she decided to make the move a permanent one by moving out of the family home where she had lived as a widow for five years. We, her three children, were very relieved that she had accepted her need for full-time care, and we decided to celebrate by holding a dinner party in the family home before it was sold. I offered to cook supper, and we met at the north Buckinghamshire house early one Saturday evening in mid-February 2001. At one point John choked on a lump of food which he had not chewed properly. He had been having difficulty swallowing for a few months, and his doctor had told him it was stress-related and prescribed more tranquillizers.

On this occasion he could not clear his throat by coughing and was becoming distressed. He went to the sink, probably in case he was sick, and I followed him. I slapped him on the back but to no avail. As a trained first-aider at work I knew the Heimlich manoeuvre but had never used it in a real-life situation. I remembered what I had been taught and wrapped my arms around his fairly stout middle. As my hands grasped each other at the front I pulled back and up, hard, several times until eventually the air in John's lungs forced the obstruction out of his windpipe.

I was relieved, but I recalled an old saying: if you save someone's life you are responsible for them. He was diagnosed with MND about two weeks later, and much later a part of me wished I had let him die by choking that night, but throughout the course of his illness I did my best to live up to my responsibility. This was my big brother. This was the man who had taught me to ride a bike and play the guitar, and he was dying. The least I could do was help him to live as well as possible until the end of his life.

On the last morning of John's life, Monday 26 May 2003, Michael and I got up at four o'clock and showered and breakfasted. We knocked on John's bedroom door an hour later, and his cheery smile greeted us as it always did in the morning. He had made carefully planned changes to his routine – no food since Saturday, very little fluid after Sunday, no laxative on Sunday night and no bowel-stimulating leg exercises on Monday morning – to avoid having to empty his bladder frequently or open his bowels. For the first time in ages he took a couple of doses of codeine on Sunday, for their constipating effect as much as for pain relief, and he had more first thing on Monday morning.

Having hoisted John out of bed and dressed him in a long-sleeved casual top and tracksuit bottoms for the journey to Zurich we did a few minutes' filming for the BBC's *Video Nation* project, to which we contributed several films, while John had a breakfast of painkillers in a small amount of water – he wanted to reduce his need to pee. Shortly after five Margaret arrived with John's friend Peggy. They were accompanying us to Switzerland.

John was as cheerful and comical as always, despite the hour and the occasion. The taxi arrived on schedule at 5.30, and John was helped inside. The journey to Luton airport was straightforward– misty fields and low sun made it poetically beautiful – although John's right leg was painful and the thirty-minute journey seemed interminably long.

We arrived at the terminal at around 6.15, ahead of time, but there was already a long queue. At this point John was not afforded priority treatment, so we joined the queue and checked in at around 6.50. We were told that John and I would travel from the gate to the plane in a vehicle called an Ambi-lift and that the others would have to take their chances. The budget airline's free-seating policy meant a tremendous scramble for seats, and there was a real danger that we would be separated during boarding. The boarding passes John and I had been given had a gate and a time, 7.15, but even though those of Michael, Margaret and Peggy did not they came with us to Gate 9.

The designated time came and went, and eventually someone asked us to come with them for boarding. 'Can we come, too?' asked Margaret, and we almost cheered when the official said that they could. Just outside the gate, not far from the plane's nose, the Ambi-lift was waiting, and we were hoisted into it by a tail lift, first John and me and then Michael, Margaret and Peggy. We sat down, and John's wheelchair was secured in place.

After the three others had boarded, an aisle wheelchair was brought into the Ambi-lift. It was narrow, with very little refinement, and I pointed out that John could not keep his feet on the very thin foot strap. He was lifted between wheelchairs, a woman at his shoulders and a man at his legs, and his legs were supported as he was steered on to the plane through the door opposite the normal passenger entrance. I followed, clutching the folder of documents that John and I had taken great trouble to compile for Dignitas.

Michael, John and I sat in the front row of seats, the only place where there was room for the transfer. With our baggage stowed in the overhead lockers there was plenty of room to lift John in his seat to make him more comfortable and to give him water via the PEG. John had been transferred to a window seat so that he would be out of the way in the event of an emergency, while Margaret and Peggy sat in the row behind us.

On the flight John looked out of the window and enjoyed the scenery, pointing out boats in the Channel until the view disappeared beneath clouds. I lifted him once and gave him some water, but for the rest of the flight we did very little. John wrote in his organizer (including the joky message to me 'You can have my seat on the way back'), and Michael shot some footage for *Video Nation*, but mostly we just sat, with Margaret's and Peggy's hands coming through between the seats to pat John's shoulders – he put his hand up to pat back – or to ruffle his hair and mine reassuringly.

Take-off was awful, simply because I hate flying, and John held my hand as I wept terrified tears. I had only told him when we were on the ground, buckled up and waiting for the last passenger to board, how much I hate flying. His comforting hand was wonderful, as was Michael's on the other side of me. John and I had never been abroad together before then, so there was no way for him to know about my dislike of flying.

There was some turbulence – but very little – and we had a smooth landing at Zurich. The aisle wheelchair and Ambi-lift procedure was repeated, and we were driven across the apron to the terminal building where we were whisked through very efficiently. In no time at all we were in the arrivals area, and there was Ludwig Minelli, the founder of Dignitas. He approached us, smiling and with open arms and an extended hand. He greeted John first, then shook our hands in turn. He had ordered a wheelchair-taxi which hadn't yet arrived, so we chatted while we waited. Mr Minelli was charming, kind and very friendly.

The taxi arrived, and Michael and I squeezed into the vehicle with John, while Margaret and Peggy travelled in Mr Minelli's car. We drove out of the airport and round the edge of the city. Very soon we were in lovely countryside. John looked around and smiled his approval. The scenery was beautiful – long fields of green running away to stands of trees with hills beyond them. We drove through a couple of little villages with huge farmhouses whose wide eaves sheltered stacks of logs for the winter's fires. Old wooden doors and window-boxes gave the houses a picture-postcard appearance, and in different circumstances I would have taken photographs. I just held on to John's left foot instead.

Eventually we turned off the quiet main road and headed to the hills with some brief glimpses of Lake Zurich behind us. We passed a couple of fields of cream-coloured cows wearing traditional bells around their necks. The sight of them made John smile, but what made him really happy was the knowledge that we were heading for Forch and Mr Minelli's home which acted as the Dignitas office.

His home had a lift that led to the first floor, a light and airy *piano nobile*. Mr Minelli and I travelled up first, then John with Michael, followed by Margaret and Peggy. Our host invited us to sit at a long table standing alongside a large floor-to-ceiling window. The table would have comfortably seated twelve people, and it was almost entirely covered with books, papers and photographs. More books – on art, history and law – lined every wall except one: on that a collection of tea-pots was displayed. To their right was a large collection of videos, and an archway led to the rooms beyond.

Mr Minelli offered us tea and biscuits. John wanted indigestion remedy and pain relief as well as plain water. We sat round the table, and Mr Minelli told us that there were some formalities to go through. He required evidence of John's identity and asked John a series of questions about his physical and mental health. At the question 'Are you tired of life?' John paused and considered. He wrote 'No' on his organizer and then went on to clarify that he was tired of living in that useless body, tired of living with MND.

Mr Minelli asked the four of us to give our names, addresses and phone numbers in case the authorities needed to contact us. He then left us alone while he typed the information and photocopied John's documents. We sat and chatted. John looked tired. He kept asking what the time was, anxious that the next stage, the appointment with the doctor, should not be missed.

At around one o'clock we left the house and drove back down the hillside to Kusnacht, a sleepy lakeside village. The wheelchair-taxi disgorged us outside a block of flats. Dr Hans-Ulrich Kull's consulting-room was on the ground floor up a short flight of stairs. There was no lift, so John was carried in his wheelchair by Mr Minelli, Dr Kull and Michael. The doctor made it clear that he needed to talk to John alone for a while, so we left them together.

Margaret, Peggy, Michael and I sat in a waiting-room before the heavy door opened and Dr Kull asked for John's sisters. Margaret and I went in. I sat next to John and held his hand, while Margaret sat beside me and I held her hand, too. The doctor said how good it was to see the four of us there with John and how sorry he was that he was so ill. He asked Margaret and me about our attitude to John's wish to die. We explained that we fully supported it. Then he asked about our family in the UK, and we described our mother's frailty and generally poor health. He enquired about John's marital history, and we told him that he was divorced. He then asked some questions about the progression of John's MND, and I gave the best answers I could, checking the details with my brother.

Eventually the doctor seemed satisfied, and he said something I will never forget: 'My first duty as a doctor is to preserve life, but I also have this extra duty I can perform here in Switzerland. I am ready to do that for you. I will write the prescription for you to end your life, Mr Close.'

He left the room to write the prescription. The three of us were very relieved to have passed this hurdle. John was tired, and he sat still with his eyes closed. After about five minutes Dr Kull came back with an envelope in his hand. 'This is the prescription I will give Mr Minelli,' he said and escorted us into the hall where we rejoined Michael and Peggy. Mr Minelli arrived at the same time, and we were on our way to the Dignitas flat.

We drove on down the hillside through more fields until we came to a busy road and signs indicating that we were near Zurich. Soon we were driving in fairly heavy traffic, Mr Minelli ahead with Margaret and Peggy and the rest of us in the taxi. We crossed the River Limmat which flows into Lake Zurich and passed the market square.

We drove between neat blocks of flats with window-boxes before stopping outside a nondescript creamy-grey block four storeys high and with steps up to the front door. Erika Luley, tall and grey-haired, was Dignitas's Dying Assistant. She had arrived at the same time, and we greeted one another on the pavement in the late spring sunshine.

Mr Minelli indicated that I should go up to the apartment with him first to prepare for John's arrival. We used the tiny lift, and Mr Minelli commented that John's wheelchair probably would not fit into it: he would have to use the one stored in the flat instead. Mr Minelli used the lift to take the wheelchair to John while I ran down the stairs. By the time I got to the ground floor John had been carried into the building in his wheelchair and was ready to be transferred to the smaller one.

Erika got into the lift with John, and I ran back upstairs. As I arrived, so did they, and I now had the opportunity to meet Erika properly. She wheeled John into the flat, and his own wheelchair followed shortly. Erika lifted John from one to the other, and I slipped a cushion under him.

While Erika, John and I were getting acquainted, Mr Minelli escorted Michael, Margaret and Peggy on foot to the nearby hotel he had booked for us. Erika left the two of us alone, and John and I looked around. Although the room we were in represented about half the floor space of the flat, it was quite small. There was a window across one end of the room with a great many plants in front of it. Looking out, between other blocks of flats, one could see a distant tree-covered hillside.

There were two single beds on the left wall – one looked typically Swiss, with flowers painted on the pale-green wooden headboard and footboard; the other was more like a hospital bed. Both were covered with blankets in muted pastel shades and had several pillows. Above the bed nearest the window hung an abstract painting of a nude in bright colours. On the wall opposite the window hung a picture (that may have been biblical or allegorical) showing a man with some animals. Looking at photographs of the new Dignitas premises in Pfäffikon I am pleased to see that at least some of those paintings adorn the walls.

The door to the kitchen led from the wall opposite the nude, furthest from the window, and between the door and the window hung a painting of a typical Swiss country scene with lush meadows and mountains. I put John's bag on the floor under that painting, beside a Z-bed and folded-up wheelchair.

In the middle of the room stood a round table and four rustic-looking but comfortable wooden chairs. The table was covered with a cloth, and in the centre was a vase of flowers. Erika put a bowl of tiny bars of plain Swiss chocolate on the table, as well as some of the round delicacies known as Mozart Balls. At the sight of them John's eyes lit up – he had had nothing to eat for thirty-six hours – so I offered him a ball.

Plain chocolate wrapped around marzipan is not my favourite treat, but John seemed to enjoy it as he held it to his lips and licked it, large quantities of saliva running from his mouth as he tasted the chocolate. He gave it back to me sucked but not much smaller. He indicated that we should try one of the plain bars, so I unwrapped one and handed it to him. Again he licked and sucked it before handing it back to me to eat the rest. The PEG feeding tube meant that he had not tried to eat chocolate for several months, and I'm glad the taste of chocolate was in his mouth when he died.

John asked the time again: it was shortly after three o'clock. Michael, Margaret and Peggy returned around fifteen minutes later, and Erika offered us tea which we accepted gratefully. While we were drinking it she appeared with a syringe of anti-emetic which John took at 3.35. We had been told that it would take twenty minutes to take effect, so John knew that the earliest he could have the barbiturates was 3.55. He asked if we would leave him alone for five minutes before that time came.

That left us with fifteen minutes of John's company to enjoy. Even later that night I could not remember what we had talked about. John was in his wheelchair near the table, I was beside him, Peggy poured the tea and Michael and Margaret were sitting on the beds. John was keen not to waste a moment after 3.55 – he wanted to take the overdose as soon as possible.

We drank our tea and chatted, and, yes, I do remember that we laughed during those fifteen minutes. When I told John it was 3.50 I asked him whether he wanted us to leave him alone. He indicated, 'Yes please, and turn me round to face the window.'

We went out into the kitchen, and Erika was there with the papers John and Mr Minelli had completed earlier. We told her that our brother wanted five minutes alone. When he knocked his organizer on the wheelchair we returned to him.

He indicated that he wanted to be turned around again to face the room. The position of the wheelchair meant that the table was slightly in front of him, to his left, and one of the single beds was to his right. Erika had followed us into the room, and she had a syringeful of barbiturate in her hand. John held out his hand for it, but I grasped his hand and said, 'Please, let us all say goodbye properly.'

He agreed, and we took turns to hold him and kiss him. I told him that all I could say was how much I would miss him. Margaret, Peggy and Michael said their goodbyes, and then we sat down beside him. I sat on one of the chairs to John's left, in the angle between him and the table, and Peggy, Margaret and Michael sat on the bed.

Erika approached again, and John extended his hand for the syringe. I connected it to the end of the PEG feeding tube and, at a strong, determined gesture from John, took my hands away. We had removed the tape holding the tube close to his belly earlier to make it easier for him to push with his left hand against the resistance of his right. John undid the clip on the PEG tube and pushed down on the plunger of the syringe. He pushed with such strength of purpose and determination that there could not be a moment's doubt: he wanted death more than anything.

At that point a voice inside my head started screaming that I wanted the process to stop. I wanted John to take an antidote – there isn't one as far as I know – and I wanted him back because I would miss him. But I quickly realized that this wasn't about me and what I wanted: it was John's choice to die. I also realized that what I really wanted was the fit, strong, funny, creative brother I had once known, not this weakened man who was unable to stand, speak, swallow or turn over in bed.

When he had pushed the plunger all the way in he closed the clip on the tube and I removed the syringe. We adjusted our positions around John, holding on to whatever part of him we could. I had his left hand in mine, and my right hand was on his left shoulder. We had previously discussed the fact that he was so strong that he would need a rhinoceros-sized dose to see him off, and now he made one last joke with his face and hands, pulling a puzzled expression and starting to count down the minutes on his fingers. The drug did its job, and within a couple of minutes he started to lose consciousness. We said goodbye to him again.

I was crying loudly and openly as John drifted into death, and it still troubles me that the last sound my dear brother heard was not tranquil music or birdsong but his snivelling sister. Erika came in and put a blanket around my shoulders and another around the three sitting on the bed. She came back a couple of times over the next ten minutes to make sure the five of us were OK.

John's head, which sagged because his neck muscles had become so weak, started to droop further forward than usual as his breathing got deeper and deeper. At one point Erika pointed out a pulse beating in the side of his neck. This became an object of fascination for me, and I found that if I stared hard it was very difficult to see any change. If I looked away and looked back I thought it was easier to detect a change in his pulse – or was I imagining it?

After twenty minutes Erika confirmed that John had died. I think we knew that already, but it was good to have it confirmed. She then followed a Swiss custom – she opened the windows and lowered but did not close the blinds. By this lovely gesture she let the outside world with its noises and scents of life into the room. We continued to sit around John in his wheelchair. Erika said she had to phone the police and left us with him.

After another twenty minutes or so John's body started to slip sideways, and we propped him up with a pillow and one of the cushions Erika had slipped under me on the wooden chair as I wept. We continued to sit with him, and I watched the changing colours of his left hand with fascination. His fingers had started to go blue-grey even before his breathing had stopped, and his colour continued to change as his body cooled.

When the three police – including the local chief – and four medics had arrived, and they were ready to start their work, we four left the room. Erika told us that they would remove all of John's clothes, and she asked what we wanted to do with them. 'We will take them with us,' I told her, as the alternative was for Erika to throw them away.

We sat in silence until I remembered that John had written something on his organizer. I turned it on, and the message appeared. It started, 'i am tired.' I read the words before passing the device to Peggy and Margaret. Michael chose not to read it until later. Erika chatted to us, and Michael asked about the man who had been at the flat earlier with her. Erika told us that he was soon to be her husband and that they had met when his late wife came to the flat to die two years before. The four of us were deeply moved.

After around twenty minutes the authorities, satisfied that there was no foul play, were ready to leave. The only woman among them, who was also the only one who spoke good English, told us that everything was in order. They left, and we went back into the room.

John's body had been removed from the wheelchair. It was lying on the bed by the window covered with the blanket that Erika had draped around Michael, Margaret and Peggy. One of his big toes was just visible, as was the top of his head. I pulled the blanket down, and we saw the changes to his face for the first time. When he was dying, sitting in the wheelchair, his head had drooped a long way down towards his chest and his face had been hidden. We could now see that his skin was blotchy and a waxen-yellow. His lips were also blotchy, stained a livid deep purple where they were not pale and bloodless. As I held up the blanket a tiny fly crawled across John's top lip, and I was about to wave it away when I remembered that he couldn't feel it. We all kissed or touched John's face to say goodbye one final time.

Peggy recently told me that, after returning home, she mentally wrapped the Zurich experience up in a bubble and put it in a different compartment of her mind. It was the first time she had seen anyone die. She now wonders how we got through the sequence of events that resulted in our being with John as he died, but she knows that it was the right thing for him. 'The only shame was that it brought his death forward because he had to be able to make the journey to Switzerland.' From not having thought about assisted dying until John raised the topic in January 2003 she now supports a change in the law.

There are some mental images from that day I cannot believe will ever fade and some things I cannot remember at all. I recall carrying John's empty wheelchair down the stairs, as it was easier than putting it in the lift, but I cannot recollect saying goodbye to Erika. I hope we did; she was a wonderful person.

Margaret, Peggy, Michael and I walked out of the building into the warm late-May afternoon in a kind of daze. As I had not been to the hotel, Michael pointed it out. We could see the building from the corner of the street, and I realized that we could see the flat from our room. I found that comforting, especially as Erika had told us that John's body would be there for some time until the undertakers came to take it away.

I wanted to lie in a hot bath with a stiff drink for an hour, but instead I had one of the tots of brandy Margaret handed out then washed my face and made some phone calls. I left a message for our mother at the residential home where she lived and I rang John's friends Sue, Pete and Di. When I had passed on the news they were waiting for that everything had gone to plan and John had died peacefully the four of us went to eat. We took a tram to the river and ate at a waterfront restaurant. We ate good food and drank a toast to John's memory before going back to the hotel confident that, in doing so, we had behaved as he would have wanted us to. It all felt slightly unreal.

I started writing this account of John's last day in the middle of the night after he died, sitting on the tiny balcony of our room and writing in the illumination provided by the street lights. I finished it four weeks later, after an informal get-together with his friends in Milton Keynes at which we scattered some of his ashes. In the intervening time I had forgotten some details, and I am glad that I wrote the most difficult part almost immediately. Rereading it I am reminded of the tremendous stress of the day.

This is what John wrote about Dignitas. By this stage he no longer bothered about punctuation as just getting the letters on the screen was an effort.

i saw an article online. this may be food 4 thought. i can't kill myself. i'm too scared of failure, of being in a hospital afterwards under some smart young doc intent on keeping me alive to show what a clever chap he is. i'd rather go to switzerland if i have to. i have to draw a line. i know i have only had 2 years of mnd but it has started to reach a point where i question the value of my life. i've had a good run so far with all my musical activity but it won't last that much longer and i am becoming more and more like a thing than a human being.

And he wrote the following in the five minutes we left him alone while he was waiting for the anti-emetic to take effect shortly before he died. I have transcribed it exactly, and the lack of capitals and punctuation reflect his weak and tired state.

i am tired in the spirit and the body
if they carried me back to the taxi
i would soon be a corpse anyway
no more faxes
no more emails
no more reasons for living
to think through
it seems sad to have come
to such a grand city
and such good people
only to die
– these thoughts are those
of a weary, terminally ill man out of joint
they have no proper form
or ending
but thankfully
his life has . . .

I still have the clothes and slippers John was wearing when he died. When Erika gave them to me I put them in the bag John had taken to Dignitas, and ten years on I have not yet unpacked it. It also contains one of his syringes, two of the little squares of plain Swiss chocolate that made his eyes light up twice – once when he spotted it and again when he tasted it – a can of Deep Heat spray, his disabled person's blue parking permit, a urine bottle and his wallet. I seldom open the bag in an effort to preserve the now-faint smell of my dear brother, but I have promised myself that I will unpack it when the law is changed to allow terminally ill, mentally competent people to ask for help to die.

2
A HISTORY OF ASSISTED DYING IN THE UK
by Jo Cartwright

As he lay comatose on his deathbed in 1936 George V was injected with fatal doses of morphine and cocaine to assure him a painless death.[1] This fact was kept secret for the next fifty years. The truth that George V was helped to die by injections of lethal drugs was revealed on publication of the medical notes that his physician, Lord Dawson, took at the time. These stated that the King died less than an hour after the injections. What is not clear is whether the King was consulted on the decision to hasten the end of his life, but it was noted that Queen Mary had asked that the King's life was not needlessly prolonged if he was terminally ill with no chance of recovery.

Shortly after George V's death, and a year after the formation of the UK Voluntary Euthanasia Legalisation Society (VELS), euthanasia was debated in the House of Lords. With a view not dissimilar to many we hear in today's debates, the King's physician spoke against the legalization of euthanasia, not because he thought it was wrong but because he believed that the matter was best left to the conscience of the physician; the doctor knows best. He said:

> One should make the act of dying more gentle and more peaceful even if it does involve curtailment of the length of life; that has become increasingly the custom. This may be taken as something accepted . . . If we cannot cure, for heaven's sake let us do our best to lighten the pain.[2]

The Archbishop of Canterbury, Cosmo Gordon Lang, prayed at the bedside of the King the night he died. In the parliamentary debate ten months later the Archbishop praised Lord Dawson's speech, effectively endorsing the doctrine of double effect that would be formally established at a later date.

VELS, which has been through a number of iterations to become Dignity in Dying, was formed in 1935 by two healthcare professionals based in Leicester, Mr Charles Bond and Dr Killick Millard. The organization quickly found national support, with Lord Moynihan becoming its first president, and the first UK Bill seeking to allow a form of assistance to die was drafted by VELS during its first year.

That Bill, if passed, would have allowed a person over twenty-one and suffering from a terminal disease causing severe pain to ask for help to achieve a peaceful death by a doctor administering life-ending medication. Subsequent attempts to change the law, including Lord Falconer's 2013–2014 Assisted Dying Bill, have developed detailed safeguards around the proposed law change. These have largely been based on experience in – and research from – places where some form of assistance to die is legal. However, two significant changes to the original legislation proposed in England and Wales have been made. First, the age limit has been lowered to eighteen, in line with changes in views on when a person has the capacity to make decisions about his or her life. Second, as a final safeguard the patient must be able to self-administer the life-ending medication. This ensures that it is the patient rather than the doctor who carries out the final act that ends his or her life.

In 1936 there was a further debate in the House of Lords on the Voluntary Euthanasia Bill proposed by Lord Ponsonby of Shulbrede. The Bill was rejected at its second reading by a sizeable majority, and Lord Ponsonby said:

> I am perfectly certain that the time will come when Parliament will have to regulate this matter. I am perfectly certain that a measure of this kind will in time be accepted and that those who are opposing it now will in time to come feel that they look back, as we look back upon those who opposed the use of chloroform in childbirth, to a time when there was a less enlightened view taken on these crucial matters.[3]

The measure was not substantively discussed in Parliament again until 1950 when Lord Chorley introduced a Bill that was later withdrawn to avoid 'dividing the House'.[4]

The issue arose again in 1969 when Lord Raglan introduced a Voluntary Euthanasia Bill. This Bill was defeated at its second reading.

In February 1993 the House of Lords Medical Ethics Select Committee was set up to look at the issue of voluntary euthanasia. Its 1994 report recognized the force of the argument for euthanasia but recommended that there be no change in legislation.

In the same year that the select committee was set up there was a ground-breaking legal case. The case of Tony Bland challenged our laws governing the right to die and paved the way for a number of other legal challenges on the laws of murder and assisted suicide.

Anthony (Tony) Bland was one of the Liverpool Football Club supporters injured in the Hillsborough disaster of 1989. He suffered severe brain damage which left him in a persistent vegetative state.

In 1992, three years after his injury, the hospital, with the support of his family, applied for a court order to allow his artificial hydration and nutrition and life-sustaining treatment to be withdrawn so that he could be allowed to die.[5] The severity of his injuries – both his lungs were punctured in the crush – led to his brain being starved of oxygen. This caused irreversible damage which meant there was no reasonable possibility of his recovering from his persistent vegetative state. His medical team attempted to establish a reaction from him, but he showed no sign of being aware of anything that took place around him. His body was being kept alive by artificial nutrition and hydration as well as artificial ventilation.

In a legal challenge Airedale NHS Trust applied to the courts for a declaration that they might lawfully discontinue all life-sustaining treatment and medical support measures including ventilation, nutrition and hydration by artificial means. In addition they sought a ruling that, if he died, his death should be attributed to his injuries and should not be seen as a consequence of the withdrawal of life-sustaining treatment.

Prior to this landmark legal case the non-treatment of patients was limited to newborn babies where their healthcare team considered it to be in their best interest. The court decided in favour of the trust and considered it to be in Tony Bland's best interests that his treatment should be withheld. Acting on his behalf the Official Solicitor appealed against this decision.

The Court of Appeal decision to allow him to die by withdrawal of life-sustaining treatment was appealed against in the House of Lords. Each of the five Law Lords dismissed the appeal, and the Airedale NHS Trust was legally permitted to withdraw his treatment, including artificial hydration and nutrition. Lord Goff of Chieveley said:

I agree that the doctor's conduct in discontinuing life support can properly be categorized as an omission ... as a matter of general principle an omission such as this will not be unlawful ... The distinction appears, therefore, to be useful in the present context in that it can be invoked to explain how discontinuance of life support can be differentiated from ending a patient's life by a lethal injection. But in the end the reason for that difference is that, whereas the law considers that discontinuance of life support may be consistent with the doctor's duty to care for his patient, it does not, for reasons of policy, consider that it forms any part of his duty to give his patient a lethal injection to put him out of his agony.[6]

Tony Bland died on 3 March 1993, and on 21 December 1993 the coroner recorded a verdict of accidental death.

In 1996, three years after the death of Tony Bland, Annie Lindsell challenged the law on voluntary euthanasia. A woman in the late stages of motor neurone disease (MND) diagnosed four years earlier, she feared death by choking or suffocating.

Lord Lester, QC, took up her case to try to win her the legal right to have help to die. Annie Lindsell, who was in a wheelchair at the time she started her legal case and was unable to feed herself or comb her hair, wanted to die

when I can't speak any more and finally lose all use of my hands. The prospect of not being able to move a muscle, of constantly having dribble wiped from my face because I can't swallow, of being incapable of dealing with my intimate personal needs, is just not acceptable.[7]

She argued that unless she could count on being given help to die she would be forced to consider ending her life before she wanted to while she was still able to do so without help. Her legal challenge asked the court to allow a doctor to intervene if she found herself suffering at the end of her life and to administer a high dose of diamorphine, without fear of prosecution, even if the medication resulted in her life being shortened.

She withdrew her case in October 1997 after it was established that doctors could legally administer potentially life-shortening drugs, not only for the relief of physical distress but also to alleviate her mental distress. She was assured that her doctor would not allow her to suffer unnecessarily, and a treatment plan was agreed which followed best medical practice.

This case clarified the law over the doctrine of double effect, and Annie Lindsell died of MND in December 1997.

Dr David Moor was a GP who was tried in 1999 for ending the life of a patient, thereby becoming the first doctor in Britain to be tried for mercy killing, which counts as murder under the law.

George Liddell, a widower of eighty-five, was suffering from terminal bowel cancer which had spread to his liver. He was living with his daughter and being treated at her home by a team of healthcare professionals, including Dr Moor. George Liddell became distressed and his condition deteriorated. The healthcare team agreed to send him to a hospice, and Dr Moor set up a syringe driver to administer diamorphine to his patient. His breathing deteriorated, and Dr Moor administered an injection of diamorphine and chlorpromazine, a painkiller and an anti-anxiety drug. Not long after this injection George Liddell died.

This case came to light when Dr Moor gave an interview to the *Sunday Times* and said that he had given many patients overdoses of diamorphine, a comment he repeated in a follow-up broadcast interview.

This admission led to Dr Moor's criminal trial in April 1999, with the jury taking just over an hour to find Dr Moor not guilty of murder.

In 2001 a patient known as Ms B sought a declaration from the court to force her doctors to comply with her wish to have her ventilator switched off, although she knew this would result in her death. The case was heard at Ms B's hospital bedside, the first time in legal history that a case has been heard in this way.

Ms B, who was forty-three years old, was paralysed from the neck down following a secondary haemorrhage into the spinal column in her neck. The initial haemorrhage had occurred in 1999. When she was told that she was at risk of a further bleed she made a living will, now known as an advance decision. This stated that if she lost the capacity to make decisions about her care she wanted all life-sustaining treatment to be withdrawn if she was suffering from a life-threatening condition. In February 2001 the secondary haemorrhage left her unable to breathe without artificial ventilation. In March 2001, following unsuccessful surgery, she asked for her ventilator to be switched off.

Ms B's wishes were not adhered to. She made further requests over the next two months and eventually instructed her solicitor to issue formal instructions to the hospital demanding that her wishes be respected. Between April and August 2001 her mental capacity was assessed, and, although initially she had been judged incapable of refusing treatment, an independent assessment by a second psychiatrist found that she had the mental capacity to choose to discontinue life-sustaining treatment. From August 2001 she was deemed to have mental capacity. Her medical team, however, refused to discontinue her ventilation; they felt unable to switch off her ventilator because they believed they would be directly responsible for her death. Because the medical team and Ms B could not agree on a suitable way forward, and because the NHS Trust involved did not have an ethics committee, her case was referred to the High Court.

The main issue for the court to rule on was whether Ms B had capacity to make an informed decision to refuse treatment. If she did, it would be unlawful to continue treating her against her will. The court found that Ms B did have capacity and that she had been treated unlawfully by the hospital trust since August 2001.[8]

She was moved to a different hospital where she exercised her right to refuse treatment. Her ventilator was switched off, and she died on Monday 29 April 2002.

Diane Pretty was diagnosed with motor neurone disease in 1999. By 2001 the disease had left her mind as sharp as ever but had gradually destroyed her ability to move or speak, making it hard for her to communicate with her family. She was in a wheelchair, catheterized and fed through a tube. She was fully conscious of what the future was likely to hold, given her diagnosis, and decided to refuse artificial ventilation.

Rather than spend her remaining days terrified of dying by choking or suffocation, she wanted a doctor to help her to die when she was no longer able to communicate with her family and friends and her suffering became too much to bear. She discussed this with her husband of twenty-five years, Brian, who has since become a Patron of Dignity in Dying.[9] He respected her decision and wanted his wife to be able to have the good death she so desperately wanted, a quick death without suffering, at home and surrounded by her family.

She said that if she had been physically able she would have taken steps to end her life, which would not have been illegal, but because of her physical deterioration this was not possible.

Her case began in July 2001 when she sent a letter, written on her behalf, to the Director of Public Prosecutions (DPP) asking him not to prosecute her husband

Brian if, at her request, he assisted her to end her life. A few weeks later the DPP replied, refusing to agree to Diane's request, so she applied for a judicial review of the decision.

On 17 October 2001 the Divisional Court refused Diane Pretty's judicial review on the grounds that the DPP did not have the power to provide the immunity she requested for her husband. She appealed this decision to the House of Lords, who dismissed her appeal on 29 November 2001 and upheld the judgement of the Divisional Court.[10] These proceedings were expedited due to the time-sensitive nature of her request. She then took her case to the European Court of Human Rights.

On 21 December 2001 she lodged her application to the European Court under several Articles in the European Convention on Human Rights (known as the ECHR). Her appeal referred to Article 2 (the right to life), Article 3 (prohibiting torture and inhuman and degrading treatment), Article 8 (respect for a private and family life), Article 9 (the right to freedom of thought, conscience and religion) and Article 14 (which prohibits discrimination). Diane's legal team argued that her fundamental rights under the ECHR had been violated by the refusal of the DPP to provide immunity to her husband if he were to assist her to end her life and by outdated English law that made assistance to die, at the request of the dying person, a criminal offence.

On her Article 2 application the European Court ruled that no right to die, whether by a third party or with the assistance of the state, can be derived from Article 2 of the ECHR and that denying Diane the right to assistance to die did not imply a violation of Article 2 of the ECHR.[11]

On her Article 3 application the European Court concluded that the UK government was under no positive obligation to undertake not to prosecute Diane's husband if he assisted her to commit suicide. They also found that the government had no obligation to provide a lawful opportunity for any other form of assistance to die and that, in denying Diane the right to assistance to die, there had been no violation of her Article 3 rights.

On her Article 8 application the European Court would not exclude the possibility that Diane's situation constituted an interference with her right to respect for private life (as guaranteed under Article 8, subsection 1, of the ECHR). Unfortunately for Diane and for her case an interference with the exercise of an Article 8 right would not be compatible with Article 8 subsection 2 unless it is 'in accordance with the law', has an aim or aims that is or are legitimate under that paragraph and is 'necessary in a democratic society' for the aforesaid aim or aims. The European Court therefore found that the blanket nature of the ban on assistance to die was not disproportionate and that the protection of the law should override Diane's right in this instance.

On her Article 9 application the European Court concluded that there had been no violation of her conscience or religion.

On her discrimination claim under Article 14 the European Court found, after some deliberation, that there need not be an adjustment in the law to allow for assistance to disabled people to commit suicide, despite access to suicide being limited by their disability. This concluded the European Court's ruling, and Diane had taken her case as far as it could go.

Diane died at a hospice near her home on Saturday 11 May 2002 aged forty-three. She had begun experiencing breathing difficulties ten days previously, just three days after she lost her right-to-die court challenge in the European Court of Human Rights.

In February 2003, with the support of the Voluntary Euthanasia Society, Lord Joffe introduced the first of his Private Member's Bills, the Patient Assisted Dying Bill, which sought to legalize assisted dying.

After deliberation by a House of Lords Select Committee the Bill was put forward again in November 2005. On 12 May 2006 an amended version of the Bill, now called the Assisted Dying for the Terminally Ill Bill, was debated again in the House of Lords before being defeated at second reading by a margin of 148 to 100.[12] This Bill would have legalized assisted dying for terminally ill, mentally competent adults and was limited to assisted dying whereby the patient would have to self-administer the life-ending medication. It would not have legalized voluntary euthanasia.

During this period Voluntary Euthanasia Society members voted to change the name of the organization to Dignity in Dying. Alongside the change of name the organization's core aim was refined to focus on assisted dying for terminally ill, mentally competent adults rather than voluntary euthanasia with potentially broader eligibility criteria.

The Mental Capacity Act (MCA) 2005, which came into force in 2007, was brought in to provide a legal framework for decision-making on behalf of adults who are considered to lack capacity.[13] This is of particular importance to people approaching the end of their lives, as that is often a time when a person lacks the capacity, either mentally or physically, to communicate their wishes and treatment preferences.

The MCA assumes five key principles:

1. A person must be assumed to have capacity unless it is established that he or she lacks capacity.
2. A person is not to be treated as unable to make a decision unless all practicable steps to help him or her do so have been taken without success.
3. A person is not to be treated as unable to make a decision merely because he or she makes a decision that someone else may deem unwise.
4. An act done, or decision made, under this Act for or on behalf of a person who lacks capacity must be done, or made, in his or her best interests.
5. Before the act is done, or the decision is made, regard must be had to whether the purpose for which it is needed can be as effectively achieved in a way that is less restrictive of the person's rights and freedom of action.[14]

This Act made advance decisions to refuse treatment, colloquially known as living wills, legally binding under statutory law. They had been legal in common law for some decades. The Act also created lasting powers of attorney (LPAs), similar to the enduring powers of attorney which formerly existed.

An advance decision allows any person with capacity to set out their wishes for end-of-life treatment in a way that is legally binding.[15] An advance decision allows doctors to know what treatment the individual would want to refuse if they could not communicate for any reason, for instance if they had severe dementia or were in a coma. Advance decisions work well if they apply to the specific circumstances a person is in.

An LPA is more flexible. There are two types of LPA: property and finance and health and welfare. Health and welfare LPAs can cover end-of-life decision-making. A health and welfare LPA gives the person appointed the power to make decisions on behalf of the person who made the appointment if they lose the ability to make those decisions for themselves.

Debbie Purdy is a campaigner, born in London and living in Bradford, who has primary progressive multiple sclerosis. She would like to be allowed to choose an assisted death at home if her suffering becomes unbearable. In the absence of a law permitting such assistance she was keen to know whether a person – most likely her husband Omar Puente – who gave her assistance to end her life would face prosecution after she died. She wanted reassurance that her choice to die would not implicate her husband.

Through her legal team of Lord Pannick, QC, Paul Bowen, QC, and Saimo Chahal, Debbie argued that the Director of Public Prosecutions (DPP) was infringing her human rights by failing to clarify how the Suicide Act 1961 is enforced. This argument was particularly important given that there had been no prosecutions of amateurs compassionately assisting the death of a loved one, at their request, under that Act in recent years.

The counsel for the DPP argued that the law does not require the director to make any further clarification on his factors for or against prosecution under the Suicide Act and that the Code for Crown Prosecutors provides sufficient information.

Debbie's particular concern began with wanting to know which – if any – of the actions taken by her husband in assisting her death would lead to his prosecution. Armed with that information she could avoid those actions and die safe in the knowledge that he would not face prosecution on her behalf. For her the case ended up being about much more than her right to retain control over the end of her life; she was fighting for clarity for all Britons facing difficult end-of-life decisions.

The current penalty for those who encourage or assist a suicide is a maximum of fourteen years' imprisonment.[16] No family member of the almost two hundred and forty Britons who to date have gone abroad for help to die has been prosecuted. Many have faced questioning and have waited months or even years before finding out that they will not face prosecution at a time when they should be coming to terms with the grief of losing a loved one. Debbie said that if her husband could face prosecution for helping her travel to Switzerland to obtain help to die, for example, she would make the journey sooner while she was able to travel unassisted. This would save him from potential imprisonment, but it meant that Debbie would die without her loved ones around her. It would also have forced her to make a decision to die before her suffering became unbearable for her.

Debbie's High Court hearing began on 2 October 2008. In the High Court the DPP said that she could not be given any reassurance that her husband would not be prosecuted as the law was clear that assisting suicide is an offence. Her case was then heard in the Court of Appeal in 2009 where again she was given no reassurance.[17] The case was finally heard on 2 June 2009 in the highest court in the land, the House of Lords. The decision in the Debbie Purdy case was the final judgement to be handed down before the Law Lords moved to the Supreme Court.

In a historic ruling the Law Lords ruled in her favour. They said that the law was not as clear as it should be. The five Law Lords unanimously backed her call for a policy statement from the DPP clarifying which factors are taken into consideration when deciding whether or not to prosecute for assisting the death of another, for example, by helping a loved one to end their life abroad.[18] Lord Hope of Craighead said:

> The code will normally provide sufficient guidance to Crown Prosecutors and to the public as to how decisions should or are likely to be taken whether or not, in a given case, it will be in the public interest to prosecute . . . In most cases its application will ensure predictability and consistency of decision-taking, and people will know where they stand. But that cannot be said of cases where the offence in contemplation is aiding or abetting the suicide of a person who is terminally ill or severely and incurably disabled who wishes to be helped to travel to a country where assisted suicide is lawful and who, having the capacity to take such a decision, does so freely and with a full understanding of the consequences. There is already an obvious gulf between what section 2 (1) says and the way that the subsection is being applied in practice in compassionate cases of that kind.[19]

Following a public consultation and the publication of interim guidance on 25 February 2010 the DPP issued the final version of his prosecuting policy on cases of encouraging or assisting suicide.[20]

The prosecuting policy makes it clear that there is a distinction between compassionate acts to assist someone to end his or her life which, subject to a number of factors, are unlikely to be prosecuted and malicious encouragement or assistance of suicide which will be prosecuted.

The prosecuting policy also makes clear that a distinction will be made between amateur assistance, such as by a loved one or friend who has no medical background, and professional assistance to die. The former is unlikely to result in a prosecution whereas the latter is more likely to do so.

However, while the policy gives individuals much clearer indications of how they are likely to be treated under the law, it does not change the law or provide immunity from prosecution. Assisting suicide is still a crime, and cases of mercy killing – where one person ends the life of another person at his or her request –

will still be prosecuted as murder or manslaughter. This is because the DPP has discretion only in cases that fall into the remit of the law on assisted suicide. There is no such discretion in cases which fall under the law of murder or manslaughter.

Several factors will influence whether a case is more or less likely to lead to prosecution. A prosecution is less likely if the assisted person made a voluntary well-informed decision to commit suicide, if the assister was wholly motivated by compassion and if the assister had sought to dissuade the person from committing suicide.

A prosecution is more likely if the person committing suicide was under eighteen, if he or she did not have mental capacity or had not made a voluntary decision. A prosecution is also more likely if the assister has a history of violence or abuse towards the assisted person, if they assisted or encouraged several people's suicides or were paid for their assistance.

Prosecutions are more likely if the assisted person was physically able to undertake the act that constituted assistance and if the assister assisted or encouraged someone he or she did not know to commit suicide. This effectively recognizes that assistance is more likely to be compassionately motivated when a person needs physical help to commit suicide and when the assister knows the person being assisted.

The policy instructs police and prosecutors to adopt a common-sense approach to the issue of financial gain. If it is shown that compassion was the only driving force behind the assister's actions, the fact that he or she may have gained some financial benefit will not usually be treated as a factor in favour of prosecution.

The policy covers actions carried out in England and Wales to assist suicide, but the suicide itself could take place in England, Wales or any other country.

The law in Northern Ireland on assisted suicide is the same as the law in England and Wales. The Director of Public Prosecutions in Northern Ireland published the same prosecuting policy on assisted suicide cases in Northern Ireland.

In 2010 Lord Advocate Elish Angiolini, QC, the Scottish equivalent of the DPP, said that similar guidance will not be issued in Scotland. There is no specific crime of assisted suicide in Scotland, but people who assist suicide may face prosecution for the crime of culpable homicide.

Debbie Purdy's victory and the subsequent prosecuting policy on assisted suicide were undoubtedly a turning point in the campaign for greater choice at the end of life. These guidelines and the principle that compassionate amateur assistance will not result in prosecution were endorsed unanimously in a House of Commons Backbench Business Committee debate in March 2012 on a motion tabled by Richard Ottaway, MP. If MPs consider it appropriate not to prosecute those who compassionately assist another to die at his or her request it must only be a matter of time before safeguards are added to this currently unregulated practice. Such safeguards would mean that people would have the legal option of asking for medical help to end their lives if they are approaching death and their suffering becomes unbearable.

The most recent legal challenges were started by the late Tony Nicklinson and a man known initially as AM and, later, as Martin.

Tony Nicklinson was fifty-eight when he started his legal battle for the right to die. He had locked-in syndrome following a stroke in 2005. While he was not asking for help to die immediately, he wanted to know that if he chose to die he could ask someone to help him to do so as he was physically unable to end his life. His case was effectively asking for legal protection for a doctor who would help him to end his life - which would be voluntary euthanasia, and therefore murder, under the law.

In the High Court in June 2012 his legal team argued that it would not be unlawful to grant this protection to a doctor ahead of time on the grounds of necessity. If the case had been won this decision would only have applied to him.

The second key argument was that the UK's existing law on murder and/or assisted suicide is incompatible with his right to respect for private life under Article 8 of the ECHR. This had previously been argued and conceded to on some level in Diane Pretty's and Debbie Purdy's legal challenges.

He was told he had lost his case on 15 August 2012, and he died at home on 22 August, having taken the decision to stop eating and drinking and to refuse treatment for a lung infection. His wife Jane appealed against the judgement, and his legal case was continued with a new appellant, Paul Lamb, who was injured and left paralysed by a car accident in 1990 and whose suffering has become more than he is willing to bear.

Paul Lamb's case was heard in the Court of Appeal, which ruled that his appeal had been unsuccessful on 31 July 2013. The judgement gave permission for the case to go forward to the Supreme Court.

A separate case had been launched by a man known as AM, who wanted to challenge a different area of the law. AM, now referred to as Martin, is almost completely paralysed following a stroke in 2008 and was forty-six when his legal battle began in 2011.

Martin wants the option to travel to Dignitas in order to have an assisted death, but he would need significant help to get there. His wife understands and respects his decision but is not willing to help him to die, so he would need the support of someone else. That person must be someone who is likely to be protected under the policy of the DPP. They cannot be one of his carers or a member of his medical team, given that prosecution could be more likely if the person involved is 'acting in his or her capacity as a medical doctor, nurse, other healthcare professional, a professional carer (whether for payment or not), or as a person in authority . . .'[21] As Martin does not have a close family member who is willing to give him the assistance he wants he is challenging the policy. His solicitors say he is being discriminated against.

Martin's initial application to the High Court sought an assurance that his legal representatives and other experts will not face prosecution or professional disciplinary procedures as a result of helping him. The High Court decided to hear Tony Nicklinson and Martin's cases in the same sitting.

Martin's lawyers argued that the policy of the DPP is not sufficiently clear and specific, especially factor 14 which states that prosecution is likely in the case of a healthcare professional who provides assistance.

Martin's case was lost in the High Court and was heard in the Court of Appeal alongside the Nicklinson/Lamb case in May 2013. In a split decision on 31 July 2013 Martin won his case by a majority of two to one. The ruling requires the DPP to provide further clarification on what professionals *can* do when asked by a patient or client for support in ending their life at their request. The DPP appealed against this decision, and the case was heard in the Supreme Court in December 2013. A decision is expected in spring 2014.

This brings us to the Commission on Assisted Dying and to Lord Falconer's Bill, currently awaiting its second reading in the House of Lords. This Bill should have a positive impact on the campaign to legalize assisted dying in the UK.

Individuals and their families have made a huge difference to the campaign for assisted dying, and the progress that can result from one person's contribution to the battle is evident. I am certain that when that law does change it will be down to the courage and tenacity of a number of individuals who have made a stand against enforced suffering at the end of life.

3
THREE SUICIDES, THREE REASONS TO DIE
Liz Smith's parents: 'We just sat there, waiting for this great moment'

Liz Smith's parents were born just sixty days apart: Barbara was a New Year's Eve baby, born on the last day of 1927, and Don, born at the end of February 1928, was a Leap Day baby. They met in the De Grey Ballroom in York when Don, who was from Liverpool, was training to be a teacher at York's St John's College. He did not get on with his first career choice, so he transferred to the police where he was very successful, culminating in promotion to superintendent.

Liz says her parents made a lovely couple, and they set her and her brother Chris a very good example of parenthood. Their father was a practising Methodist, but Barbara wasn't religious. She had worked in a bookshop in the Shambles in York when she was young, but she stopped when the children were born. When Chris and Liz started school she took a course in hairdressing, and with that qualification she taught at a youth club because she loved young people.

Barbara's mother had an unidentified form of dementia, and, before she died in 1961, she spent some time in York's Bootham Park psychiatric hospital. Liz remembers the stories Barbara told about visiting the hospital and seeing her mother being restrained for her own protection, screaming, pulling her hair out and trying to hurt herself. Witnessing these scenes had a profound effect on Barbara and left her with a lifelong fear of being in the same situation in later life.

When she was in her sixties Barbara started to develop dementia. Liz says her mother was aware what was happening to her and that most of the time she was perfectly 'with it', although her memory was becoming erratic and confused. Even right at the end of her life Barbara could dress and feed herself – she just couldn't remember anything. She found this very distressing and was convinced that some imaginary events were real. She also had phantom pains in her tongue and her leg, so Don 'took her everywhere for all sorts of tests', but no cause was ever found. At Barbara's request Don enrolled her on several Alzheimer's drug trials in an attempt to slow the progress of the disease, but none was successful.

Because of the nature of the treatment Barbara witnessed her mother undergoing at Bootham Park she made a radical decision. From a relatively young age she would ask family members, 'When it comes to my time, will you help me to kill myself?' Liz's first memory of her mother asking her this was when Liz was around ten.

'I know that sounds awful, but we were brought up with it, and I just never thought anything of it really. Mum's biggest fear was that she would become demented like her mother, so I always used to say "Yes, Mum" then toddle off to play. Interestingly my brother Chris only remembers Mum telling him that she would kill herself when the time was right – she never asked him to help her.'

In the early 1990s Liz went to live in the USA for three years with her husband and sons. About a year before they were scheduled to return to the UK Liz got a phone call to say that her mother was in a coma. She returned to York as quickly as she could, and by the time she got to the hospital her mother had been an in-patient for a couple of days.

Barbara was there because Don had found her with white powder around her mouth. She told him she had taken what she thought was a lethal dose of paracetamol. She said she had lived long enough with the dementia and she wanted to end her life. She vomited not long after taking the tablets, but she was determined to die so she prepared to take another overdose the next day.

Some time before this Chris had arranged to take his parents to a Christmas concert at the school where he taught drama. It took place on the evening Barbara took the first overdose, and Chris remembers vividly what happened when he arrived at his parents' home that evening.

Although it had been just a couple of weeks since Chris had last seen his father he was shocked by his appearance. Don was bent over and looked stressed and suddenly very old. He had also lost weight. After greeting Chris, Don told him that he would have to go to the concert without them as Barbara had taken an overdose.

Chris had heard his mother talk about ending her life often enough to know that she meant it. He went upstairs to see her, and they chatted for a while. Barbara told Chris that she was proud of him and that she wasn't frightened of dying. She was very calm and at peace with herself and said she just wanted her life to end. Chris had no choice but to leave his parents to attend the concert. Leaving his mother and father alone in that situation was the hardest thing he has ever done. He returned to his parents' home later that evening. At the subsequent inquest he described how he found his mother looking quite radiant and very cheerful late in the evening of that day.

Liz says that, following the second overdose, 'Mum became unconscious, but she was moaning all the time and Dad didn't know what that meant or what he should do.' Because Barbara didn't die quickly and she appeared to be in distress Don was soon beside himself with anxiety. He did not know how to help his wife, so he tried to end her life by putting a pillow over her face, but he found he couldn't do that to the woman he loved.

Barbara remained at home and in this terrible unconscious, moaning condition for several hours before Don, in a moment of unimaginable despair at his wife's apparent suffering, rang their doctor. The GP rang the district hospital and arranged for Barbara to be admitted. Don wouldn't go with his wife, saying he couldn't bear it. Later he told Liz that when the ambulance crew took Barbara out of the house he saw her as she was when she was twenty-three, the age she was when they married.

Chris went to the hospital with his mother to explain what had happened. By the time Liz arrived the medical team was talking about feeding her mother. They were saying that they wanted to do everything they could for her, although Chris had told them that his mother did not want to be resuscitated. Liz was appalled. 'I was so upset at the thought that the doctors were going to try to save her life. Mum couldn't go through that again, and my family couldn't go through it again either.'

Liz talked to the doctors taking care of her mother and explained again that her mother did not want any form of resuscitation. She stressed that the whole family was in agreement about this. The doctors said that because Barbara had been admitted to hospital they had an obligation to treat her. Liz feels that the doctor treating her mother was sympathetic to the situation because the paracetamol she had taken had caused a blood clot to form in her brain, and he chose to send her for a scan. Liz thinks that taking her mother to another part of the hospital and moving her between the bed, the trolley and the scanner probably dislodged or broke up the blood clot. Barbara died later that night, although the blood clot was not mentioned as a cause of death. Liz feels that the doctor did a good thing in moving her mother around, although he could not discuss his motives for this with her or her brother. 'I can only assume that he had a suspicion that that might happen. The young nurse who went with me to the scan was saying, "How can you want your mother to die?" and all the classic things that people come out with when they don't understand. So I said, "I love her enough to let her go."'

An inquest was held into Barbara's death. Don was a police superintendent, so he was probably familiar with the procedure surrounding an inquest. Barbara's GP attended, taking a solicitor with him, but Liz's father and brother were unrepresented. They talked to the coroner and explained what had happened. Don told the court about the statement Barbara had made for years expressing her determination to kill herself if she developed dementia and her life became untenable. He also told the inquest that after his wife had told him she had taken an overdose, 'She told me not to be sad about it, and I spent some time talking to her. She was very brave. She was a fighter, someone who had spark.'

Chris told the inquest, 'When we thought she was going to survive and it would make her worse we got her to hospital as soon as we could.' The coroner was very supportive, and his verdict was that there was nothing suspicious about Barbara's death, that she had killed herself and had died of liver failure. It is a common cause of death after a paracetamol overdose, but, as Liz put it, 'It takes a long time.' There was some very sympathetic local-press coverage of the story.

Liz believes that after her mother's death on 22 December 1995 her father was interviewed by the police, but she doesn't know any details. She describes her father as a typical British gentleman and says that when her mother died he cried only once, and even then he apologized for it.

'He never really spoke about his feelings, and he didn't talk about Mum's suicide. It must have been hard to be questioned on suspicion of having committed a crime when all he had done was help the person he most loved in the world. That's what amazed me – he was a Methodist and a policeman, so for him to do what he did to help her die . . .'

Liz says that Barbara wouldn't have wanted anyone to be hurt by her actions, and it would have broken her heart to know how much her death upset her family. Liz says her mother was 'utterly selfless and generous, the sort who would have done anything to protect her family from hurt'.

It must have been frustrating for Liz's father that his beloved wife did not die at home as she had wanted, but at least she was unconscious by the time she was taken to hospital. She didn't know Liz was there, but Liz is stoical about that. She says, 'I'd been over from the USA on a recent visit and had spent a long time with her – we were incredibly close.'

After Barbara died Don continued to go to church every Sunday, and he helped to organize social events there. He joined a group that looked after the church grounds and the general upkeep of the building.

It is unsurprising that after experiencing his wife's suicide he thought long and hard about his attitude towards his own death. Liz was not aware of it at the time, but she realizes now that after Barbara died Don resolved never to let his family go through the trauma he had been through. Tragically his plans were to go awry.

In 2002 Don was diagnosed with a kidney tumour, and the cancer spread to his lungs. To start with, he coped at home, and after he had one of his kidneys removed Liz spent some time with him in York. By 2004 he was still very independent. Liz was living near London, and she would visit him as often as possible. He didn't want to impose himself on members of his family. As she put it, 'He said, in the nicest possible way, that he couldn't stand to live with us. He was a man of strict routine.'

In the spring of 2004 Liz and her family called on Don unexpectedly. They had been to the Yorkshire Dales and decided to visit him on the way home. When they arrived he was being taken away in an ambulance. His doctor had arranged for him to be admitted to a hospice in York. He had rung his doctor earlier that day after having been in too much pain to get to the toilet.

Liz went to the hospice with her father and, soon after he was settled, she asked a nurse about his prognosis. When the nurse said 'weeks' Liz nearly fell off her chair. 'I had no idea that his illness was so advanced. I hadn't given it any thought. I was really shocked because he never complained or spoke about being in pain or anything, so I just assumed he was all right.'

Very soon after he was admitted to the hospice Don told his daughter that it would be nice if the family could all spend the following bank-holiday weekend together at his house. Liz didn't pick up on what he was saying, but, looking back, she realizes that he had been planning his death for a long time. She thinks that his idea was to say goodbye to his family that weekend, but she had to tell him that for all sorts of reasons it wasn't possible to make the arrangements.

When he had been in the hospice four or five days she rang to tell him she was coming up for the weekend. He told her that he would like to go home to see his garden. Liz arrived to pick him up after lunch and asked what time they had tea at the hospice and was told that it was served at around five o'clock. She told a nurse that she would have him back by then.

Don didn't seem bothered about anything other than getting home. They drove past the shops, and Liz suggested stopping to buy milk, but he vetoed the idea. Liz told him, 'I can't make you a cup of tea without milk', but he wanted to press on. She dropped him off at the house because, of course, she had to go back to the shops.

'When I returned with the milk, as soon as I opened the front door I saw a note on the floor in the hall. I knew instinctively what it was going to say. I went to the kitchen, and there was Dad, in tears, shouting at me not to come in. I can't describe how unlike him that was and how shocking it was to see him like that. It was almost like dealing with a frightened animal. I had to stand back and say, "Look, it's OK. I'm not going to stop you. Just calm down. It will be fine." I noticed the vacuum cleaner was in the kitchen, and I asked him what it was doing there. He told me that he'd carried it into the kitchen and tried to suffocate himself with a plastic bag, but he couldn't go through with it.'

Don told Liz that he had taken some of the analgesics the hospital had given him and that he had also drunk some liquid painkiller. He was worried that he might vomit like Barbara had the first time she had taken an overdose. Liz says that the liquid painkiller was really thick treacly stuff and if anything was going to make you sick that would. She suggested he sit in his favourite chair, and they moved to the lounge. Don sat in the chair facing the garden, and Liz sat on the floor beside him. They chatted. Don asked his daughter to get some sleeping tablets he had left upstairs, but he didn't take any of them in case they made him sick. 'I asked him if he wanted a cup of tea. Although he was desperate to have one he didn't dare drink it in case of being sick.'

'We just sat there, waiting for this great moment to arrive, but nothing happened. While we waited, we talked. We talked about the garden, and we talked about Mum. We talked about my family, and I told him how much I loved him. We didn't really talk about what he was doing. In fact, the only time it came up was when nothing seemed to be happening. I asked him, "How are you? What's going on?" and he just said he felt sleepy. When he was still awake at about four I started thinking: What am I going to do? Tea's at five! I was getting in a bit of a state, so I rang the hospice and told them he had taken an overdose. The woman who took my call said, "Get him back here as soon as you can." I told her I wasn't willing to take him back to the hospice if they were going to pump his stomach. I didn't want them to resuscitate him.'

Because of what had happened to her mother Liz didn't want to involve her brother, but her father felt differently. When he was settled in the car he insisted that Liz should ring Chris. Leaving her father in the car, she went back inside to make a hurried call before returning him to the hospice. When they got there a doctor gave Don what Liz presumes was an antidote. She says she felt like a traitor, and she thought: This is not what Dad wants. She felt very upset and frustrated.

Don had never mentioned his decision to end his life, but he was always very well organized and had written letters – for the coroner, the police, Liz and Chris – which were laid out on the kitchen table.

'He had organized all his accounts. He had planned everything down to the last detail, but his plans were going wrong because he didn't know how much of what to take. He couldn't ask anyone for help, so he'd had to plan it entirely on his own. The previous week, while he appeared to be coping well at home, I'd stayed with him for a few days. He made me go out with him to buy new towels and a microwave. Looking back, I can see that it was almost as if he was covering his tracks, disguising his plans. I can imagine him thinking: If I send Liz out to buy things they won't suspect.'

She certainly didn't suspect. When asked whether her father had ever talked about his suffering she said no. 'There was only one time he came close to saying anything about the situation. He'd always loved all sports and enjoyed reading the newspaper. When I rang one morning his tone had changed, and my sports-mad father was saying that reading the paper and watching sport on TV wasn't enough any more. That's the only time he said anything that suggested he was less than happy. I assumed he was getting a bit depressed. I never dreamt that this was going to happen.'

Later she found out that their father would phone Chris asking him to come over because he was having a panic attack. Apparently these occurred quite frequently, and although her brother visited their father as often as he could he wasn't always able to leave work and go there at a moment's notice. Chris had suggested that Don should live with him and his family in the guesthouse they ran. That way someone would be on hand to help him on a daily basis, but Don was too independent to accept his offer. Chris now feels these panic attacks contributed to the decision their father made to end his life. He thinks Don couldn't cope with not having complete control over his life and his future.

Before their father took the overdose, Chris and Liz had discussed the possibility that he might kill himself. They decided that he wouldn't, mainly because he was so religious.

Don took the overdose on Friday 31 April 2004. When Liz went back to the hospice on the Saturday morning there was a nurse with her father who was from a country that permits assisted suicide. The nurse was upset, and she told Liz that when she had gone to see Don that morning that she had found him with his belt round his neck and wrists. He had been blue, and she had taken the belt away from him. Liz cannot imagine why he had the belt round his wrists.

'He was obviously in a hell of a state. While the nurse was telling me this, in Dad's room, he came round from his doped-up state. The expression on his face was horrendous – he just looked terrified, that's the only way I can describe it. I think he looked that way because he realized he was still alive. He didn't say anything or make any noise, but he was struggling to get out of bed, thrashing about. I had to lie on top of him and hold him down. The nurse rang a bell, and when no one came to help she went to find someone. Eventually they gave him something that calmed him down – knocked him out.'

While Liz was with Don that Saturday evening he came round from his sedation in a state of terror again. She remembers going to the nurses' station and screaming at them that they were torturing him and asking why didn't they leave him alone.

Liz stayed in her father's house that night. Because she had witnessed his second episode of coming round terrified before she left the hospice she was unable to sleep. Seeking reassurance, she rang the hospice at three in the morning, and the nurse on duty was one Liz had not spoken to before.

'She told me that my father was incontinent, that it was a sign that he was on the way out and that she'd had to change the bedlinen. She also told me that Dad was fully aware of what was going on. What hurt me was the tone of her voice. It was as if she was telling me off, as if she didn't approve of what he'd done in taking the overdose. At least, that's how it came across. Her attitude knocked me for six.' Liz wondered at the time why the nurse was telling her about her father's suffering in such graphic detail. She says that she thought: OK, so he's really ill, but why put him through all that?

After a sleepless night Liz and Chris went back to the hospice at dawn on Sunday 2 May. Shortly after they arrived their father once again came round from sedation looking terrified. A nurse gave him an injection to calm him down, which eventually worked, and he fell asleep. His breathing was very erratic. On several occasions she and Chris thought he had died, but then he would start breathing again.

Liz was not in her father's room when he died, aged seventy-four, but she is comforted by the thought that he was not aware of her absence or presence after that final injection.

She is angry with the hospice. 'I felt that the treatment Dad was given in the hospice after his overdose was inappropriate, and I know it went against his wishes. Quite a long time afterwards someone from the hospice rang and asked whether I had any complaints. I was still in such a state that I said no, but I've been kicking myself ever since. It could well have been somebody trying to stop that sort of thing happening in the future. I was shocked by the look I saw on Dad's face when he came round. If he had been able to discuss his fears about what might happen – and what he wanted to happen – at the end of his life he would have been able to talk about it properly and ask for help. If it had been possible to ask for an assisted death I think he would have done that. When we were sitting in the lounge waiting for the overdose to take effect he told me that he had been planning it for ages and that he couldn't think how he could kill himself. He'd thought about taking the car out and smashing it into something, but he was worried about hurting someone. So he was desperately looking for a way out, and this was it. Being able to have an assisted death would have made a huge difference to him and the family. He knew he had terminal cancer and that he had nothing to look forward to other than a slow and very painful death.'

Chris was very badly affected by his mother's death. He was so traumatized by everything that had happened that he was prescribed tranquillizers by his GP and he felt unable to work. He suffered depression from then on, and for years after he experienced persistent nightmares. He had more and more time off work and was eventually given the option to hand in his notice or be sacked. The head teacher felt that Chris's students were suffering as a result of his repeated absences. He duly gave his notice and left the teaching profession.

He has only recently felt well enough to come off the antidepressants he had been taking since his mother's death. It is understandable that, although ten years had passed since Barbara's suicide, when their father took an overdose Liz's first instinct was to try to protect her brother. She said that if her father hadn't asked her to ring him she would not have done so.

The ashes of Liz's parents are interred in the garden of their former home. After Don died a friend of the family bought the house, and Liz knows she was aware of the cremated remains in the garden. Her mother's ashes were scattered round a rose bush, and Liz says that it is hard to know what to do in such circumstances if people haven't stated their desires. That statement applies to every situation we face in life as well as those unique questions we need to answer as we approach death. One way to make sure our wishes are known is to talk about the subject in advance: events such as the annual Dying Matters Week in the UK can act as a stimulus to those difficult conversations.

The deaths of Barbara and Don have not been talked about very much within

Liz and Chris's family. Tragically their parents, two lovely people whose lives ended horribly, did not feel able to talk about their intentions with their loved ones for fear of incriminating them. Chris was initially very reluctant to tell his side of the story. Even after all this time he is still worried about being prosecuted for the part he played in his mother's suicide. He eventually decided to talk about the events he had witnessed, as he feels strongly that the law on assistance with suicide should be changed.

Neil Love: 'Time to go while it's my choice'

Neil Love was born in Glasgow in 1942 to a warm and creative family. His grandfather was a music-hall comedian and musician, his mother had played the cello in her youth and his maternal aunt had been a violinist on ocean liners between the wars. Neil's father had suffered lung damage as a soldier in Italy and was never well, but he worked as a clerk and doted on his family.

Neil was an odd child, eager to join in with family involvement in amateur dramatics and musical activities but at other times withdrawn, going camping alone or simply curling up on his bed and shutting out the world. There were tantrums, too, and hair-raising solo adventures oblivious of his safety. 'He has an artistic temperament,' the doctor told his mother – or at least that's what she thought he said.

He was highly intelligent but admitted to Lizzie, his second wife, that he had not been academically inclined and had wasted his schooldays, something he partially remedied in later years. He was good with his hands and at technical drawing. On leaving school he took up an apprenticeship with Yarrow's shipyard on the Clyde. He married his first wife, Edda, at nineteen. A son and a daughter quickly followed; they were born close on the heels of Neil's youngest sister, his mother's 'surprise' baby who was a joy to all. Neil did well at Yarrow, but shipbuilding was in decline, and as soon as he finished his apprenticeship he was laid off and never worked in a shipyard again.

Jobs were scarce, and after some time spent working on Glasgow's trolley-buses he moved south and joined the Metropolitan Police. With a regular income and police married quarters he had a measure of security at last, so Edda and the children joined him.

In 1974 Lizzie, the woman who would become Neil's second wife, arrived in

London from north-west Scotland where she and her husband had combined a folk-singing career with running a hostel for climbers and backpackers in Glen Torridon. When the lease expired they parted, and, with the business closed and their musical career at an end, Lizzie took a fortnight's break to stay with a friend in London . . . and remained for eighteen years.

Working first for MENCAP and later for a regional health authority Lizzie became a neighbour of the Love family in Earl's Court. She rarely saw Neil, but she got to know Edda and the children as well as their relatives who visited from Scotland.

Neil and Edda were married for seventeen years. Early in 1979, realizing she had not seen Edda for some time, Lizzie dropped a note through the door asking if she was ill and could she be of any help. Neil called by and explained that Edda had left. The kids were with him, he said, and he was coping fine . . . but he wasn't.

It was some weeks before Lizzie saw Neil again. When she did it was obvious that all was not well. Depression and self-neglect meant he had lost a lot of weight, and soon after he spent some weeks in the Metropolitan Police's convalescent facility at Hove while Lizzie kept a neighbourly eye on the two teenagers.

Neil returned to work in Scotland Yard's information room late in 1979. Lizzie relates what happened next. 'One evening, coming off the late shift, he announced that he had put in for a police flat in Richmond. "I need to move the kids out of the city," he said. "Do you fancy coming with us?" I was a bit askance. Our connection had scarcely become a grand passion, hardly possible in a house with two teenagers and a possessive dachshund! "Edda and I will get divorced eventually," he added, "and I've been paying into the widow's pension fund all these years. If I die without a wife nobody gets the money. So come with us, and if we're OK in a couple of years maybe you'd marry me." Not the world's most romantic proposal but typical of his pragmatic approach. So I gave up work and moved in, inheriting an entire family including a wonderful mother-in-law and three sisters.'

Neil and Lizzie moved to Richmond in 1980 and were married the following year. She developed sarcoidosis and was very ill for a time, and Neil nursed her with great devotion. They developed an interest in houseplants and spent hours bird-watching in Richmond and Bushey Parks. Neil was involved in the Iranian and Libyan Embassy sieges, among other major events, and his odd moods were put down to the stress of his job and the loss of his mother who died in 1983. In 1984 they moved again, to a police house with a 'real' garden in Hampton Hill. They grew organic vegetables in deep beds. Neil learnt to dig and trench and discovered the joys of compost. All seemed well.

In 1988 Neil's high-street optician, suspecting a problem, gave him a letter for his GP. Referral to an ophthalmologist and a brain scan followed. While they waited for a definitive diagnosis there were many frightening possibilities, some with a short life expectancy, and at one point Neil covered his face with his hands saying, 'Help me, Lizzie, help me!' But it was to be none of the things they feared most, and over the next fifteen years he never showed such anxiety again and faced his future with great stoicism.

What the scan – and further examinations – at the National Hospital for Neurology and Neurosurgery in Queen's Square, London, revealed was an epidermoid cyst in the centre of Neil's brain. 'It's the size of a golfball,' he told Lizzie cheerfully. 'I was wheeled into the lecture theatre and shown to the students. Fame at last!' The repercussions temporarily escaped them both, relieved as they were that it seemed to be nothing worse.

According to the website of the American Epidermoid Brain Tumor Community, an epidermoid cyst is a rare and benign tumour of the brain which consists of skin cells that create a sac filled with fatty acids and flaky keratin. It is a congenital condition that forms during the third to fifth week of foetal growth when normal developmental cells are trapped within the brain. It is slow growing, so patients often do not have many symptoms or a diagnosis until the second to fourth decade of life when the tumour becomes apparent owing to its size or location.

Many epidermoid cysts form outside the brain just inside the skull where they grow until they are big enough to cause headaches. In that position they are relatively easy to remove. But Neil's cyst was in the fourth ventricle, deep within the skull and impossible to access without great risk. It was deemed inoperable, and no one could predict his future level of disability or the order in which his symptoms would appear. 'I've got between five and twenty years,' said Neil, and he shrugged. 'Well, so have most people my age.'

The four ventricles form an intricate, fluid-filled cave-like system within the brain. Cerebrospinal fluid (CSF) constantly filters into them, flowing down from two lateral chambers to a third central one and on through the fourth to circulate around the spinal cord. From there the CSF returns around the outside of the brain, re-entering it through a sinus between the hemispheres at the top. CSF cushions the brain and spinal cord, delivers nutrients and carries away waste products. A free flow and stable internal pressure of CSF is essential to our well-being.

The fourth ventricle, the site of Neil's cyst, is the smallest. It is situated between the cerebellum (which fine-tunes movement) and the brainstem (where the roots of many functions lie). Immediately above the fourth ventricle the main cranial nerves spread out to serve most of the body, and it is one of the worst positions for a large cyst. Fortunately for Neil the cyst was soft enough at this stage for the CSF to flow freely round it, although there was pressure on the sixth cranial nerve which restricted lateral movement of one eye. This was what had alerted the optician and, at diagnosis, was his only symptom.

He was not expected to have fits or seizures, so, with prisms to correct his double vision, he continued to drive. He kept his job with the Metropolitan Police for several more years, long enough to qualify for a full pension. His retirement after thirty years' service was scheduled for 1996, but one day in 1991 his boss called Lizzie at home. 'Do you think he wants to go?' he asked. 'I'm not going to suggest it to him, but if you think he wants to go I can recommend him to the Medical Officer.' Lizzie agreed, and Neil's retirement was brought forward to 1992.

Police houses are tied accommodation, so Neil and Lizzie had to move. Neither of them wanted to stay in London, so they explored England and fell in love with Derbyshire's Peak District. They converted a quarter of Neil's pension to a lump sum and took out a small mortgage to buy a cottage in Taddington, a tiny village of about a hundred houses high on the moors. Lizzie can think of nowhere that could have given Neil such joy and support as he had there over the next eleven years.

The people of Taddington took Neil to their hearts right away, although they soon spotted that all was not well. One night leaving the pub with a neighbour Neil turned to speak and sat down suddenly in the road, the way a baby does when learning to walk.

Lizzie says, 'Our neighbour looked shocked, and the next lunchtime I was summoned to the pub. "What's up wi' Neil?" asked someone. "Drunks don't fall down like that, and he only had half a pint." I explained, and from that day on they couldn't do enough for us. I swear we owed Taddington our sanity.'

Nevertheless, Neil had difficulty adjusting not just to his condition but to no longer being a policeman. He would disappear for days on end, sleeping in the car by the Ladybower Dam or on the hillside above the village. He seemed unable to grasp that Lizzie found this alarming or that she was worried he might harm himself. He just needed space, he said, and Lizzie tried to understand. His older sister said that he had been like that as a lad. 'I used to wonder if he was a bit autistic,' she said, and for Lizzie the penny dropped!

In his teens Neil's mother had consulted their GP about his strange withdrawals. 'The doctor says he's a wee bit artistic and might need some extra schooling,' she reported before booking him in for classes at Glasgow School of Art. A doctor of that era, aware that autism could be mild, seems way ahead of his time, but what parent in the 1950s had heard the word 'autistic'? Even if they had, they would only have pictured unreachable children in institutions veering from panic to silence and back. Lizzie thought the same but phoned the National Autistic Society anyway. 'Have you heard of Asperger's syndrome?' someone there asked.

'I hadn't, so they sent me a book about it, and they were there for me over the coming years.' Slowly Neil's oddities fell into place: his refusal to eat because the meat was on the wrong side of the plate; a sandwich that had been moved and 'isn't mine any more'; an inability to read the menu in an Indian restaurant because there were too many sparkly things on the walls; the sudden bouts of shouting; and the need to withdraw from information overload and clear his head.

Asperger's syndrome (AS) presents uniquely with each individual according to his or her nature and circumstances. Individuals may demonstrate few or many from a whole raft of behaviours, but the commonest include an inability to empathize or pick up on cues such as facial expressions; social awkwardness or naïveté; a need for strict routines and rules, which leads to a tendency to adopt the behaviour of others (sometimes inappropriately); and anxiety when routines are interrupted or rules are unclear. People with AS are often highly intelligent, but they usually cannot anticipate the unexpected. They tend to adopt concentrated interests that dominate their conversations and exclude other activities. They withdraw in the face of sensory overload, and they are often stereotyped as geeks, loners, nutty academics, people with odd collections of things, lovable eccentrics – or just the quiet guy in the corner who never speaks. They are not mad or dangerous . . . just different.

There could be no definitive diagnosis of AS, but Lizzie was convinced. 'I radically adjusted my expectations. I learnt to stand back, to give Neil space, and it worked. He became calmer and able to enjoy our new life. For me it was frustrating and distressing at first. I had lost the Neil I thought I had and needed to reconnect with a different Neil altogether. I understood at last why he left all decisions to me. Financial transactions, house purchase, insurance and so on were beyond his ken, a confusion of regulations that overloaded his mind and closed it down.'

As a policeman Neil had known where he stood. He had known what clothes to wear and when to leave for work. There was a number on his shoulder saying who he was and numbered sheets for reporting each kind of incident. There was even a numbered sheet for things that didn't have their own sheet! Within this framework all hell could be let loose, but as long as the framework held he knew what to do.

'I realized I needed to give him structure but freedom within it. I did my best. I felt very alone at times, frustrated and afraid of getting it wrong, but my heart went out to him, and I felt deeply protective. It was love but of a different kind. Sometimes it felt quite fierce.'

While preparing for retirement Neil had qualified in holistic massage and kinesiology, intending to start a practice and gaining a detailed knowledge of anatomy. He loved the orderly connection of bone, muscle and nerve and, with typical pragmatism, began to treat his ailing body as a personal crime scene. He asked questions and learnt about the cyst. What was happening? Why? What might it do next? 'Once he understood,' Lizzie says, 'he was very cool about it.'

Neil was often effusively affectionate. 'He was five feet nine inches tall, and the little hollow under his collarbone was just where my head fitted when he hugged me. If he upset me he would throw his arms around me and say, "Oh, darlin', darlin', I'm a big ogre. Forgive me."' Lizzie laughs as she imitates his Glasgow accent.

In Taddington he was a popular figure, and although he never practised professionally his massage skills were welcome on sore backs and necks and eased many an ageing knee. He devised mixtures of essential oils and would talk for hours on the subject to anyone who would listen. Once a month he visited Alma, an elderly friend in London with whom he had studied, and they would spend a long weekend 'talking and eating a lot of ice cream', as he told Lizzie. While he was away Lizzie would clean the house, cook and freeze a month's meals and do all the things that Neil found so disorienting. Outside the house Neil was the life and soul of the party, but at home he needed peace to recharge his batteries.

Neil became ataxic soon after the move, beginning to lose voluntary coordination of his muscle movements. Although the planned hill walks never happened there was plenty to see from the car. He revelled in the hills and woods, the light through the trees, the valleys spread out beneath him, picnics on hilltops, birds, horses . . . and there were brass bands and male-voice choirs to listen to, harvest suppers and well dressings to attend as well as Buxton Opera House. He had a social life for the first time. Neil and Lizzie amassed a huge collection of CDs, which he found a solace, and they joined the village quiz team. They developed an interest in family history, and Neil enjoyed spending days in archives and libraries patiently trawling through the records. He cheerfully drove those without cars to appointments and supermarkets and was a willing helper at village events.

Neil's condition slowly deteriorated as new symptoms appeared. His left hand developed a tremor, and he could use it only with the fingers clamped together like a mitten. Sometimes that arm waved about vaguely when he tried to reach out. He staggered, too, and his legs would occasionally stop moving mid-stride while his body continued forward, crashing him to the ground. He took to using a stick. He developed a slight head tremor of which he was unaware – his dentist and his hairdresser agreed not to mention it.

As his health grew worse there were misunderstandings with medics. His GP believed the cyst should affect only Neil's eye and that his other symptoms were psychosomatic, so he referred him to the mental-health team.

Lizzie describes the consequences. 'It was a couple of years before we could disentangle ourselves from that. Eventually we asked for a change of key worker. Her first question was "Why do you let your wife speak for you?" "Pen!" demanded Neil waving a hand. He wrote, "I can find words to write but not to speak. Lizzie knows me and fills in the gaps." Light dawned, and the nurse said, "You should never have been sent to us. What do you really need?" I spoke for Neil, knowing his needs. "Cutlery he can use, a seat for the bath, help with speaking and physio-therapy."' Everything was in place within a week, and Neil was discharged from the mental health team's care.

Life in Taddington went on. In 2001 Lizzie became coordinator of the week-long well-dressing festival, a huge communal effort which, after months of preparation, occurs in August. Neil willingly involved himself and his car in activities outside, while she kept disruption at home to a minimum. Lizzie was again coordinator in 2002, but early in 2003 she felt the need to resign. 'Things were changing,' she says. 'I could see Neil would need me more, and I was worried that I might let him or the village down. I couldn't do just half a job for either of them.'

Neil, meanwhile, had progressed from a stick to an elbow crutch. He fell more often, sometimes knocking out his dental crowns. His smile had become lopsided, the wasting visible even beneath his beard. His tongue pulled to one side, and his speech was comprehensible only by those who knew him well. In June that year he paid his last visit to a shop, buying family greetings cards. From then on he stayed in the car while Lizzie shopped. Driving was his one remaining contri-bution, a vital one, as Lizzie never learnt. She wondered how he would cope if he had to stop driving.

Once seated in the car Neil's driving was unimpaired. The monthly visits to Alma in London continued, Lizzie loading him into the car at her end and Alma extracting him at the other. 'He insisted on showering without help, but he sometimes fell. He needed help with dressing, toenail-cutting and other more personal aspects of daily living. Mostly he made a joke of it, but having me cut his food up in public really hit a nerve. We often ate at the Eyre Arms in Hassop, and Nick, the landlord, watched us struggle the first time. We were both close to tears. After that Nick took to cutting Neil's food up before our meals were served. Bless him!'

'I'm for the knacker's yard,' he said in mid-2003, and 'I shan't see Christmas.' Lizzie thought his bleak outlook was premature, but she realized they were entering a new phase and that serious disability was around the corner. She quietly put her mind to aids and adaptations – a bed in the dining-room perhaps; a downstairs shower.

Afraid that speech might soon desert him, Neil asked his daughter and her partner to visit during the well dressing in late August 2003. He wanted to talk to her while he still could and give her a gift for her fortieth birthday in October. Lizzie says she could feel the tail end of summer in more than one sense.

As September commenced Neil announced that he would stop driving in a month's time. Lizzie's heart sank. It was the one thing he could still do for people, and he would not take such a decision lightly. A final visit to Alma was planned. The day before he left he fell in the bathroom, his ribs hitting the front of the lavatory bowl with some force. Lizzie was sure they were cracked or broken. 'But there was no way he wasn't going to Alma's.' He asked Lizzie to strap him up with a folded towel around his ribs, tied with dressing-gown cords, and he drove to London and back as usual.

By this time he was using a Zimmer frame. The reflexes on his left side began overreacting, throwing the arm up or jerking his leg violently to the right as he took a step. He advanced just a few inches at a time with Lizzie walking sideways with him, holding down the left side of the frame, and Neil worried about the strain on her knees.

More worrying was the change in his breathing and swallowing. 'It was obvious to me that something would go terribly wrong. His breathing had changed, the in-breath coming in three short bursts. The muscles were not working as they should. He had some problems swallowing and sometimes breathed food into his windpipe. It was a pea the first time I saw it. He coughed, and the pea shot across the room. He just laughed and said, "Oh, that's nothing. At Alma's it was a chocolate-coated brazil nut." "What! A whole one?" "Yeah! It shot out and stuck in the curtains." He was downright gleeful. I was horrified and frightened, but I couldn't let him know.'

Neil announced that his last driving day would be 9 October. 'We'll do a big shop,' he said, 'then send the car back to Motability.' He told Lizzie that she could sign up for grocery shopping online and that they could use his mobility allowance for taxis, even having a day out now and again. Lizzie said OK.

They spent that day shopping in Buxton, Neil waiting in the car as usual. They stuffed themselves with hot sausages from Lomas's, and the girls from the shop came out to hug Neil as they always did. At the supermarket Lizzie loaded the boot, and they spoke cheerfully to some friends who were about to go on holiday. Neil was very laid back and jolly, and Lizzie was relieved that he was so positive on his last driving day.

Back at home Neil said, 'Now I can tell you why I've stopped driving. I'm getting fizzing sensations in my head . . . and it hurts when I turn my neck.' While Neil was very matter-of-fact Lizzie says that her own feelings defied description.

They only wanted a light supper, and Neil suggested sharing a big prawn omelette from a single plate. He went to bed shortly afterwards, asking Lizzie to bring him a mug of milk. Unknown to her, when she took up her husband's drink she would see him alive for the last time.

Because of his need for quietness and space Neil had his own bedroom. The arrangement was that if Neil's door was open in the morning Lizzie was to wake him. If it was merely ajar he was to be left until breakfast was ready. On the morning of 10 October 2003 the door was ajar, so Lizzie boiled the kettle and put out their cereal. Then she went to wake Neil.

'I pushed the door open, and he was lying there in this weird position. He'd half fallen out of bed. His face was on the floor, his legs were still in the bed and one arm was under him. His left arm lay beside him. It wasn't trembling. It was the first time I'd seen it still in years. My first thought was: Why is his hair so shiny? It was the sun reflecting off the plastic bag he had put over his head.

'On television when someone sees a body they scream. Well, I didn't, but maybe that's just me. In an emergency the first thing I think is: What can I do? Is there something I can do? I felt for a pulse. There was none. His arms were mottled and his face purple. I knew not to touch anything else. I walked back to my room and sat on the bed. I thought: If I sit here very quietly like a good girl for five minutes I can walk back in there and it won't have happened. That was my first reaction. But after a couple of minutes I thought: No, there are things I must do.

Neil had explained the procedure long ago in case he should die in his sleep. Don't call a doctor; don't touch anything; call the police. But I didn't call the police first, I rang our friend John Slyfield, who was vicar of Edensor, and he said he and his wife would come at once.

'John said later that he'd had a gut feeling that Neil was near the end when he'd visited a few days earlier. He said, "Neil stood up to shake hands with me as we were leaving, which he didn't do as a rule. He looked me in the eye, and I had a feeling he was saying goodbye."'

Beside the bed was an envelope with a brief note. 'I love you darling. Time to go while it's my choice. Thank you, Taddington. Look after my Lizzie. Love, Neil.' There were two kisses and a PS: 'See disc.'

As the Slyfields drove over Lizzie phoned the police. Eventually there were eleven people in her tiny house.

'There were scenes of crime officers, paramedics, a detective inspector, a pathologist, regular constables, the Rev. and Mrs Slyfield and me. There were boots up and down the stairs all morning. I knew from Neil's police experience that this wasn't exceptional, that all this activity was standard procedure. Eventually they said they'd finished and I could go up. They'd laid him on the floor with the duvet up to his chin. His face was like ice, but his tummy was still warm. I laid my cheek on it and wept. It was standing room only at the bottom of the stairs, but I didn't give a damn who heard me. I didn't weep for long. People had jobs to do. I snipped a lock of his hair, kissed him goodbye and stood back while they took him away.'

The day after Neil died Lizzie was questioned at home. With the phone constantly ringing the interview took many hours. The police were in no doubt that he had taken his own life, but they had to be sure that Lizzie had not helped him nor known that he intended to commit suicide (the criteria for 'aiding or abetting'). It was five or six weeks before the attending detective inspector returned to tell her she was in the clear. 'I didn't see myself as some kind of suspect,' she says, 'but I suppose I was.'

It is very difficult to kill oneself through asphyxiation alone because the body's natural reaction is to remove any obstruction to one's breathing, so a question arose as to whether Neil had taken any drugs.

'There were pill packets, and the toxicology report showed that he'd taken at least two, perhaps three, types of painkiller. The police told me that as an ex-policeman Neil would have known exactly what to do to effect his suicide. He took the painkillers to make himself numb and woozy. He would have known when to put the bag over his head, at a point when he was unlikely to remove it. He knew not to eat much prior to taking the overdose. He would have understood the value of having milk in his stomach and taken into account the average speed of the digestive process so that he could predict the time of his death. I was grateful to have been given that information. His death probably occurred at about six in the morning. He knew my alarm went off soon after that, and he was still warm when I found him just after seven. He would not have wanted me to find him cold and stiff.'

It is obvious how much planning went into Neil's suicide, and the degree of consideration he showed Lizzie confirms that the tragic stories recounted in this book are, at heart, ones of love and compassion. Lizzie is quite clear about why her husband of twenty-two years ended his life when he did: the document on his computer disk made it plain.

'He wrote that he was worried about losing control of his life; of someone taking it out of his hands. He was afraid that stress might make me ill or that my knees would be damaged as I helped him walk. I had tried not to make him feel responsible, but he worried just the same. He had a great fear of being taken to hospital in an emergency and being kept alive against his will. It was the thing he most wanted to avoid. He must have spent hours jabbing away with one finger to write that explanation. His limited speech made you forget his facility with the written word, and it comes as a surprise to many people.'

A police pathologist's brief is merely to ascertain cause of death, but the surgeon who performed Neil's post-mortem rang Lizzie later. 'I had a little look,' he told her. 'I thought you might like to know that the cyst had become quite dense and expanded in a way that pressed his cerebellum down and to the side. He would probably have lived only a few more months.' The pathologist wondered if Neil had worked that out for himself.

Lizzie knew that those months would have been gruelling and distressing for Neil, involving terrible muscle spasms and pain. Eventually his brain would have prolapsed under the edge of his skull, killing him instantly, but the suffering involved in reaching that point would have been terrible to endure and to witness.

The due process of the law required input from many people, not only on the day Neil died but for a long time afterwards. The coroner's officer questioned Lizzie at length but with great sensitivity. The plastic bag was checked for fingerprints. Then there was the post-mortem. Tests were done and reports written and eventually, in March 2004, there was a brief but painful inquest at which the coroner said something like 'Having an incurable illness and not wishing to cause his family further distress, Neil Love took his own life.' None of this comes cheap in terms of public money and precious time, and most of it would have been unnecessary if Neil had been able to talk to his doctor about having an assisted death. He would then have been able to make his wishes known and die in peace and dignity with his family at his side.

The practicalities are awkward, but it is the emotional effects that ripple on, spreading beyond those most closely involved. Taddington is a tiny village, mostly on a single street slanting across a hillside. Two ambulances and four police cars blocking the road did not go unnoticed, especially at that time of the morning, as people were leaving for work.

Says Lizzie, 'I was outside avoiding the crowd indoors when the first neighbour pulled up. "Is it Mrs Davies? Is she OK?" It was hard to find words. "No, Rita. It's Neil. He's dead. He did it himself." I could say nothing else. Cars were queuing behind her, and Rita had to move. I'm told people gathered in a lay-by just beyond the village, sharing their shock and gathering their wits. Many of them remember that morning whenever they pass the spot. My opposite neighbour heard when she arrived for work at Bakewell Police Station. After immediately signing herself off duty she came to the cottage, took over the tea-making and made me sit down.'

People from small villages often work in the wider community, and, later that morning and twenty miles away in the police call centre in Chesterfield, Lizzie's neighbour Jean was at her workstation when information relating to Neil's death floated up on the screen in front of her. She froze and had to be helped from her chair. Jean's policeman husband Phil served at Bakewell and had trained as a family liaison officer. His help and friendship in the coming months kept Lizzie from despair.

'When Phil brought Jean to see me she was still in shock. We stood speechless with our arms around each other. I nearly cracked at that point, but it wouldn't have helped either of us. Somehow I managed to call Neil's family. Those were the hardest moments. Meanwhile neighbours came and went for days, making me eat, lending extra coffee mugs and vases, tactfully melting away in the presence of vicars, undertakers and police but making sure I was never alone unless I wanted to be. I can never thank them enough.'

In Taddington the consensus was that Neil had done a very brave thing – the turn-out for his funeral showed that. A couple living opposite the church reported that the street, both up and down the hill, filled with knots of people on foot converging on St Michael's, much as folk had done for a thousand years or more. There were over two hundred people at the service. Neil's dentist and hairdresser came . . . as well as girls from Bakewell Post Office, Lomas's the butcher and Safeway in Buxton. Many of the congregation stood. Derbyshire Constabulary sent an officer in dress uniform who saluted at the church gate, and Lizzie and Neil's neighbours clubbed together for a piper. The Reverends John and Mary Goldsmith conducted the funeral jointly with great tenderness. The sun shone.

Lizzie's first wedding anniversary without Neil was 2 November 2003, and two days later a woman from the Department of Work and Pensions came to collect his pension book. It had lain in its drawer since the day before he died after that last shopping expedition. On top of it was an envelope that Neil had somehow put in the drawer on that last evening. It was marked 'For Lizzie Nov 2' and inside was an anniversary card. Neil had written, 'With you in spirit'. His last visit to a shop was back in June, and Lizzie feels sure he bought the card then and that he had already made his decision to die.

'I've still got it. I put it out every November for a couple of days. It was one of several loving booby-traps Neil laid for me. Most telling were two marked quotes in Tolkien's *Lord of the Rings*. Neil loved being read to, and he had me read that book to him every couple of years. I noticed the bookmark had been moved to the Appendices to the tale of Arwen and Aragorn. Aragorn's line of kings has the option of dying at will before old age assails them, and Arwen is distressed when he tells her it is time. There was a shaky pencil line in the margin marking two passages. "Take counsel with yourself, beloved, and ask whether you would indeed have me wait until I wither and fall from my high seat unmanned and witless" and, further down the page, "I speak no comfort to you, for there is no comfort for such pain within the circles of the world." I think Neil meant my pain, the pain of my grief.'

Not long before he died Neil worked out that he had Asperger's syndrome. He told Lizzie, and she confessed that she had suspected for years and been in touch with the National Autistic Society. 'Who's a clever girl, then?' he said and hugged her. He asked that the proceeds of the memorial concert he wanted to be held be divided between the church and the National Autistic Society. 'I want you to sing . . . and I want the children to play.'

The concert was held a year after Neil's death. Several of Taddington's fine young musicians played solos – a sixteen-year-old French-horn player, her thirteen-year-old sister, who played viola, and a fifteen-year-old trombonist who played both Bach and jazz. Older professional and amateur performers contributed, and Lizzie sang 'Hello, Young Lovers' from *The King and I*. It was a wild wet night, but people came from miles around, and they raised almost £400.

'A neighbour once told me about seeing Neil fall on the ice three times in succession but just get up and carry on. "That man knows no fear," she said. Neil's cremated ashes are interred in Taddington churchyard, close to the spot where the tea tent is pitched at well-dressing time and next to Annie Needham whose cakes and pies were one of his joys. On his gravestone it says, "He knew no fear."'

Fearless as Neil was in all else, his one great anxiety was that he might be kept alive against his will, his family forced to endure his suffering and with public resources expended to no avail. How different the end of his life would have been had the law allowed him to seek medical help to die.

4

A FAITH VIEW OF ASSISTED DYING

by Reverend John Cartwright

God, by definition, is likely to be good. Being good, God almost certainly dislikes unnecessary suffering. This is not a chapter about theodicy, the theology of how a god of perfection can allow suffering at all. It is about consistency. Elsewhere in this book many views are expressed, and many stories are told about personal experiences of end-of-life matters. I am going to conduct a thought experiment looking for consistency.

While not true of all human suffering, there are some situations wherein the suffering involved is a matter of our choosing. I have to say that, for myself, I am content that a perfect God must allow suffering in order to also respect choice.

The subject of assisted dying is beset with strongly held views and poorly reasoned arguments. Let us use this thought experiment to look at one particular situation and see what can be observed clearly.

A hypothetical 'I' is dying slowly enough to realize that there will be a wait for death. That 'I' is being treated for the pain arising from a disease that will kill 'me' but not very soon.

In reality we find that some patients *are* in the sort of situation described above. They sometimes die sooner than their disease would kill them from the unwanted side-effects of attempts to control their pain. This is the doctrine of double effect. An example of its use in practice would be a patient with untreatable cancer who is supplied with diamorphine.[1] Diamorphine is among the most effective painkillers in the repertoire of modern medicine, but it is also lethal. This patient may be in more pain than is treatable with a low dose of diamorphine, and in order to manage the pain the patient is, over time, given diamorphine in lethal quantities with the primary intention of relieving pain.

Wikipedia defines the doctrine of double effect as a set of ethical criteria that Christians and some others use for evaluating the permissibility of acting when one's otherwise legitimate act (for example, relieving a terminally ill patient's pain) may also cause an effect one would normally be obliged to avoid (in this instance sedation and a slightly shortened life). Double effect originates in Thomas Aquinas's treatment of homicidal self-defence in his work *Summa Theologiae*.[2]

In 1999 Dr David Moor, a British doctor, was tried for the murder of a terminally ill patient (see Chapter 2). He administered what turned out to be a lethal dose of diamorphine to a victim of bowel cancer, and the patient, who was eighty-five years old, died. He had been discharged from hospital into the care of his family, supported by a team that included his GP Dr Moor. When the patient's condition deteriorated and he was screaming with pain his daughter called their family doctor. Dr Moor gave him a lethal dose of diamorphine, although he intended only the attenuation of pain.

The case would not have been tried except that Dr Moor spoke openly to the press about his end-of-life care experience. Dr Moor said that he had been involved in such cases on average ten times a year for his entire thirty-year career. He was found not guilty of murder.

This case established the doctrine of double effect as legally acceptable in England and Wales. Healthcare professionals will give different answers when asked whether they are aware of the doctrine of double effect being used in practice. However, enough respondents say unequivocally that it *is* used that way for us to be confident that people die from lethal doses of analgesics quite often and that the intention was not their deaths but the alleviation of their suffering.

I argue that this is sufficient to allow us to use the doctrine of double effect as the basis for establishing a relevantly similar practice available to some patients who can decide for themselves when the lethal event should occur. Before I do that I want to return to the question of God's approbation.

Would God approve of Dr Moor's actions in administering a lethal dose of analgesic to a terminally ill cancer patient in great pain? I suggest that of course God would approve. You may not accept that approval as a defining characteristic of God and thus perhaps superfluous. So I will argue the point as follows.

My conclusion is that God approves of helping people to die when the person being helped is near to death, is in great distress and their death is the unavoidable consequence of trying to alleviate pain. I say this because, in any religion with a concept of God, God is not – by definition – malicious, and it would be malicious to *withhold* pain relief. The patient's death is inevitable and it will happen soon.

Despite the claim that God sometimes uses suffering for some beneficial reason, under the particular conditions of imminent painful death there can be no beneficial outcome. Indeed, as an aside I would find it surprising if any religious person relied upon a God concept that included such torture. So God approves of the doctrine of double effect.

It is important to note that there have been no complaints about the doctrine of double effect from any religious body, even those normally outspoken on issues dubbed 'pro-life'.

It seems to me to be quite clear that people of faith are in accord with the legal guidance on the matter of the doctrine of double effect. They accept that unintended deaths will occur while trying to alleviate intolerable suffering in those who are terminally ill. It is important to grasp that point because the principles established thereby will help us in deciding the morality of assisted dying, which I shall return to shortly.

Let us consider the conclusion stated above and the legal position it reflects. Note that the patient's wishes are not taken into consideration at this stage.

It might be reasonable to suppose that a patient's wishes are evident when the person is screaming from pain, but their screaming is likely to have ceased by the time the analgesic becomes lethal. By then it will already have at least dulled the pain. My point does not concern the morality or practicalities of obtaining informed consent. The point that needs to be considered here is this: if the patient was able to give informed consent his or her involvement would increase the moral weight of the doctrine of double effect.

You may not concur. So the next move is to consider that possibility.

There is an alternative to it being morally persuasive that a patient consents to treatment, but it is at least odd and at worst paternalistic. If the claim is made that, in the conditions described above relating to helping a terminally ill patient die, it is better that the person is helped to die *without* their consent, then some very specific conditions must be applied to prevent this looking like a slippery slope to non-consensual treatment in other areas. For example, it might be possible covertly to sterilize people with congenital disorders without their consent and 'for their own good' on a similar basis. To prevent such a slippery slope it would be necessary to say that it is justifiable to *kill* a patient without consent but not to *treat* that individual without his or her consent. The fact that this situation does not occur should be noted.

That is of course exactly the 'slippery slope' outcome that opponents of assisted dying use as an appeal to fear without any clear justification for so doing.

My thought experiment has some very simple components. I am not suggesting that healthcare professionals routinely kill patients against their will. All I want to consider is the hypothesis that if informed consent were available to physicians administering potentially life-ending levels of diamorphine would that not add to the moral and legal justification for death being an unintended outcome of pain relief in some cases? I believe I demonstrated above that the answer must be 'yes', as the alternative is unconscionable.

Let us summarize what we have established so far:

1. The doctrine of double effect is fully justifiable when lethal doses of painkiller are administered to people who are dying and in unbearable pain.
2. Patients are not always consulted before such courses of action are initiated: there is no need to ask patients whether they want to be released from avoidable suffering, even if the treatment might bring about their demise more quickly than if they were simply left with their disease.
3. It seems quite likely that a benevolent God would approve of this sort of treatment.

I am a Christian, and my understanding of God is inevitably conditioned by that. I have formally studied some of the world's religions, and I see no reason to believe that anyone's view of divine intervention assumes asymmetry. What I mean is this: no one seriously believes that his or her God disapproves of all medical interventions. Even those who do believe that such intervention should be limited also accept that God would approve of such things as first aid, dentistry and midwifery. People of faith are generally content to accept that God is also quite keen on advanced medical interventions, such as organ transplantation, to extend life expectancy.

What seems very odd is that such an advanced intervention to prolong life is considered to be consistent with the will of God while any suggestion that life could be curtailed is be said to be a violation of the sanctity of life and thus *against* the will of God.

Let us return to the single issue we are evaluating here, the unintended death that happens when the doctrine of double effect is applied. Many patients who present with serious diseases are treated in such a way as to extend their lives beyond the expectations of similar patients who are not treated. An intervention has prolonged their life, but that intervention, even when successful, will often not cure the condition. For example, forms of aggressive cancers can be attenuated so that a longer life is available, but the disease will, eventually, kill the patient.

The doctrine of double effect works because of that. Treatment extends life, which is said to be good, but the disease is not eradicated and eventually overwhelms the treatment. Suffering ensues, and the patient dies painfully. No good can be gained from the pain that would arise from extended treatment, and without the medical interventions already provided the patient would probably be dead by this stage anyway. So it is quite acceptable to administer increasing doses of analgesic to deal with suffering knowing that the treatment could well be fatal.

No reasonable version of any sort of god could want a patient to be kept alive, shortly to die, without pain relief in those circumstances. So your God and mine must approve of the death that occurs as a consequence of the doctrine of double effect.

Now let us consider the ethical problem of choice. In the matter of unintended death resulting from therapy the patient is not asked whether that person chooses to have his or her life put at risk by treatment aimed at mitigating suffering.

It seems to me that there are only two reasons for this lack of consultation. The first is that it is self-evident that a patient would choose to die rather than to persist in great pain when death is inevitable and imminent. The second is that it is immoral to ask someone to consent to his or her own death. Any other explanation of which I am aware is simply a variation of one of these two. For example, 'We can't consult the patient because it might upset them' implies self-evidence, and 'No one should be asked to agree to being put at great risk' implies a moral claim.

For me this is the crux of the search for consistency, which was my goal. The first reason, 'It is self-evident that a patient would choose to die rather than to persist in great pain', straightforwardly supports a conclusion that someone who is terminally ill and who is suffering intolerably ought to be allowed to choose to die rather than to persist in his or her suffering *unless* the second reason is also valid.

So we have established that neither God nor man has any reason to oppose the doctrine of double effect. In practice the doctrine does not consider the choice a patient might make. That could be because it is plain that the patient would definitely choose death over suffering, or it might be because it is morally wrong to ask someone to agree to stop living rather than to suffer when there is no hope of recovery.

Consistency requires that assisted dying must be justifiable if it is self-evident that a patient would choose to die rather than to suffer without hope of recovery.

The significant difference between two patients who are suffering, one of whom has a long time to wait and another who is close to dying, is that of informed choice being available.

Thus if we are to oppose assisted dying the basis for doing so would be that it is wrong for a patient who is terminally ill to be involved in the medical decision that shortens his or her life so as to avoid suffering. Let us examine that idea in more detail.

The doctrine of double effect seems to rely on the principle that a patient does not need to be advised that treatment designed to mitigate suffering is also likely to be fatally toxic. In the search for consistency we are trying to find out whether the principles established in the relevantly similar situation of the doctrine of double effect can be used to support a case for it being morally right to facilitate assisted dying. I have involved God so that the idea of moral good can be scrutinized, and I will return to God's likely views later. It seems, however, that helping people to die when they are terminally ill and in pain is both morally and legally justifiable. That principle could be utilized to justify assisted dying except that, in that situation, the patient must definitively be both informed of and involved in the process.

The question to be addressed is this: does being *unaware* of the fatal effect of treatment make that treatment morally acceptable in a way that being *aware* of its dangers would not? To put it differently, if a patient with a painful life-ending condition knows that the pain alleviation they need is going to kill them should the treatment be withheld? And, since this is the crux of the matter, I shall illustrate the question by exemplification.

If I were to contract untreatable cancer I would know that the mutation would probably kill me and that the disease would likely be very painful. I would ask for pain relief to be available to minimize the pain, and, in the late stages of the disease, I would ask for a syringe driver or pump to be set up so that I was in control of providing whatever dose I needed to make the pain bearable. If, knowing about the doctrine of double effect, I chose to self-administer a fatal dose (thereby making an informed choice to die) should I be denied a treatment that is widely available to the uninformed? Of course not.

There may be an argument for not making the probability of dying known to someone who does not understand how diamorphine works. Grounds for withholding that information – such as not increasing the patient's distress, their incapacity to comprehend and so on – are all important, but their discussion would be a digression here.

No reasonable person would prevent me from receiving pain relief, in the circumstances described, simply because I understand that I am making a choice that will result in my death.

Before looking at how God might feel about all of this, let us see how this might look if applied to assisted dying. I will return to my hypothetical medical condition, but will vary it just enough so that I am not going to die in the short term.

Imagine that I have a slow-developing but none the less untreatable and painful fatal disease. I put my affairs in order, make my peace with my family and God and decide that I want to shorten the time until my inevitable demise. Why may I not simply ask for medical help to die?

The sole difference between these two scenarios is that, in this variation of my thought experiment, I do not want to prolong my discomfort. If the disease were fast-acting I could expect to die quite soon (but it is not). I know that I'm going to suffer and die *quite* soon but not *very* soon. Can it be anything short of cruel to make me stay alive in those circumstances?

I have written this exemplification in the first person for a reason that is not morbid. This is a thought experiment designed to focus on the problem without digression. In these specific circumstances, given that the doctrine of double effect is already accepted, it would be hard to defend an insistence that a hypothetical 'I' must be forced to suffer living for the sole reason that 'my' disease is slow to kill.

Typically opponents of assisted dying worry about a slide from a principle to remote and unwanted outcomes. For example, if it was legal for the hypothetical 'I' to ask a doctor to end 'my' life in the circumstances described, concerns would be expressed that coercion might be applied. Under that malign influence other terminally ill people might feel compelled to ask for assisted death *against* their will. For example, given the limited resources available to the NHS, patients with no realistic chance of a successful outcome might be subjected to pressure to ask for an early death simply to release scarce facilities.

This is a good example of the wrong thinking that accompanies arguments based on slippery slopes. It might be reasonable to think that caring doctors would be tempted to encourage patients to give up their fight for life earlier than they might want to for the possibly laudable motive of allowing scarce resources to be better utilized. For example, it might be said that some people are not receiving proper treatment for conditions that could lead to long-term recovery while others with no hope of recovery are absorbing resources. Why not encourage the latter to ask for an assisted death? The slope then becomes a toboggan run. Doctors would be involved in involuntary euthanasia. Those malign doctors would use a similar justification to please mean-minded administrators and 'put down' patients who are unable to earn a living or children with disabilities.

These concerns are well aired, widely reported and also quite wrong. Slippery slopes like this rely upon an unreasonable appeal to fear. If resources could be saved this way surely the doctrine of double effect would already be being used to justify it?

As there is no need to ask patients for consent to treatment that falls under the doctrine of double effect, beds could be vacated at any time by medics killing the most ailing on the grounds of the unintended consequences of adequate pain relief. I can find no evidence at all that this has ever occurred in the UK.

To restate the case, scrutiny of the proper care of terminally ill patients reveals that some die as a result of their medication because, in the effort to control pain, the drug used is lethal. Patients are not always told this: their consent to be treated for their disease is deemed to be enough to permit the administration of drugs that have no therapeutic effect against the disease itself. These drugs are used to deal with the pain alone, and no consent needs to be elicited from patients about the use of increasing doses of powerful painkilling drugs that are likely to result in their death.

Two points arise from this. First, there is no claim that a slippery slope has arisen from the doctrine of double effect. If scarce resources were to be saved, as in the example above, then an early death could easily be facilitated once strong analgesics are in use. I have talked about this with practitioners and have been given the impression that the contrary is the case: I have been told that scrupulous care is taken to minimize the use of drugs such as diamorphine. It is possible that this is the result of concerns about negligence, or it might be that there is an ideological view that life should be preserved. The fact that we cannot work out why this is the case from the limited and hearsay evidence available to us does not detract from the point that end-of-life management sometimes brings about death. The doctrine of double effect has not led to claims that unwanted outcomes are already happening, and there is no evidence of a slippery slope.

Second, patients who are subject to the doctrine of double effect are not, at present, involved in choosing a potentially life-ending course of action. A slippery slope to unwanted outcomes is more likely when the sufferer is unaware of their probably early demise because they cannot express a strong objection.

The moral difference between the application of the doctrine of double effect and assisted dying is that of the patient's informed choice, which becomes visibly more important now. Let us return to my thought experiment to see why this is so.

'I' have been diagnosed with a painful and terminal disease. It will not kill me for some time. I want to end my life sooner than would be the case if the disease and the pain relief were managed so as to maximize my life. My choice to die sooner rather than later has to be convincing.

To avoid unnecessary complexity I will not digress into a discussion of who it is that needs to be convinced. It is enough to draw your attention to the point that in cases of assisted dying the patient must be convincing before the means of dying can be made available to them. The actual mechanism might involve two practitioners, as with abortion. For our purpose it is not important to say exactly who has to be persuaded, but it is vital to state that persuasion is necessary.

If practitioners are expected to demonstrate that the patient understands that the assistance they want will bring about their death, and that the patient's reason for wanting to die is to avoid protracted and intolerable suffering, the matter becomes one of medical competence. Diligence in medical practice avoids any realistic possibility of there being a slippery slope. All that is needed is that a patient is seen to have been properly informed.

Opponents of assisted dying often appeal to a fear of coercion, saying that it produces a slippery slope. If patients were being coerced to ask for an early death that would become obvious by virtue of having a properly drafted process. For example, in order to obtain the means of dying under the supervision of a medical doctor a patient might have to convince not only the doctor involved but a third party recognized by legislation as being relevantly competent. This might be the family's lawyer or priest or it might be an independent counsellor. It is not difficult to see how society could use an appeal to the legal process to provide protection from sinister or malevolent practices. It is certainly not necessary to abandon the desire for proper choices to be available at the end of one's life because of an emotional claim such as 'Hospital administrators will save money by killing off vulnerable patients.' On the contrary, a properly formulated process whereby a patient is able to coherently argue for control over the final part of his or her life (which is about to be truncated anyway) can only enhance the end-of-life experience of that patient. An improvement in the experience of patients who want to manage the end of their life is important.

This issue, which is already metaphorically awash with equivocation, is especially prone to confusion. I will list some of the more common ones before explaining what I propose doing to avoid them.

Whose god? People of faith can always resist reason by identifying characteristics of their own view of God that specifically support a belief or opinion they held *prior* to encountering the argument. For example, 'God is supreme, and it is for God to decide when life is over.' That approach falls quite easily to the search for consistency: in the example I give such a God would disapprove of efforts to *prolong* life on the same basis.

God uses suffering. While it is true that many people of faith – and indeed the founders of faiths – have suffered in the process of living their faith, that does not amount to proof that God used that suffering. It simply states that many have suffered for their beliefs. People in terminal illness are not in that condition *because* of their beliefs; they are simply very ill. While I can see that people of faith often suffer because of their beliefs, such as Jews during the Third Reich, that is not relevantly similar to it being wrong to bring about the end of the life of someone who is suffering from a disease. I can also see that God might be pleased that someone of faith chose to continue in their faith rather than renounce it just to avoid suffering. What I really cannot comprehend is a conception of the divine that includes a requirement that people be kept alive, against their will, in hopeless suffering and pain. That seems to me to be a wholly wrong understanding, and it looks as though some religious humans have invented an evil being that requires some humans to torture others.

The gods of the various religions have different requirements. While it is the case that the followers of the various religions have different rules and perceptions to those of other interpretations, it might be possible to say that all of the main religions have a god-view that includes ultimate good. It seems to me that this is plainly the case for all three religions of 'the book', Christianity, Islam and Judaism, and Buddhists, Hindus and Sikhs also follow teachings that lead them to a version of the divine that is good.

In fact, it seems foolish to want to worship an entity that is anything but good. So, to avoid a sustained narrative of comparative religions, God is by definition good. Let us see if that statement can be of any use in our investigation into the possibility that God approves of assisted dying.

Philosophers and theologians have disagreed with each other for thousands of years and in millions of words about what counts as good. That is not the pertinent point for my purpose here. My question is: *Can a god who is good also approve of my desire to die under some very specific circumstances?*

To clarify this point my thought experiment asks whether any reasonable understanding of divine goodness would be offended by my hypothetical position.

In an enhancement of my experiment I am hypothesizing that 'I' have been diagnosed with a fatal disease and that there is no possible cure for my disease. It will be increasingly debilitating but will not kill me very soon. I have months of pain and indignity to endure before I can expect to die. I make my peace with God and those about me and decide to choose to end my life earlier than the disease and its treatment allow. Does my choice conflict with the goodness of God? To put it another way, what good can possibly be achieved by making my intolerable life continue?

Let us consider some possible responses:

1. My family – and anyone else who cares about me – might be upset if I chose to die rather than wait to die.
2. My decision is cowardly. I should grin and bear it as an example of my faith to others.
3. If I trust God, there may yet be a miraculous cure.
4. Suicide is a mortal sin.

I am quite sure there are other similar responses, but I will deal with these because a general point emerges.

1. If my family and those close to me thought my dying was premature, this would perhaps be the most telling point. Of course it is inconsistent with the notion of a loving God that we go out of our way to upset those close to us. However, if my wish to die were *actually* premature, then, assuming that we have a well-crafted and visible procedure for dealing with assisted dying, my request would not be granted. I anticipate that people close to me would, knowing my views, be considerably more upset by my being made to suffer against my will than by my demise.
2. I do not enjoy pain. A religious view that says I should grin and bear it worries me. If it is cowardly, from God's perception, to avoid pain there is another asymmetry involved. For example, it would also be cowardly to have an infected tooth removed. That is simply not credible, and it requires a peculiar view of God.
3. Spontaneous remission of tumours does happen, as does recovery from deep coma. Part of my faith – and I suppose that other people who believe in God share this – is that I will find myself in an afterlife. I can see this point about the slight possibility of a recovery against

the odds best from the point of view of a non-believer: if one is entirely materialistic and expects that there is no resurrection or rebirth or reincarnation, perhaps it might be worth suffering a few extra days of pain. Not for me, though. I know where I'm going. That is . . .

4. . . . Unless, of course, I am preventing my access to heaven by having offended God in my decision to ask for help to die. Although assisted dying is definitively different from suicide in a variety of ways – for example, one has to demonstrate one's well-balanced mental state – I will allow that some people might see assisted dying as a form of suicide. Two things would need to happen to allow that perception to prevent this thought experiment resulting in my death, and I reject them both. The first is that such a tortured definition of the term 'suicide' is so inaccurate as to encompass any death that is avoidable and envisaged. By that definition a great many icons of godliness would be included: Christ himself could have avoided being crucified, for example, and other religions have their martyrs. The second is that, although believing that suicide is morally wrong, I can find no justification for believing it to be any more especially or singularly abhorrent to God than, say, pride. Adding those points together, I do not expect to be barred from heaven.

What I set out to do in my thought experiment was to demonstrate that

1. there are circumstances wherein assisted dying can be seen as relevantly similar to the already accepted practices justified by the doctrine of double effect;
2. persons of faith need not reject either assisted dying or the doctrine of double effect on the grounds of their faith; *and*
3. in at least one set of hypothetical conditions not only is assisted dying acceptable to the godly but is positively recommended.

I expect that you will have knowledge or experience of some actual cases. People whose end-of-life experiences propel them to campaign for the legalization of assisted dying frequently make the point that it is not the case that they want to die now; rather, they say, the life that is left to them would be enhanced if they knew they could choose to die at their own volition. I do not think this point can be overemphasized.

Along with Dylan Thomas I intend to expend a great deal of effort raging against the dying of the light. I have not the slightest intention of 'giving up the ghost'. If I contract some unpleasant, fatal disease I propose to attempt to beat it. But what I want – and want very much – is to be able to decide for how long and under what circumstances I live with that illness.

Having watched several people, including members of my own family, die slowly and with increasing debilities (including incontinence) I can state quite plainly that I fear living badly more than I fear dying.

This chapter turns out to be a personal plea. Were I to find myself in the position of the hypothetical 'I' to whom I have alluded in my thought experiment, I would very definitely not want the additional anguish of being made to endure my condition beyond the limit of my own choice to die.

In my thought experiment 'I' am dying slowly and in increasing pain and indignity. I cannot be cured. The treatment consists of pain management and nursing support. My condition is going to kill me, but that will not happen for a significant period.

There are still many things that 'I' can – and am able to – do. My life remains worth living, for now. However, I am well aware that eventually I shall become, say, immobile, incontinent and generally unable to enjoy a life with any dignity, and dignity is important to me.

Because 'I' am currently unable to decide for myself the point at which my life ceases to be of value, on my terms and to me, I become fixated on that issue alone.

This realization takes away from 'me' the enjoyment that I would otherwise obtain from being able to do the many things still available to me. The point at which my life ceases to have value to me is thus brought forward. The remaining part of my life becomes tortuous, not because of my illness but because I am not allowed to manage my own end-of-life to suit me.

Being denied access to assisted dying therefore *removes* part of my life from me – the opposite of the outcome that opponents of assisted dying want to achieve.

I have not argued that assisted dying ought to be applicable in all pertinent end-of-life situations. My argument is not that assisted dying should be commonplace. My case is simply that society should not deny me the life-enhancing choice of managing my own death in the event that an incurable illness afflicts me. The law needs to change to reflect that choice so I can be assured that no repercussions will affect anyone involved in helping me to implement my decision.

I have argued that any understanding of God cannot include the notion that such a being would want to promote avoidable suffering. That argument provides people of faith with a justification for accepting the doctrine of double effect.

I have further argued that a patient would not offend God if they were to accept treatment with lethal unintended effects simply because they were aware of the probable side-effect.

The last variable to reflect upon is whether or not God is offended by my choosing an assisted death to curtail inevitable suffering prior to an equally inevitable demise.

It is *my* choice, hypothetical though it presently is. I am not trying to argue a general principle. I am arguing that under specific circumstances I, a Christian who wants to live well for as long as possible, should have the legal right to medical assistance when – and only when – I find that I am going to die of an incurable disease that will involve my suffering for a prolonged period.

I am going to die anyway. I am not being involuntarily euthanized. My nearest and dearest sympathize with my decision. I have tried very hard to beat the disease, but I have had enough and want – quite literally in my case – to go and meet my maker.

When I arrive at that meeting, will the maker be displeased by my action in choosing to die? I am quite sure that I shall be welcomed by a God whose characteristics are arranged around the concepts of love.

As the writer of Ecclesiastes put it, 'there is a time to be born and a time to die' (Eccl. 3:2). When it's time, it's time, and, in my thought experiment, the time I stand before God is my choice.

5
AIDING AND ABETTING SUICIDE
Nigel Goodman: 'I am suffering and I want to die'

In 1969, when Heather Pratten's first husband Ken Goodman's behaviour started to become what she calls 'a little bit bizarre', she had only the ordinary reasons to be concerned for her five young children. Ken would put cigarettes down and leave them burning or turn taps on and leave the sink to overflow. He worked as a mechanical engineer, and he lost job after job. Then one day he simply came home and announced, 'I'm not going to work any more.'

Their oldest child Stephen was fifteen, Nigel was eleven, Philip was eight, Tina was seven and Deborah was six. Whether or not all of the children were initially aware of the difficulties their parents were going through, they would be compelled to deal with the consequences once the cause of Ken's strange behaviour was discovered.

Heather says that if they had known what was wrong with Ken their lives would have been a lot better. The strain of not knowing why he was behaving so oddly led to tension and many arguments. For example, after collecting the unemployment benefit he was given to take care of his family Ken sometimes lost the cash on the way home. If it hadn't been for her father's financial and practical support Heather doesn't know how she and the children would have coped.

Eventually she told Ken that she couldn't stand his behaviour any longer and that either she would leave the family home or he had to. She says that at heart he was a kind and loving man who would not allow his children to be moved out of their home, and he told Heather, 'No, you stay here, and I'll move out.'

'Ken moved into a boarding-house. When he'd been there six weeks the owner rang me, saying, "There's something wrong with Ken. He hasn't paid me for four weeks. I've made an appointment for him to see a doctor." I was pleased to hear that because Ken had always refused to see a doctor when I suggested it. When I raised my concerns with our GP his response was, "If Ken won't come to see me, there's nothing wrong with him."'

The woman who owned the boarding-house suggested that Heather should go to see the doctor with Ken. She also told Heather that she had given Ken an ultimatum, saying, 'You do this, or you're on the streets.' When Heather explained to the doctor what had been happening the GP suggested that Ken should attend Goodmayes Hospital for a neurological assessment. Knowing he had no real choice Ken agreed.

Heather gained an insight into Ken's illness from an unexpected source: his best friend lived opposite Heather's mother, and he made the comment, 'Ken's got that same funny walk his dad had.' Heather asked Ken's older brother Harry about the cause of his father's death, and he told her that he had been in a psychiatric hospital after a nervous breakdown. Heather told the neurologist about this, and he sent off for Ken's father's medical records. When they arrived they revealed that two years before Heather met Ken his father had died of Huntington's chorea. The medical records showed that Ken's grandfather had died of the same illness some time earlier, and they ended with the words 'Family not to be told.'

Heather was left to face the uncomfortable fact that before she married Ken her future mother-in-law Ivy – who had been a friend of the family before marrying into it – had known that her father-in-had law died of the same dreadful disease which had later ended her husband's life. Despite knowing this Ivy gave strict instructions that nobody was to tell her children what it was that killed their father and grandfather.

Huntington's disease (HD) is a disorder of the central nervous system. It is caused by a faulty gene and is normally inherited, although the mutation that causes HD can occur spontaneously. It affects both men and women, men often later in life than women. The first symptoms usually appear in adulthood and can be very varied.

The Huntington's Disease Association website explains that the faulty gene affects the way the brain functions. As the disease progresses the affected person can change emotionally (they may become short-tempered and angry), physically (they may have jerky movements and their speech may be difficult to understand) and cognitively (they may find it hard to concentrate and remember things).

The association had recently been formed when Heather found out that her husband had the disease, and research into causes and cures was only just getting under way. Despite the scarcity of good information about HD Heather quickly realized that Ken's sister – who had a two-year-old son – also had the disease and that Harry, their older brother, did not. She also realized that her children might – or might not – have inherited the faulty gene.

Like many HD patients at the time Ken spent the last years of his life in a psychiatric hospital. Heather says that his sole aim was to live at home again, but she couldn't cope with his irrational behaviour and look after their children at the same time. She says that it was particularly bad in the early days when, after visits home, he would refuse to go back to the hospital. Sometimes she had to call the police to take him away because he could be very aggressive – one day he smashed every downstairs window in their home.

Heather says that HD makes people do really bizarre things and that sufferers don't understand the consequences of what they do. She defends Ken, saying that he wasn't really like the person he became, and she ascribes some of his behaviour to what she calls 'HD rages'. Ken once said to her, 'I'm so frustrated because I can't do anything and you can still do everything.' Sometimes, she says, he would just stand in the street and shout. Heather is very grateful to her next-door neighbour, who would come out to talk to Ken and calm him down. He always responded to her.

It was partly because of the upset Ken caused on his visits home that Heather asked for him to be moved. He was transferred to the hospital in Surrey that was caring for his sister. Heather remembers, sadly, that Ken's sister was in the next ward, but the siblings with HD in common never met unless Heather was there. Her father would take her and the children to visit Ken at least once a month. Much later the children told her that they had hated going to the hospital and didn't like seeing their father there.

Ken was only forty-four when he died of heart failure. Heather thinks he died early because he was given a lot of inappropriate treatment. She says he had electric shocks and other therapies he would never have been given if the doctors had known he had HD.

When Ken was diagnosed there was no test for HD or any other genetic disease. If one of your parents had HD you knew you stood a chance of developing it, but all you could do was wait for the symptoms to appear – or not. Heather thinks the length of time the illness lasts is the worst thing, saying that her sister had cancer and died in five years: most HD patients live between fifteen and twenty years after diagnosis. Heather understands that the younger you are diagnosed with HD the faster it progresses. Some people don't get HD until their seventies, but Heather has seen a baby, a two-year-old and a child of thirteen with it. Everyone with HD gets movement problems: their legs become uncontrollable and it is that dance-like movement – the swaying, swaggering walk which is a distinctive feature of the disease – that led to it being called a chorea, from the Greek word for dance. Sufferers' arms either become rigid or they flail around ('cartwheeling', Heather calls it). Their eyes flicker, so reading and watching television are not comfortable. They are eventually unable to talk or to swallow and are doubly incontinent. Everyone with HD experiences psychological changes, but it is the degree of those changes that makes the difference. And in the majority of cases all of these problems, physical and mental, escalate to a certain extent before a form of apathy descends.

Heather's attitude to the news of the genetic time bomb potentially ticking away in her children's bodies was very different from that of her mother-in-law Ivy. Heather says that, as a result of some family-history research, she was contacted by someone in Canada whose mother was Ken's father's sister. He told Heather that, when his mother became ill two years before Ivy's husband (Ken's father) died, he wrote to Ivy telling her that his mother had HD. Ivy wrote back, saying, 'Don't ever contact me again. You are telling lies. You are never to speak to my children. You are never to contact them.' Heather recognizes that Ivy wanted to protect her children but feels that in the end her action simply made the situation a lot harder for them. Heather says that some families still don't talk about HD, but she took a different decision.

'Of course I had to tell the children what was wrong with their father. The girls were quite young and they took it in without really understanding. It came to them later, and gradually. Philip didn't say anything, and Nigel said, "I'll just go and shoot myself."'

Because Heather's eldest son Stephen wanted to be a doctor he understood the implications of HD all too clearly. Heather thinks that his father's diagnosis destroyed his chances of doing well at A-level, but she is pleased that he joined the police service and has had a good career.

At one point Deborah went to see their family doctor because she was really upset that she might develop HD. He told her, 'It doesn't affect women' and, as a Roman Catholic, advised her to go home and have a baby. Deborah's response was to refute his so-called knowledge, saying, 'My aunt's got HD!' That was when Heather decided to change doctors.

Nigel responded to the possibility of developing HD by saying, 'I'm never going to live like that. I don't want to go into hospital. I don't want to be looked after by anyone. I'm just going to live my life.' He told Heather that he was never going to get married and, although he had girlfriends, as soon as a relationship started to get serious he would end it.

He had started his career working as a sign writer for British Telecom, and when the company stopped using those skilled craftsmen he became an outside linesman. When British Telecom offered him redundancy he took it, although Heather told him he was too young for that. He replied, 'Oh, things are happening.'

Nigel had been living in his own flat for some time when suddenly he started phoning home more often, which Heather says wasn't like him. She started to see a lot more of him, too. She told him that his sisters, who were both coming up for thirty, were getting worried about developing HD. Nigel's answer was always, 'I'm all right. Don't worry about me,' but Heather was concerned because he was walking oddly. Unofficial confirmation of her suspicion that Nigel had HD came on her birthday. He always sent hand-drawn birthday and Christmas cards, and then one year she got a shop-bought birthday card.

At around that time some of his friends phoned Heather saying, 'Nigel won't open the door to us. We know he's in, but he won't open the door.' She spoke to him about it, enquiring, 'Don't you want to see them?' and he said, 'Sometimes they get on my nerves.' This reply was uncharacteristic, but Heather accepted it. When he added, 'I'm going to see my friend in Scotland, and I've given my cat to Deborah,' she didn't think he would do it; she didn't believe he would actually get on a train. For a while they had been going out together once a week – to London's museums and art galleries – but he wouldn't travel by train as he could no longer bear to be in a crowd of people. Instead, they started going to Southend or Lakeside or the cinema in her car. Heather didn't believe that Nigel would go to Scotland.

Over the next five weeks Heather rang Nigel many times, but there was no answer. Finally he picked up the phone and simply said, 'Help me!' Heather and her second husband Ron went to Nigel's flat, and when they opened the door . . .

'He'd been starving himself and he just looked like a skeleton. He'd been drinking vodka to keep himself unconscious, but he'd run out. We called an ambulance, and he was furious. Afterwards he said, "If you ever do that again I'll never speak to you. If you'd got me some vodka I would have been dead in a couple of weeks."'

The psychiatric hospital to which Nigel was admitted made sure he started eating again. Heather saw him at least once a week after that, and they had more days out together. At this stage Nigel had not been diagnosed with HD or any other condition. The hospital treated him as an alcoholic, and they didn't listen to anything Heather said about HD.

Shortly after being discharged from hospital Nigel seems to have taken some pills. Heather doesn't know what they were, nor does she know why he took them. She thinks that he might have been trying to shut out the life that was going on around him by becoming unconscious. Whatever his motivation, after taking them he ran down the street naked and was taken back to the psychiatric hospital. Following that episode she finally got Nigel to talk about HD, and he agreed to take the test. Dr Rosser from the neurological hospital knew Nigel and was aware that he wouldn't go to London for the test, so she visited the psychiatric hospital where he was an in-patient. Before taking the samples needed for the test she said to Heather, 'I don't think the test will show us anything we don't already know.' Heather agreed and made sure the doctor was aware that she wanted to be with Nigel when he got the result.

Shortly afterwards Heather arrived at the hospital to take Nigel out for the day and was told, 'He's gone to get the result of his test.' When she said that she had wanted to be with him she was told that he had gone in a taxi with a nurse. Dr Rosser told Heather afterwards that she knew she wanted to be with her son when he had his diagnosis of HD confirmed, but, she said, 'I didn't know what else to do. He insisted that I tell him the result.'

Heather had not known that the results were due that day, and she was glad that she was there when Nigel got back to the hospital knowing that he had HD. She could see a difference in him. 'He threw his arms round me and clung there. Then he said, "No, I'm all right, I'm all right." At least now we could talk about it.' They still went for days out, and Nigel would still laugh and joke, but their conversation kept coming back to how he would die. He had been diagnosed with HD at thirty-six, and Heather had known for two years that he had it.

Now when they had days out Heather could tell that the illness was beginning to affect him. She says that what he hated most was his changing personality. They were in a café at lunchtime one day when the queue stopped moving and Nigel asked very loudly, 'Why has it stopped? It's those two old ladies up there. Why are they holding up the queue? Why don't they get their meal and move on?' When the queue had resolved and mother and son were sitting down he looked at her and said, 'Wasn't I awful? Wasn't I dreadful and rude? I've really shown you up – I didn't mean to do it.' She told him not to worry about it.

The genetic fault in Ken's family leads to rigidity, and Nigel's fingers were no longer working properly. He was finding it difficult to hold a knife and fork, so he had started eating with his hands. To make him feel less awkward Heather would also eat with her fingers. 'You can imagine what people thought . . .' Then she discovered that Ikea sold meatballs and chips, which could be picked up easily.

When they were out they often visited a branch of Little Chef because Nigel loved their ice cream. On one visit he had an ice cream then said, 'I want another one.' People with HD sometimes get stuck in a loop, so Heather wasn't surprised. After eating the second one he told her, 'I want another one, but I'll be sick if I have another one, and I want another one, but I'm going to be sick, and I want another one.' Heather tried to distract Nigel's thinking from the loop in which he was stuck by suggesting that it would be fun to act like Bonnie and Clyde, running up to the till and dumping the money before running off. It was going well until Nigel got to the till, when he started shouting, 'No, no, I've got to have another ice cream!' Heather remembers that a woman standing nearby remarked, 'I wouldn't let anyone treat me like that . . .' Heather didn't say anything; she just thought to herself: If only you knew . . .

They went back to their seats, and the waitress brought Nigel another ice cream. Heather ate most of it while she tried to work out how to break the loop. One of his favourite programmes was *Mission: Impossible*, so she said, 'Right. Here are the car keys. Your mission is to get out of here and unlock the car before I get out.' To her relief this worked, and he left as she paid for the three ice creams. When she got to the car he was standing there, and they looked at each other and just laughed. He said, 'Oh no – aren't I awful?' and again Heather told him not to worry about it.

He had an occupational therapist called Jany who Heather says was marvellous. By this time he wouldn't let anyone except his mother into his flat as he was so independent, but Jany rode a motorbike and wore leathers, so Nigel was impressed by her. On the days when Heather couldn't get to Plaistow to visit Nigel, Jany would make sure he was all right. Heather says her attitude towards him was fantastic 'although he could be quite nasty to her when he had one of his moods'. Jany told her, 'I know he gets a bit moody, but I like him.'

Heather recalls that during the last two years of Nigel's life their conversations always came back to one subject – how was he going to die? 'Nigel told me he had been round the railway station twice, thinking about killing himself by throwing himself under a train, but he didn't want to make people late for work. He was also thinking of the driver. He didn't want a violent death. So when he talked about going to Southend, taking a boat out and jumping off because he couldn't swim I said, "You don't like cold water." He answered, "Yes, but it is an option."'

By this time he had cut himself off from all his friends saying, 'I'm not comfortable around people.' He had stopped eating again and he got himself into what Heather regarded as 'a terrible state'. One day she visited when Jany was there.

Nigel was pacing up and down. He had stabbed his settee with a knife, ripping it to pieces, so Heather and Jany decided to call an ambulance. When Nigel refused to get into it the paramedics called the police. Nigel was Tasered because he would not put down the knife the officers could see in his hand. He was taken into custody at Stratford police station, where he was known and where officers knew his brother was in the police. Later that day Heather and Ron were told that Nigel had settled down. He had been given something to eat and had been outside for a walk, partly to help him recover from being Tasered.

Following this episode Nigel returned to the psychiatric hospital. Shortly afterwards Heather arranged to take him to Southend on his forty-second birthday, 31 March 2000. Before then a couple of friends had visited him, and he said the same thing to them that he said to everyone, 'I want to die.'

Heather had planned to take Nigel to her home before going to Southend on his birthday, but when she collected him he said, 'No, no – I want to go back to my flat. I love my flat.' When Nigel said that Heather didn't have any cause for concern. She knew how much he liked being at home, and she saw it as a treat for his birthday. His home reflected his personality: when he lost the ability to hold a pencil and draw he would cut pictures from magazines and stick them on the walls instead. When he could no longer hold scissors he took to arranging bits of material. Heather says he always had to be doing something creative.

But, however much Nigel loved being in his flat, his HD movements meant that he couldn't put videos in the player and he had broken the music centre. Heather recognized that his quality of life was deteriorating. Pain wasn't really an issue with the HD, but he was enduring mental agony because he was becoming dependent on others and he was losing the ability to talk as well as having trouble swallowing. Losing the ability to draw meant that he was deprived of one of most enjoyable activities in his life. Heather knew that he didn't want to keep on going in and out of hospital, but he didn't want anyone to look after him in the flat either.

On the way there Nigel said, 'Let's eat chicken, sweet potatoes and sweetcorn – it's my favourite meal.' Heather had his birthday cards with her, and when they got to the flat she suggested opening them. He said, 'No, no, I'm not interested in that. It's too late for that. This is the best day of my life. My friends have got me what I want.' He left the room and came back with a syringe and a packet about two inches square containing a pink substance. He said, 'This is enough heroin to kill me, and I want to die. This is what I want, and this is how it's going to be.' Heather realized that he was serious about ending his life, so to distract him she said, 'Fine, fine, but let's open your birthday cards first.' She could see that he wasn't really interested in them. She sang 'Happy Birthday' to him, but he just said, 'Let's get on with it. They told me to put it in a spoon over the stove with some water.' He got some of the liquid into the syringe, but Heather says his movements were so bad that there was no way he could inject it.

'I knew that this was the best way for him to go – I didn't want him to die under a train. He kept dropping the syringe, and every time I picked it up and gave it back to him. In the end he looked at me and said, "Oh, I can't be bothered with all this." He'd used about a third of the powder to fill the syringe, and he just tipped all the heroin that was left on to the spoon and swallowed it. Then he looked at me and said, "Yuck. That was disgusting!" We laughed, and he said, "Promise me I won't leave the flat alive." I promised. He said, "If you call an ambulance I'll never speak to you again." I said, "Nige, if I don't call an ambulance you're never going to speak to me again anyway," and we laughed, and he hugged me.'

They lay down together on a futon in the lounge and talked about Nigel's life for a while before they both fell asleep. Heather says she had no problem with what Nigel was doing – she knew it was the best thing for him if it worked. She doesn't know why she slept so long – about four hours – but when she woke up she could see that her son's life was nearly over. His face was waxy white, his lips were blue, and he was taking a breath only every now and again. She heard the downstairs tenant arrive home and realized that Nigel's flat should be empty; any noises would arouse suspicion. Then she remembered that Nigel should have been back at the hospital and wondered whether they would send anyone round to the flat.

'I thought: I can't stand it any longer. I picked up a pillow and put it over his face. I knew very well that if I'd waited a short time he would have been dead, but I couldn't stand it any longer – it just had to end. I don't think I held the pillow there very long, but when I took it away he didn't take any more breaths. The doctor who did the post-mortem said that Nigel had been so close to death that my actions didn't really make any difference, which was fortunate for me because it made a difference to the charges I faced.'

When asked how it felt when she picked up that pillow Heather said she didn't think she was in her right mind at the time. She and her son had talked about how he would die for two years, and when she woke up to find him nearly dead beside her she remembers thinking: It's got to end. She was afraid that someone would come to the flat looking for him, and there was a nagging fear at the back of her mind that although she thought he was nearly dead the heroin might not work. She was horribly conscious of that fear and of the fact that she had promised her son he wouldn't leave his flat alive.

'It can only have been a very brief time that the pillow was over his face. I've got terribly arthritic knees, and there's no way I could have stayed on them for very long. It was very short – I would say under a minute, but I don't know. I knew he was very close to death. I just sat for a little while afterwards. It was a peaceful time, because all the suffering, all those problems, had ended. He'd gone to sleep with his arms crossed over his chest, and he looked so peaceful.'

For the next half-hour Heather sat with her son's body. She then phoned the police and told them, 'My son has taken an overdose, and he's died.' The police arrived, followed by an ambulance crew: the paramedics had been to Nigel's flat before, and he was known to the police officers. After his body had been taken away she went to the police station. She admitted that she had been with Nigel when he tried and failed to inject the heroin and when he had swallowed it, but she did not mention the pillow. Heather told the police that Nigel had killed himself because he had HD and gave them two of his suicide notes.

'Nigel was always writing notes, and they always said the same thing: "I am suffering and I want to die." I used to pick them up and bin them, but fortunately he'd left one in his flat and I had an old one in my bag. He wrote the same thing every time: "I am suffering and I want to die."'

The police interviewed Heather for what she considered quite a long time. She felt exhausted, but the officers were very good to her. She told them that she was very claustrophobic and couldn't stay in a locked interview room. She promised not to leave if the door was left open. They agreed, and a policewoman stayed with her. When Ron arrived they interviewed him, too.

Nigel died on the Friday, and Heather was told to go back to the police station on the Monday. Over the weekend she told her family about the pillow. Her policeman son Stephen and her husband Ron accompanied her when she returned to the police station. She was offered a duty solicitor but didn't take it up. She decided to tell them 'absolutely everything, because I've never been a liar and it's not something you can keep inside – it was such a big thing'. To her there was nothing to be afraid of. The police had always been her friends. They were not the enemy, HD was the enemy.

'When I told them about the pillow I could tell that they were really amazed. I could see them looking at each other, and then they brought in the murder squad. They came and searched our house.'

After the search the police took away a very old newspaper clipping about an HD sufferer in Scotland whose family had helped him obtain something to end his life. At this point Ron decided to get a lawyer. A friend of his told him about two good criminal lawyers in Romford. One would be kind and sympathetic. The other, Ben, was known to be extremely good but wouldn't offer Heather much in the way of sympathy. She chose Ben and says that the minute she met him she felt much better. He instilled confidence in Heather, and she feels certain that he made a difference to the outcome of the case.

Initially Heather was on bail for murder, but, despite that coming on top of her grief and with her other son Philip being ill at the same time, Heather just 'let it go'. 'My biggest worry was that they would not let me see Philip.'

Ben gathered a great deal of evidence. He obtained copies of Ken's father's medical records, the ones that said 'Family not to be told', and of everything that had been written about Ken. At that time medical records were handwritten and weren't easy to read. Ben also told Heather that she needed to gather as many character references as she could. The barrister said that women normally get references from other women and that judges are prone to dismiss those. Heather had lots of references from men because she had been a youth worker and hers was a police family.

The case was heard at the Old Bailey in October 2000. There was no trial because Heather pleaded guilty. 'I would never have pleaded guilty to murder, but I always intended to plead guilty to aiding and abetting Nigel's suicide.' She knew that she faced a penalty of up to fourteen years in prison but says that she felt convinced that she was going to be all right. 'And in a sense I was all right. I got a one-year conditional discharge. That was amazing, and I was very lucky. The judge said that other cases would not be treated so leniently and that nobody should take my sentence as a precedent, that it wasn't what he would give to everybody else. He couldn't give me community work because I was already doing that. He said he wasn't going to hand me over to the probation service because he knew I wouldn't do it again.'

Heather's case was doubly gruelling because the HD tragedy in her family was not yet over. 'I felt guilty about Ken going into hospital. Other people look after their partners with HD, but I knew I couldn't manage him and the children. I don't feel any guilt about Nigel because he lived his life exactly as he wanted to. He made his own decisions, and I never had any problems with that – he was in charge and would have achieved his death without me, but he didn't want to die alone. Philip, my other son who died of HD, was different to Nigel. You could wait on Philip hand and foot, and he loved it. I don't think he suffered so badly. He died very differently.'

Philip was nearly two years younger than Nigel. Heather says he had an odd sense of humour. She was called to his school one day because he had nailed the carpentry teacher's slippers to the floor! She says he often did things like that. On his way home from a party one night he removed every gate that could be lifted off its hinges and swapped it with another one: good gates were replaced with shabby ones, but someone spotted him and called the police. One day Philip and some of his friends stood each side of the road and pretended to pull up a rope in front of passing cars: there was nothing in their hands – they just mimed – but they had chosen a place only just down the road from the police station, and they were caught.

Philip was really upset when Heather remarried after Ken's death, and she thinks he had HD from a younger age than Nigel. If there was an argument Philip was always involved – 'It was like he was swimming upstream when everyone else was floating downstream.' He was very good with his hands and loved cars. But, like his father, he was always in and out of work.

Philip moved in with one of his friends, but that didn't work out. He moved around quite a bit and eventually had a nervous breakdown. 'I truly believe it was a nervous breakdown rather than the start of HD – Philip didn't feel safe on his own. He went into a psychiatric hospital, and the nurses were fantastic. But one day when I got there he was sitting outside. He wouldn't talk to me, so I asked him what was wrong. Philip told me he had asked one of the doctors, "Do you think I've got HD?" The doctor had looked at Philip and said yes. But that doctor didn't tell the nurses what had happened, and for three days Philip didn't say a word to anyone. The staff didn't know what was going on, why he wasn't talking. That was when we started looking for homes for him.'

Philip was first admitted to a psychiatric hospital when he was thirty-six, and he was about thirty-nine when Heather and Ron started to search for a suitable residential home for him. He got a place in a new home in Colchester, but he was the only patient there, and he hated it. Another man moved in, but he was from Colchester which meant he could go out and meet friends. Philip was in the home on his own, and in the end he smashed up his room and had another short spell in hospital. He then moved to a home in Kent that catered for all sorts of illnesses, but he didn't settle there either and went back to the hospital. There were very few specialist HD residential homes at that time, but someone told Heather about St Andrews in Northampton. They said it was really good, so Heather asked her local authority to fund it. They declined to pay because it was too expensive.

Heather recalled that Ken's father's medical records had 'Family not to be told' written at the bottom. Assuming this was the doctor's decision, she told the council, 'It was your doctor who withheld this information and gave my family all this trauma. We didn't know what we were dealing with.' She told them that the least they could do was to make some effort to put things right or she would go to court. Within ten minutes the local authority had decided to fund Philip's place at St Andrews.

Heather got to know the St Andrews' doctors and nurses very well because she visited Philip regularly and would spend the whole day there. After he had lived in St Andrews for some time Philip suffered a series of chest infections which eventually led to him losing all function. One day in 2008 St Andrews phoned to say that she should visit her son as soon as possible. She went to Northampton with her daughter Deborah. Philip had lost the ability to swallow, so the staff and the two women put drops of iced water in his mouth. A doctor suggested that Philip could go into an ordinary hospital and be put on a drip, but Heather said, 'If he goes to hospital, what will that achieve? It will just prolong his death for a few days, and he'll be among people he doesn't know.' At St Andrews Philip was never left alone; if she went out for a walk a nurse would stay in the room with him. Heather told the doctor that she didn't want him taken to another hospital. After around a week of giving him nothing but sips of water Heather realized that Philip was starving to death. She felt certain that he must be in pain, and she was aware that he couldn't tell anyone. She asked for Philip to be given a morphine patch. She was glad that his suffering was ameliorated, even though he died during the night after it was applied. He was forty-eight.

Philip never talked about ending his life. Heather thinks that a long time before his brother died someone must have said something like, 'If you feel like that, why don't you die?' to him. He told his mother, 'I'll never commit suicide', and she says that she knew he meant it. For this reason it was much more difficult for her to be with him dying than it had been with Nigel. Heather says it was 'really horrendous', and she thought that Philip could have gone on for a few more days. She even wonders whether she may have shortened his life by asking for the morphine patch. 'But he couldn't talk, and I don't think he would have wanted to live any longer.'

Even if Nigel had been able to ask his doctor for help to die, Heather says he would have died when he did: he couldn't wait. He died at a time when he was capable of acting alone to end his life. 'Nigel told me, "I might even have to end up hanging myself." You wouldn't want anyone to go through that. That's why I thought the friends who got him the heroin did the best thing for him. I knew they'd been to the hospital and talked to him. They listened to him and knew what he wanted.'

Heather thinks that heroin was the best help Nigel could have had because it gave him a peaceful death. All the other ways he had considered were violent and unpleasant, and Nigel wasn't a violent person. She knows that he had some good friends and that at the end they came through for him. At his funeral she overheard something that made her realize who had obtained the heroin. She was reassured because it was one of Nigel's oldest friends.

When asked whether if Nigel had been able to talk to his doctor about having an assisted death with prescribed medication he would have done so she said that it was hard to know. He was annoyed at himself because he was unable to control his behaviour. Once he could no longer draw, life didn't hold much meaning for him. He was petrified that someone would have to look after him round the clock. He could have lived another eight years with HD. Ken died at forty-four, Philip died at forty-eight and Ken's sister died at fifty. Nigel was forty-two when he died, and he had already reached a stage he found intolerable. He did not find pleasure in anything. 'He used to like going round museums and art galleries and going to the pub with his friends, but there was just nothing left for him to enjoy.'

Heather is glad she helped Nigel to die, calling it the best thing she ever did for him. She says she doesn't feel sad when she thinks about his death – she thinks of it as a happy thing because he was so happy that day. He had actually smiled.

Nigel had no trouble telling people that he wanted to die. And he didn't have a problem with the heroin because it was better than going under a train or drowning or hanging. He knew he would just go to sleep. 'And yet people ask whether I feel sad or regretful – I don't, because it was a peaceful day. Nigel would be amazed that so many people are interested in him and that we are still talking about him thirteen years after he died. There is a comforting element to knowing that someone died peacefully after suffering terribly like he did. It was what he wanted. It was what he got. If you saw someone at the end stage of Huntington's . . . Nigel wasn't a coward to avoid those last years. He was brave enough to say, "I'd rather die than live like that."'

6
ASSISTED DYING AROUND THE WORLD TODAY
by Davina Hehir and Philip Satherley

There are certain places where assistance to die can legally be provided. Our main focus is on Oregon in the USA, which has a wealth of data and research on practice since legalization in 1997 and which closely resembles the system for which Dignity in Dying campaigns in the UK. We will also discuss practice in the Netherlands, which formally legalized voluntary euthanasia and assisted suicide in 2002, as well as examining practice in Washington State, Belgium and Switzerland.

Three different types of legal assistance-to-die practice are permitted in eight jurisdictions across Europe and the USA. In all of these the patient is at the centre of the decision-making process: the patient must satisfy various criteria to qualify for assistance to die, and safeguards are in place to ensure the patient's protection.

The first situation is that the patient has a terminal illness with a typical prognosis of six months or less and takes doctor-prescribed life-ending medication by himself or herself. This – assisted dying – is the system in the US states of Oregon, Washington, Vermont and Montana.

The second is that the patient has an incurable condition *or* faces unbearable suffering *or* has a terminal illness (that is, they may not necessarily be dying) and takes the life-ending medication by himself or herself. This – assisted suicide – is the system in Switzerland.

Third, the patient typically has an incurable condition *or* faces unbearable suffering *or* has a terminal illness (that is, they may not necessarily be dying) and their life is ended by a doctor administering an injection of medication. This – voluntary euthanasia – is the system in the Netherlands (which also practises assisted suicide to a lesser extent), Belgium and Luxembourg.

The State of Oregon was the first place in the world to legalize assistance to die. In 1994 the Death with Dignity Act (DWDA) was established, legalizing assisted dying for people who are terminally ill. Patients requesting assistance must satisfy a number of criteria, which are checked by two doctors, and only then can they receive the life-ending prescription.

A 1994 vote by the general public in Oregon found that 51.3 per cent were in favour of assisted dying and 48.7 per cent were against. A second vote in February 1997 found that 61 per cent of the public were in favour. This change in the law was spearheaded by a group of proactive campaigners and supporters. A key group was Compassion & Choices, a USA-wide pro-choice organization that focuses its efforts on the legalization of assisted dying for terminally ill people. In addition, Compassion & Choices supports people around their wider end-of-life rights, such as the advance refusal of life-prolonging treatments, and works with patients who have requested assisted dying in US states where it is legal. Implementation of the Oregon DWDA was tied up for a few years, but it was eventually enacted in October 1997. There have been several attempts to block the DWDA. Around the time of implementation in 1997 there were efforts to repeal it, but these failed. Similarly, a move to suspend the licence for prescribing the life-ending medications needed for the DWDA was prevented by Oregon's federal judge. A further challenge to the DWDA by President George W. Bush's administration in 2005 was also unsuccessful.

All this pro-assisted dying activity in Oregon stood in sharp contrast to the New York State case of Vacco v. Quill (1997). This focused on a 'right to die', the outcome being that the current ban on assisted dying in the State of New York was constitutional and that doctors should not be allowed to assist dying patients to end their lives.

Oregon residents feel that it is important to stress the distinction between 'assisted suicide' and 'assisted dying' to reflect the safeguards and practice of the DWDA in their state. Medical and legal experts in the USA have recognized that the term 'suicide' or 'assisted suicide' is inappropriate when discussing the choice of a terminally ill, mentally competent patient seeking a peaceful and dignified death. The DWDA states that deaths under the law do not 'constitute suicide, assisted suicide, mercy killing or homicide'.

The American Public Health Association (APHA) conducts health-promotion and disease-prevention activities and represents a broad range of health-care professionals. Its policy called 'Patients' Rights to Self-Determination at the End of Life' focuses on the importance of language when describing assisted dying.

The APHA recognizes the importance of using accurate language to describe care options. The choice of a mentally competent terminally ill patient to self-administer medications to bring about a peaceful death is accurately reflected in the term 'aid in dying'. APHA does not support the use of inaccurate terms such as 'suicide' or 'assisted suicide' to refer to the choice of a mentally competent terminally ill patient to seek medications to bring about a peaceful and dignified death.[1]

Before we discuss the assisted dying process it is essential to spell out exactly who is eligible for assistance in Oregon. As well as being a resident of Oregon, the DWDA requires that the patient has a terminal illness with a prognosis of six months or less, is an adult aged eighteen or older, has the capacity to make the decision and is making the request entirely voluntarily and without coercion. Two doctors assess the patient: one is the 'attending' doctor (who may be the family's doctor or a specialist who has cared for the patient since diagnosis) and the other is the 'consultant' (or second doctor) who may have specialist knowledge of end-of-life care that the attending doctor lacks. Patients who fall short of the standards are turned down. Importantly, the patient must take the life-ending medication – a barbiturate – which comes in the form of a liquid which he or she drinks. This ensures that the final act is entirely the patient's own doing, in contrast to voluntary euthanasia.

... it is possible that placing responsibility for the final act on the individual rather than the physician serves to prevent individuals ending their lives prematurely. Indeed, it may be that the setting of a date with a physician for euthanasia constitutes a form of passive pressure to end life, in so far as individuals feel that they are unable to back out once a date has been set.[2]

The patient must be the first person to raise the issue of assisted dying – no care professional can raise the topic with a patient – usually with the family doctor or the specialist clinician in charge of care since his or her terminal diagnosis. The attending doctor must explore the physical and psychological reasons for the request and discuss all the available palliative and supportive care options. If either of the doctors is uncertain about the patient's capacity or ability to make decisions, the individual will be referred to a psychiatrist or psychologist. Counselling is available as well. Under the law the doctors have to formally report all activity to the Oregon State Public Health Division to ensure that the procedure has been followed correctly, data which is published in an annual report.

The patient must submit two oral requests (the second just before the attending doctor writes the prescription for the life-ending medication) and a written request (signed in the presence of two witnesses). The patient can cancel his or her request orally or in writing at any time during the process. There is a fifteen-day waiting period after the first oral request, and there is a mandatory two-day wait after the patient makes the written request. This means that the soonest the process could be completed would be approximately three weeks. However, the time from the first request to the patient's death is usually between forty and fifty days. Any time after the prescription has been written the patient can collect the life-ending medication and keep it at home. Like all care professionals pharmacists can opt out of engaging with the assisted dying process, but the evidence suggests that most don't do so. Pharmacists have to comply with strict guidance – ensuring that whoever picks up the medication is fully informed of its side-effects and how to take it – as well as reporting to the Oregon State Public Health Division which over-sees the process and gathers data.

There is no legal obligation for the attending doctor to be present when the patient takes the medication, although this is always an option. Often a trained volunteer from Compassion & Choices of Oregon (many of whom are social workers or other care professionals) will be available throughout the process. They will help the patient and his or her family with any emotional or practical issues, such as picking up the medication. In many cases the volunteer is present when the patient dies, both to ensure the person takes the medication correctly and to give bereavement support. The patient will become unconscious about five minutes after taking the medication and usually dies within twenty minutes.

The DWDA does not authorize either euthanasia or mercy killing, and anyone who used coercion on a patient would be prosecuted.

While social workers, nurses and other non-medical care professionals have no legal role in assisted dying in Oregon there is an emphasis – should they not conscientiously object – on them providing clear information and support to patients if they are asked. They should be aware of what the DWDA is and how to refer patients to their doctors or to an organization such as Compassion & Choices of Oregon.

The number of terminally ill patients who had an assisted death was very low for the first few years. This was to be expected as people adapted to this radical change in the law and as awareness of the choice for terminally ill people grew. In 1998 there were sixteen deaths (0.05 per cent of all deaths in Oregon that year), and it wasn't until 2002 that the figure reached 0.13 per cent of all deaths. The figure rose slowly until 2008: that year it was 0.19 per cent, and it has remained at around this level since then, with seventy-seven deaths (0.24 per cent) in 2012. Opponents of assisted dying often cite this as a four-fold rise in numbers. While this is true, the figure has actually gone from 'extremely low' to 'still low' and accounts for a small, steady number of deaths per year. Since the law was passed over fifteen years ago a total of 1,050 DWDA prescriptions have been written and 673 patients have died from ingesting medications prescribed under the DWDA.[3]

The Oregon Health Authority produces an annual report that can be accessed on its website. This gives the number of deaths from assisted dying, the characteristics of the people dying and their reasons for requesting assistance.[4] The overwhelming majority of people are aged sixty-five to eighty-four and are white. There is an even split between men and women, and most have some form of higher education. In 2012 almost 100 per cent were enrolled in hospice care, a figure that has shown a steady increase since 1998 when it was about two-thirds. Most people have cancer (approximately 80 per cent), and the rest have terminal conditions such as motor neurone disease or chronic obstructive pulmonary disease.

The annual report also allows us to see the reasons that patients give for requesting assistance to die. For over 90 per cent of patients 'loss of autonomy' is a key reason. 'Less able to engage in activities making life enjoyable' and 'loss of dignity' are cited as reasons for between 80 and 90 per cent of patients. 'Losing control of bodily functions' occurs about 50 per cent of the time, and concerns about being a burden are a factor for about 40 per cent of patients. 'Inadequate pain control or concern about it' is cited much less frequently at around 25 per cent.

A Compassion & Choices blog, which discusses how the DWDA allows patients and doctors to have honest conversations about dying, quotes its President, Barbara Coombs Lee, as saying, 'The conversations have more to do with peace of mind and quality of life than a desire to die.'[5]

What these figures indicate is that the majority of patients are concerned with the more personal and qualitative aspects of dying rather than physical care. The issue of burden requires some examination, as, quite rightly, many people have genuine concerns that some patients might choose assisted dying because they don't want to be a bother. Research by Linda Ganzini is helpful in understanding this issue: she concludes that the fear of being a burden may reflect a patient's reactions to the thought of being dependent during the dying process rather than their reaction to communication with their families.[6] It is worth reminding ourselves that in Oregon patients must express a persistent desire for assistance to die and that they are assessed by two doctors. If either doctor (or indeed any other health- or social-care professional involved in their care) suspects the patient is being coerced in any way the matter is investigated further with the potential of prohibiting assistance to die.

Research by the Hastings Center found that the hospices' role is largely confined to providing information about the DWDA in a 'neutral' manner.[7] Patients must find two doctors who are willing to evaluate whether they are eligible and, if they are, to assist. As in the UK, hospice care in the USA is delivered across a variety of settings (usually the home but also in specialist units), and the majority of people who have an assisted death die at home. Many hospices in Oregon, however, do not allow their staff to have conversations with patients who ask about assisted dying. Instead, patients are referred to their doctor without any of the discussions you would expect to accompany such a life-changing request. Considering the important role hospices play in the care of terminal patients and their families, this is something that should be addressed.

There is a conscientious objection clause in the DWDA which allows all care professionals to opt out of engaging with the assisted dying process. There are no figures available for the number of doctors who opt out, but the data shows that sixty-one doctors wrote the 115 life-ending prescriptions in 2012. This strongly suggests that concerns about 'doctor shopping' (whereby the patient will seek out a sympathetic doctor who might somehow ignore the legal safeguards in order to help that person die) are unfounded. Doctors who ignore the safeguards and legal requirements are subject to prosecution.

The annual reports also tell us that many patients who receive the life-ending prescription do not use it but die of their underlying condition. The DWDA brings comfort and peace of mind to many more people than the few who end up taking the life-ending prescription. Many thousands of patients are empowered to discuss the option openly and in detail with their doctor without any untoward legal implications.

In the years following the implementation of the DWDA there was a flurry of research activity that centred on patients' safety, their reasons for requesting assistance, the impact of assisted dying on palliative care and how care professionals view the DWDA. Of central importance was a 2007 paper by Margaret

Battin et al. that examined the impact assisted dying had on potentially vulnerable groups (including adults aged eighty-five and over, disabled people, people of lower socio-economic status and those with mental health problems).[8] This research found that those vulnerable groups had not been adversely affected by the legislation and were, in fact, under-represented in the numbers of assisted deaths. This research has been pivotal in convincing people who were concerned about the safety of assisted dying in Oregon.

Families are encouraged to become part of the process of assisted dying, although the decision is entirely the patient's. Some care professionals indicate that, at first, many families are opposed to their loved one having assistance but eventually come around to the dying person's way of thinking. Research indicates that the families of those who have had a assisted death are not negatively affected by the process and feel better prepared for their loved one's death.[9]

Evidence strongly suggests that the DWDA in Oregon is working well, safely and effectively and that, crucially, vulnerable people are being protected. Overall support for assisted dying is strong in Oregon, with the DWDA acting as a good template for practice elsewhere.

After several failed attempts, and with a majority of 58 per cent of voters backing it, the Washington Death with Dignity Act (DWDA) came into force in 2009. It closely follows the Oregon model in that the patient must have a terminal illness with a prognosis of six months or less, the person must have mental capacity, the request must be voluntary and without coercion, the individual has to be a resident of Washington State, the process is verified by two doctors, palliative and supportive care options are explored and the patient can opt out at any time. As with Oregon, an alliance of end-of-life rights organizations, politicians and care professionals campaigned for the Washington DWDA with the main opposition coming from the Coalition Against Assisted Suicide made up of disability rights advocates, Christian organizations from a number of denominations, politicians and right-to-life organizations.

Assisted deaths in 2012 accounted for 0.17 per cent of all deaths, so the figures are close to those in Oregon.[10] Similarly, many patients do not end up taking the life-ending medication but have it as 'emotional insurance'. Most patients have a diagnosis of terminal cancer, and most of them cite loss of autonomy, dignity and the ability to participate in life as key reasons for their request. As with Oregon, care professionals can opt out of engagement with the DWDA, and no patient can be denied other medical care or treatment because of his or her request for assisted dying. Compassion & Choices Washington serves a similar function to the organization in Oregon, giving support and information to patients who request assisted dying. Little academic research has been conducted in Washington, probably because Oregon has been seen as a 'test bed' for assisted dying, and the lessons learnt from that research have been applied to Washington.

At the end of 2009 Montana became the third state in the USA to allow assisted dying. The way it was legalized in Montana differed from Oregon and Washington in that the Supreme Court ruled by five votes to two that nothing in the state's law actually prevents terminally ill, mentally competent patients seeking medical assistance to die. Some critics, although supportive of this ruling, thought that the Supreme Court did not go far enough, almost washing their hands of the topic as if the right to die didn't have anything to do with them.

What this ruling means is that doctors in Montana can now prescribe the necessary drugs to terminally ill people who request assistance to die without fear of prosecution. The patient has to self-administer the life-ending medication. Several Bills have been introduced since 2009 to try to prohibit assisted dying, but none has been successful.

In 2013 Vermont legalized assisted dying for terminally ill people, emulating the Death with Dignity Acts in Oregon and Washington, although the application of the law here differs slightly from that in those states. For the first three years the practice will follow Oregon and Washington, but after this it will be overseen by professional standards similar to those governing other aspects of medicine instead of by a DWDA. It is thought that this two-step approach was taken to allow the practice to be formally introduced and to allay fears that the government was interfering in individuals' end-of-life decisions.

The Netherlands, Belgium and Luxembourg all passed voluntary euthanasia and/or assisted suicide Acts in the first decade of the new millennium. They all have a wider remit than the criteria set out in the USA.

The Termination of Life on Request and Assisted Suicide (Review Procedures) Act took effect in the Netherlands on 1 April 2002. It legalized voluntary euthanasia and assisted suicide under very specific circumstances. Patients who have an incurable condition, face unbearable suffering and who are mentally competent may be eligible.

Theoretically this was practised before April 2002 through court law which developed the 'defence of necessity'. This enabled doctors who faced a conflict between the duty to preserve life and the duty to relieve suffering to practise voluntary euthanasia as long as certain criteria were met. These specified that the patient must have consistently expressed a wish to die; the individual was suffering unbearably (as defined by the patient and agreed by the doctor); there was ongoing consultation and a strong relationship between doctor and patient; the ending of life was practised effectively; and records were kept and reported to the appropriate authorities.[11] Relevant organizations were keen to ensure effective and safe practice. For example, in 1987 the Royal Dutch Pharmaceutical Association issued guidelines on what medication should be used, who could collect and administer it and so on, advice it updates regularly.

What the Act did was to ensure that guidance was available, accurate and enforceable. It included a list of six 'due care' criteria that must be met in order to exempt the doctor from criminal liability. The attending doctor must:

1. be satisfied that the patient has made a voluntary and well-considered request;
2. be satisfied that the patient's suffering is unbearable and that there is no prospect of improvement;
3. have informed the patient about his or her situation and prospects;
4. have come to the conclusion, together with the patient, that there is no reasonable alternative in the light of the patient's situation;
5. have consulted at least one other physician who must have seen the patient and given a written opinion on the due care criteria referred to above; *and*
6. have terminated the patient's life or provided assistance with suicide with due medical care and attention.

As with Oregon, it must always be the patient who raises the possibility of assisted dying. Any care professional can conscientiously object and withdraw from the process. There is widespread support for the law among both the general public and care professionals. Historians argue that the Dutch are very open to discussing challenging issues, such as recreational drugs and prostitution. This is reflected in the way politicians guided the development of guidelines and law rather than acting to prohibit the practice outright.

The doctor must report the person's death and complete all the relevant paperwork; this is used to compile an annual report by the Regional Euthanasia

Review Committee. While there have been around forty cases where it was thought the doctor did not act in strict accordance with these due care criteria (for example, by not using the correct life-ending medication or by not being present at the moment the patient took the medication), no prosecutions have been brought and all of the doctors were found to have been acting within the law. The Dutch law includes special provisions surrounding requests from those under the age of eighteen, although this is very strictly practised.

As with Oregon, an independent doctor sees the patient and assesses the extent to which the due care criteria have been met. If the patient qualifies for assistance and still wants to go ahead, the doctor consults with the pharmacist and the medication is delivered to the doctor. In the majority of cases the patient will be assisted to die in their home with loved ones present. If the medication is not used – because the patient changes their mind or has already died – it must be returned to the pharmacist.

A state-funded project called Support and Consultation on Euthanasia in the Netherlands (SCEN) trains general practitioners in formal consultation and in giving expert advice to colleagues who have questions about euthanasia and assisted suicide. Around 80 per cent of patients who die from voluntary euthanasia are attended by a SCEN-trained doctor.[12] In these cases SCEN-trained doctors act as second independent doctors, and they enhance the safeguards by bringing in-depth knowledge and experience of end-of-life care to the assessment process.

The Netherlands is different to Oregon in that Dutch patients are allowed to record their wish for voluntary euthanasia in an advance directive. This means that their wishes could be acted on if they lose mental capacity. However, such advance directives are rarely observed because doctors are reluctant to practise euthanasia in cases where the onset of dementia has compromised a patient's ability to communicate.[13]

Research shows that a request for voluntary euthanasia starts a complex emotional process for everyone who is involved. The patient and doctor share a great deal of information and build up a good relationship in order to reach agreement on whether voluntary euthanasia is right for the patient and whether he or she is eligible. The burden placed on the doctor has to be taken into account alongside the rights of the patient.[14] Most voluntary euthanasia requests come from patients who have terminal cancer and the majority die at home, although some patients die in a hospital, care home or hospice setting.

Unlike Oregon there is no set prognosis timescale in the Netherlands, but the patient's condition must be incurable and must be causing unbearable suffering with the individual left feeling hopeless. The patient and doctors discuss in great depth what 'unbearable suffering' means and what impact the patient's condition is having on their life, as well as considering what impact it might have in the future. Good communication and shared decision-making are vital to the process, with doctors deliberating in detail with each patient about what constitutes unbearable suffering.

By far the majority of assisted deaths in the Netherlands are voluntary euthanasia, but a small number are assisted suicides. In assisted suicide the patient takes the life-ending medication, and it is usually a barbiturate which they drink. In the case of voluntary euthanasia, a strong sedative is intravenously administered to induce a coma before a lethal muscle relaxant is administered to stop breathing and cause death.

Voluntary euthanasia cases accounted for just under 3 per cent of all deaths in the Netherlands in 2010.[15] In 2005 this figure was 1.7 per cent, and in 2001 (i.e. just before the formalization of practice through the Act) the figure was 2.6 per cent. Figures have fluctuated over the years, owing in part to an increase in doctors reporting the practice. Research indicates that in 1995 only 41 per cent of doctors reported cases of voluntary euthanasia, rising to 54 per cent in 2001 and to 80 per cent in 2005.[16] The recent increase in numbers of deaths reported may also be due to an ageing population with increased co-morbidities and terminal illnesses as well as changes in the general public's ethical views.

It is interesting to compare the statistics for cases of non-voluntary euthanasia – that is, ending the patient's life without their explicit request – before the Act with more recent figures. This practice occurs much less often now: 0.7 per cent of all deaths in 2001 were brought about this way, falling to 0.4 per cent in 2005 and 0.2 per cent in 2010.[17] A 2009 study carried out in the UK by Clive Seale found that 0.3 per cent of lives were ended without an explicit request from the patient: the practice of non-voluntary euthanasia is clearly not restricted to the Netherlands.[18] It would not be a huge leap of faith to claim that the formal legalization of voluntary euthanasia in the Netherlands in 2002 has led directly to lower rates of non-voluntary euthanasia. Legalization has certainly raised awareness among doctors of what the correct end-of-life practices are and of the importance of open communication.

Jansen et al. looked at patients' and relatives' experiences of a home visit by their doctor during the assisted dying procedure.[19] Overall they found the experience helpful, increasing their trust in the consultant and being reassured by the visit that the decision-making process would be meaningful and effective. The openness of the process was also shown to help the patient and family deal with the situation.

The Netherlands is often criticized by opponents of assisted dying for not having dedicated palliative care services, implying that services are poor and that dying patients are demanding assistance because they are not getting good enough care. This is not borne out by the system in place in the Netherlands, which ranks highly in surveys of European and global palliative care.[20, 21]

There has been an increase in palliative care funding since the 2002 Act. As well as a rise in the number of hospice facilities, numerous palliative care training programmes have been introduced.[22] Palliative care is organized differently from the UK, with most healthcare professionals in the Netherlands getting general training in the issue. Of course there are specialists in palliative care, but this approach means that the healthcare community at large has a greater awareness of the end-of-life care needs of patients.

The implementation of the 2002 Act was a spur to improve end-of-life and palliative care as a whole, and it increased the importance of open and frank discussions between patients and care professionals. A 2011 report by the European Association for Palliative Care concluded that, in countries where legal assistance to die is practised, palliative care is as well developed as in those countries where it is not.[23]

All the evidence suggests that the Netherlands is delivering excellent quality palliative care and end-of-life services and that the Termination of Life on Request and Assisted Suicide (Review Procedures) Act has not had a negative impact on this.

In Belgium, as in the Netherlands, the voluntary euthanasia law is not limited to terminally ill patients but includes those who are in a medically futile state and suffering unbearably (mentally or physically) as the result of an illness or accident. The Belgian law did not legalize assisted suicide.

In 1999 a Private Member's Bill was put before the Belgian Senate and was finally passed in May 2002. The key motivation for passing the law was to regulate practice and to make sure that processing requests for assistance, carrying out the procedure and the necessary reporting were all performed correctly, with patient safety at the heart of the decision-making process. As with the Netherlands the law provided legal safety for doctors so long as they practised within the limits of the law. Although there have been attempts to expand its limits, the remit of the law has not been widened. Patients must put their request in writing, and they must have the capacity to make decisions. It must be their entirely voluntary and sustained wish, and they are assessed by two doctors to confirm that the legal requirements have been satisfied. All palliative care options must be explored. If the patient is not expected to die in the near future he or she must see a psychiatrist or another appropriate clinician.

The number of patients having voluntary euthanasia has risen over the years, and, as is the case in the Netherlands, when we examine pre- and post-legislation figures it becomes clear that the number of cases of non-voluntary euthanasia has fallen.[24, 25]

Unlike the Netherlands, where the number of patients who have assistance to die appears to be spread evenly across the country, there is a distinct split in Belgium between the Dutch-speaking part (Flanders) and the French-speaking part (Wallonia). Research found that acceptance of voluntary euthanasia was slightly higher in Flanders, while doctors in Wallonia were more likely to hold negative attitudes towards voluntary euthanasia and received fewer requests. There seem to be differences in the understanding and application of the legislation between these two regions, with doctors in Wallonia consulting less often with an independent doctor (which is required), appearing to believe that euthanasia is a matter between physician and patient and reporting the practice less often.[26]

In May 2002 a law was passed that declared that all citizens of Belgium have the right to receive palliative care, that they should receive personalized information about their illness and treatment option and that they should be given the highest possible quality of life and autonomy.[27] As a consequence of this – and the voluntary euthanasia law – being passed, central-government funding of palliative care doubled and awareness of end-of-life care (and rights) increased. Research shows that the majority of Belgian doctors who are involved in the care of dying patients thought that the voluntary euthanasia law contributed to the carefulness of wider end-of-life behaviour,[28] and only 10 per cent thought that the law impeded the development of palliative care.[29]

In 2009 Luxembourg became the third European country to decriminalize voluntary euthanasia. It follows the Netherlands system quite closely, and there have been only been a handful of cases of voluntary euthanasia, with little or no scrutiny from either academics or opponents.

Perhaps the most widely known jurisdiction where assisted suicide is practised is Switzerland. Assistance can be provided within the framework of Article 115 of the Swiss Criminal Code (1942) which does not prohibit assisted suicide in the absence of selfish motives. This means that, essentially, it is a criminal offence to assist when the person has selfish motives but not when he or she is acting out of compassion and the person dying is doing so entirely voluntarily. However, it was not until the 1980s that the first organizations for the purpose of allowing assisted suicide were founded. Active euthanasia, where the doctor injects the patient with a life-ending drug, is strictly prohibited.

Residents of Switzerland tend to use an organization called Exit (Exit Romandie in the French-speaking part of Switzerland and Exit Deutsche Schweiz in the German-speaking part). There are around three hundred cases of Swiss residents having assistance to die every year,[30] with the majority having a terminal illness (although there have been a few reported cases where the person wanted to die because they had severe depression or even blindness).

Dignitas, which is primarily used by people who are not residents of Switzerland, was founded in the late 1990s by Swiss lawyer Ludwig Minelli for the purpose of ensuring that foreign nationals seeking assistance to die could have that help somewhere safe and neutral. There are approximately 800 British members of Dignitas who pay an annual membership fee of about £60. The cost of an assisted suicide is estimated at around £5,000, and there can be additional costs involved: Dignitas's fees do not include the cost of getting to Switzerland or of accommodation, for instance. Dignitas is keen to make it clear that a reduction of (or even complete exemption from) membership fees can be agreed for members who live under what they call 'modest economic circumstances'. This provision also applies to the additional payments involved in preparing for someone's assisted suicide. The majority of people who have assistance to die at Dignitas are German, but over two hundred British citizens have died there since 2002.[31]

In order to have assistance to die with help from Dignitas the person must first be a member of the organization. He or she must have the capacity to make the decision. The individual must have a disease that will lead to death *or* be enduring incapacitating disability *or* be in unendurable or uncontrollable pain. Finally, he or she must be able to take the life-ending medication without assistance. The person who is asking for help to die has to provide, by post, a copy of his or her medical records. Once the criteria have been satisfied the individual gets a 'provisional green light' from one of the doctors associated with Dignitas. This enables the person to book an appointment during which a fuller assessment is conducted before a prescription for the life-ending medication can be written. If the person is not physically able to swallow, a gastric tube can be used. Friends and family can be present at the death, something Dignitas actively encourages.

On the whole Dignitas is supported – and seen as a good thing – by the people of Switzerland. A public referendum, held in 2011 in the Canton of Zurich, asked whether foreign nationals should continue to be able to travel there to have assistance to die. The public decided overwhelmingly that the choice of assisted suicide should not be outlawed, neither for Swiss nationals nor for foreigners. Dignitas is not without controversy, and it is often accused of making a profit out of people's deaths, even though it states that it is a non-profit organization.

We have seen that legal assistance to die in various forms exists in eight jurisdictions. Some allow assistance only for those with a terminal illness; others have a wider remit which includes those with chronic conditions or uncontrollable pain. Some laws require the individual to take the life-ending medication by himself or herself; others require the doctor to end the person's life by lethal injection.

Close attention has been paid to the practices in many of these jurisdictions, particularly Oregon, which was seen as a test bed by some campaigners and academics who were keen to explore the implementation of assisted dying, and the Netherlands, traditionally a very open society which continues to investigate all aspects of voluntary euthanasia practice.

The campaign to change the law on assisted dying in England and Wales has advocated the Oregon model of assisted dying since 2005.[32] There are clear reasons for this approach. As we have seen, the Oregon legislation enjoys wide public support and gives peace of mind to a far wider group of dying people than those who actually go on to have an assisted death. There is no evidence of abuse in Oregon, nor is there any evidence to support a 'slippery slope' argument. Investment in palliative care provision and the uptake of palliative care training by doctors and social workers have both increased since the DWDA was introduced, as has the number of terminally ill patients accessing palliative care at the end of their life. Importantly, there have been no calls in Oregon to extend the law beyond the clear eligibility criteria of terminally ill, mentally competent adults who are expected to die within six months. For campaigners in England and Wales this demonstrates the benefits of a law limited to providing choice in dying to people who are *already* dying. It also illustrates that there is not a demand for a wider law. This point is perhaps reinforced by the fact that in the Netherlands, which does have wider eligibility criteria, the vast majority of cases of voluntary euthanasia and assisted suicide involve people with terminal cancer.[33]

At present, the law in England, Wales and Northern Ireland makes clear that it is a crime to encourage or assist a suicide and that this is punishable by a maximum of fourteen years' imprisonment.[34] As a result of the ruling in the

Debbie Purdy case, in February 2010 the Director of Public Prosecutions published guidance setting out the factors that would be considered when deciding whether or not to prosecute someone for assisting suicide.[35] This prosecuting policy undoubtedly marked a step forward for patient choice: it could not (and did not) change the law, but it did clarify how decisions are likely to be made in these cases. For people such as Debbie Purdy, the policy provides clear guidance on what to expect: she wanted to be able to make an informed choice about whether or not to seek an assisted death in Switzerland, armed with a good sense of the likely implications for her husband or any other friend or family member who helped her. Essentially, the policy explains that a friend or family member, whose motivation to assist a loved one to die at his or her informed and persistent request is entirely compassionate, is unlikely to be prosecuted. In this sense the policy takes a compassionate, common-sense approach.

However, while it is undoubtedly true that as a result of the prosecuting policy some people have been able to end their lives safe in the knowledge that their loved ones will not face prison for helping them, our dying citizens do not have the medical and legal safety that an assisted dying law along the lines of that in Oregon (and that proposed by Lord Falconer's Assisted Dying Bill) would provide.

Despite the measure of clarity brought by the prosecuting policy the current law does not work well. As the real-life stories in this book demonstrate, the present situation deprives dying people of choice and can cause immense suffering. Unable to make a safe, supported choice to take control of their deaths in the UK over two hundred British people have chosen to be assisted to end their lives in Switzerland. As we have seen, this is a very expensive option, likely to cost in excess of £5,000, which means that for some it is simply *not* an option. The British people who die there, while very appreciative that they are able to do so, are not dying at home but in a foreign country and often without the company of those they would want to be with them.

Others choose to take matters into their own hands. An estimated 2 per cent of suicides in England (which equates to about 120 deaths each year) are those of people with terminal illnesses.[36] Some terminally ill people refuse food and water as this is the only way they can have any control over their death and bring an end to their anguish, while many others suffer through the last weeks and days of life, denied any choice and control.[37]

While the prosecuting policy has provided some reassurance in relation to the involvement of compassionately motivated friends and family in assisted suicide, it causes particular difficulty for healthcare professionals. This group is explicitly identified in the policy of the Director of Public Prosecutions, under factor 14 of the public-interest factors tending in favour of prosecution.

A prosecution is more likely to be required if the suspect was acting in his or her capacity as a medical doctor, nurse, other healthcare professional, a professional carer (whether for payment or not) or as a person in authority, such as prison officer, and the victim was in his or her care.

This causes real problems for patients, doctors and other healthcare professionals, primarily because it acts as a barrier to open conversation. Unlike jurisdictions where assisted dying is legal, patients in the UK feel unable to talk to their doctors about their desire for an assisted death and, as a result, may make hugely important decisions without the benefit of having open discussions with healthcare professionals. This means that people may decide to end their lives without having fully explored the alternatives, such as changes that could be made to their health and social care. It also means that people may be being assisted to die when they are not necessarily competent to make that decision. We have seen that the Oregon DWDA encourages conversations between patients and their doctors. UK patients are missing out.

In addition, patients in jurisdictions where some form of assisted dying is legal can be confident of medical involvement in their death. This might be limited to safeguards and providing a prescription, or it might include a medical professional being with them at the time of their death. In contrast, current law in the UK (and the prosecuting policy where it applies) militates against this. Even getting to Dignitas for an assisted death – where there is at least a degree of medical involvement and trained-volunteer supervision – could potentially prove difficult for some UK citizens. To access assistance to die at Dignitas a person needs to demonstrate his or her medical condition to the satisfaction of a Swiss doctor, and, for British patients, the easiest way to do this is to provide a copy of their medical records. Some UK doctors might be reluctant to hand over a patient's medical records if they think that the person wants to end his or her life for fear of being seen as assisting suicide. Healthcare professionals have legal obligations that require them to perform acts which could be seen as capable of encouraging or assisting suicide. For example, patients have the right to access their medical records under the Data Protection Act. If a healthcare professional is aware that an individual wants the records for the purpose of seeking an assisted suicide overseas, it is unclear whether releasing a patient's records would give rise to liability under the Suicide Act. Recent GMC guidance for doctors, expressly on the topic of assisted suicide, suggests that providing medical records is unlikely to be considered assistance,[38] but other aspects of the guidance suggest that providing information, in the knowledge that a patient could use it to end their life, *might* be seen as assistance.[39]

In addition, we have seen that the introduction of laws in the Netherlands and Belgium has been followed by a decrease in illegal practices such as non-voluntary euthanasia.[40, 41] Research in the UK shows that doctors are illegally ending patients' lives here with and without their explicit consent. Approximately 0.21 per cent of deaths attended by a medical practitioner in the UK are as a result of voluntary euthanasia at the patient's explicit request. That means there are around 1,000 illegal cases of assistance to die each year, with a further 1,500 deaths as a result of non-voluntary euthanasia.[42] So, enhancing patient safety – both in terms of ensuring patients have met some eligibility criteria and in regulating doctors' practice – is critical.

Another element of this concerns the timing of checks and safeguards on practice. At present in the UK any 'official' investigation into a person's reasons for wanting assisted dying – looking at his or her capacity to make a decision, how informed the individual is regarding options and the motivations of anyone who assists him or her – only happens after the patient has died. This is obviously too late to prevent abuse. In all the overseas jurisdictions we have examined there are multiple checks, investigations and safeguards that take place before a patient can be assisted to die.

Evidence from abroad shows that legal assistance to die can work safely, simultaneously protecting people and offering real choice. Research carried out in the UK demonstrates that the majority of people who are terminally ill believe that assisted dying should be available, even if they do not necessarily want it for themselves.[43, 44]

For the purpose of Dignity in Dying's campaign for terminally ill adults to have choice we turn particularly to Oregon, where assisted dying was legalized in 1997. Assisted dying has been practised safely and effectively with no alarmingly sharp rises in numbers or cause for concern about why people have requested assistance to die. There is no reason why such a safeguarded approach could not be applied here in the UK.

7
VOLUNTARILY STOPPING EATING AND DRINKING
Efstratia Tuson: 'Talk to the captain; they can just drop me overboard!'

Pamela Tuson's grandmother Angeliki was a shepherdess, born on one of the islands in the North Aegean Sea. When Angeliki was about fourteen she and her friend Katrina ran away to Cairo. Pamela tells her grandmother's story. 'When my grandfather first saw my grandmother in Cairo he decided that he wanted to talk to her, to kiss her. She said, "If you want to kiss me, you have to marry me! And you can't talk to me because my cousins will see you and you'll be in trouble – they'll come after you!" In fact, she had no cousins or any other family in Egypt. My grandmother became the local midwife, drawing on her experience as a shepherdess. Her name means "Angel", and poor neighbours who got sick would ask her to help them instead of the doctor. She was a really strong woman. My mother inherited her strength, and I suppose I have inherited it from my mother.'

Angeliki's youngest daughter Efstratia, Pamela's mother, was born in Egypt in 1924. The headmistress of her school wanted to send her to university, an unusual goal for a girl in an Arab country at that time. Efstratia was unable to continue her education because of the family's circumstances, including the fact that Efstratia's aunt was pregnant with her first child. Angeliki took Efstratia with her when she moved from Cairo to the Egyptian countryside to help with the birth.

Efstratia met her English soldier husband during the Second World War, but her parents did not want the couple to marry. They would say, 'Khaki can hide a multitude of sins – you don't know what's behind it,' because, as Pamela observes, soldiers were sometimes married. If Efstratia married a British soldier she would inevitably leave Cairo – and her parents – to move to England with her husband. In those days that could have meant never seeing her family again.

When Efstratia was around nineteen, after three years of asking the British Army and her parents for permission, she and Pamela's father were married in Egypt. Efstratia travelled to England in one of the naval convoys that crossed the Mediterranean. Despite the danger posed by torpedoes and aerial attack she enjoyed the experience greatly – as she later told Pamela, every day was treated as if it could have been the last, and there were parties on board ship almost every night.

After arriving in England in 1944 she had a very difficult time. By contrast with the sunny and warm Egyptian climate winter was particularly severe and bitter that year. She could not get Greek food, and what food she could obtain was rationed. There was no one who could speak her language. She had been educated in Greek – and, partially, in French – and she could only speak a few words of English, so she had to learn a new language. There were no formal courses, so she taught herself. In addition, she had no family or friends in England, there was a great deal of bomb damage and there was no Greek Orthodox church.

Faith had been an important component of Efstratia's upbringing, with the Greek community in Egypt being based around the church both in terms of worship and of community support. She found the experience of attending an English service quite different. Efstratia would have been made acutely aware of the difference when in 1952 her first child died of liver cancer at the age of seven. That would always be a devastating experience for any parent, but to have it happen so far from home must have been almost unbearable.

She learnt to play bridge and did voluntary translation work for a BBC radio programme for non-English-speaking Greeks. After Pamela's father died in 1984 Efstratia's life opened up. She travelled extensively and took a teaching course in English. She taught Greek for the next twenty years, and she continued to improve her spoken and written French.

Pamela knows that her mother did her best for her and her two brothers as they grew up, often under very difficult circumstances. Efstratia was quite an unusual mother for her time because she insisted on working. Pamela's father was in the army until 1961, and it was not the norm for army wives to work, but Efstratia would climb out of the window to get to her job, despite her husband's possessive nature. She was determined and strong-willed.

Efstratia believed in assisted dying and euthanasia all her life. Pamela wonders whether her mother's view that you should do whatever is needed to stop suffering came from the Greek culture. She says that, like cremation, assisted dying is one of the things the Greek church does not allow or even talk about, but Greek people who believe in cremation occasionally practise it regardless of the church's teaching.

Pamela described her mother as a very gentle person. She wouldn't hurt a fly and didn't like to cause anything to suffer. She certainly didn't like the idea that her children might witness her suffering over a long period.

Efstratia developed asthma and allergies when she and her husband moved to a house in a low-lying damp area in Surrey after he left the army. Otherwise she was well all her life until in about 2003 she felt something heavy in her left side. A consultant found that she had an ovarian cyst that was very large and needed to be removed. During the operation a great deal of mucus was found to be emanating from her appendix: it was a sign of *Pseudomyxoma peritonei*, which was otherwise asymptomatic. While she was under the anaesthetic for the cyst removal the surgeon removed as much mucus as possible.

When Efstratia was diagnosed there was no treatment for *Pseudomyxoma peritonei* other than the Sugarbaker procedure (named after the consultant who devised it). This involves attempting to remove every mucous cell before bathing the area in a form of chemotherapy. If any mucous cells are missed they will multiply. The operation requires the patient to spend about thirteen hours under general anaesthetic. It was deemed inappropriate because of Efstratia's age and her history of high cholesterol, as well as the physical and emotional trauma the procedure would inflict on her with no certainty of benefit.

In May 2008 Efstratia, in extreme pain, was admitted to hospital for investigation. Her doctor decided to aspirate the mucus: it is important to remove it while it is liquid because, if it collects and congeals, it solidifies. In that state not only is aspiration difficult but the size and weight of the collected, solidified mucus can prevent the organs working properly. Efstratia underwent the aspiration procedure a total of eight times before she died in January 2009. 'During that period she asked every doctor who attended her for help to die. Naturally they refused: they seemed awkward and scared to go into her room because it seemed they were afraid to have to say no to her pleas for their help to die. Their visits became shorter and less frequent. Once she said to me, "They're going to do it this time – don't leave me" (she was excited rather than afraid), and I said, "Look, Mummy, they're not going to do that. They won't risk their careers."'

The *Pseudomyxoma peritonei* did not stop Efstratia doing things, but the mucus distended her abdomen. In addition, sometimes it got heavy and pressed on her bladder making her need to urinate inconveniently often. Efstratia was concerned about the aesthetic aspect of her condition – she felt self-conscious about the distension of her abdomen – and she was in a lot of discomfort as the distension increased. She began to lose weight because the build-up of mucus compressed her stomach and made her feel full. She also developed a hernia and experienced unremitting acid reflux. Neither that nor her gross constipation was properly managed, and neither condition could be successfully treated with medication.

Pamela acknowledges that it was the loss of dignity that affected her mother most. 'My mother couldn't defecate unaided, and her bowel was pressing on her bladder making her urinate frequently. Her distended bowel also meant she was unable to sit comfortably, and she could no longer enjoy playing bridge.'

On top of that she had had cataract surgery. One of the lenses slipped, but the hospital admissions and recovery periods meant it was too difficult to get new glasses to enable her to read, play patience or watch TV. She also had painful degeneration and limited use of one shoulder after the joint was set badly during surgery following a road accident.

In 2008 Pamela and Efstratia went on two last cruises together: in August they toured the Nordic regions, including St Petersburg, and a second cruise took them to the Caribbean over Christmas and the New Year. Pamela arranged those cruises because she knew her mother's life was coming to an end. She chose the Cunard *Victoria* during her maiden year, as she knew there would be a higher than usual ratio of staff to passengers should help be required, and there was a hospital on board. Mother and daughter had always enjoyed cruises. Efstratia, who loved water and the sea, especially enjoyed the entertainment. Pamela has a disability, so Cunard gave mother and daughter a large cabin with a walk-in shower and a big terrace.

The second cruise involved crossing the Atlantic in late autumn, and almost everyone on board was consigned to their cabins with seasickness. Pamela says that she and her mother had looked forward to spending Christmas on board.

'You couldn't really get out of bed! Once we got to the smoother seas and sunnier climate of the Caribbean things improved, but it wasn't a happy trip. My mother stopped taking her supplements and aspirin, and she stopped drinking water. When I asked her, "What's going on?" she said she would have the water later. Perhaps she simply didn't want the trouble of getting out of bed. She cut back on everything. She came out of her cabin for Christmas dinner, but she was not drinking, and I was getting seriously worried about her. I called the on-board medical service, and a nurse decided she should be admitted to a room in the ship's hospital.'

Pamela and her mother stayed on the *Victoria* for the duration of the cruise, except for a short walk during their first port of call. On the way back to England the ship made a scheduled stop at Madeira, and Efstratia's abdomen was drained again. When the ship docked at Southampton Pamela drove her mother straight to a large private hospital in London.

'Once more she was hoping that a doctor would end her life. She had hoped that the ship's doctor would do it. She always gave me the job of talking to them. During the cruise she'd said, "Talk to the captain; they can just drop me overboard!"'

By this time, January 2009, Efstratia had been a member of Dignitas for a few months. She wanted to go to Switzerland, and Pamela advised her not to tell anybody or to say anything about it. She did not tell any of the doctors, but she did tell Pamela's two brothers. One of them started talking about it, despite being advised not to, because he thinks you should be honest about assisted dying. He said, 'Right, we'll take her to Switzerland.' Pamela found out that Efstratia could go to Dignitas by ferry and ambulance; it would be a long journey, but a special vehicle could be found.

'The problem was that there were insufficient doctors in Switzerland willing to work with Dignitas. They were under pressure owing to demand, and my mother would have to wait three months. And then there was the report we needed from the hospital, which the staff lied about. They kept saying they would give it to me, and I began to feel uncomfortable asking for it repeatedly. At first they said that the fax machine was broken. Later, if I wanted to speak to a doctor I had to try to catch them in the car park!'

In about 2007 Efstratia had written an advance decision, but it was not enforceable: the hospital's legal team pointed out that Pamela had acted as one of the witnesses. At her mother's request, and because she and her brothers knew that it was what their mother wanted, Pamela got another advance decision form. Efstratia completed it, and it was witnessed within a matter of hours, but the hospital's legal team was highly suspicious – Pamela imagines them wondering how on earth the family had got a new form completed so quickly. It was fairly straightforward to complete because in answer to every question her mother said that she wanted to die.

Efstratia's consultant commented that it was unusual to find all the members of a patient's family in agreement. He said that there are usually one or two relatives who will disagree and want the person kept alive at all costs despite their suffering.

'My mother began feeling very cold and said she'd like to go to Dignitas. It was quite difficult to start with, because nobody was answering the phone. Eventually somebody did answer, and he said something about Friends At the End. I found someone to talk to there, and they sent a woman to speak to me. She enquired, unsuccessfully, at Dignitas to see if they could bring the date forward. She then talked to my mother in private, and after that discussion my mother decided she would stop eating and drinking. When she told us this we said that she had to be very sure that was what she wanted to do: there was no going back. She was pleased to have a way out. She told us that she was going to stop eating and drinking in order to die – she was absolutely clear about that.'

Efstratia had been in hospital for about a week when she decided to stop taking food and fluids. At that point she was still suffering painful acid reflux and was grossly constipated. The doctors wanted to try various drugs, but she didn't like taking them. She was very sensitive to medication and suffered from allergies, despite having always eaten healthily. The medications, which Pamela says were considered palliative care, just made Efstratia feel worse. Pamela is angry that palliative care is seen as a panacea – it provided very little comfort to her dying mother.

Pamela reacted very calmly when her mother announced that she was going to stop eating and drinking. 'It was my mother's wish, and deciding your own fate is a human entitlement: everybody must be able to decide for themselves. It's not for other people to decide – the person dying is the one who is suffering. That type of suffering is on a different level – you have to be in that body, undergoing that unbearable suffering and with that lack of existential control, to understand it. I was focused on doing everything that was necessary, and I was concentrating on the job at hand. My role was to be compassionate, to make my mother's life as comfortable as I could, to get her the best medical attention that was available, to spend as much time as I could with her, to help give her as much peace of mind as possible and to try to make her death painless.'

Pamela's only comment on her mother's decision to stop eating and drinking was to warn, 'Mummy, you have to be really sure, because if you start eating and drinking again your kidneys may be damaged, and life could be much more difficult afterwards.' She says the risk of kidney damage was the reason there was so much emphasis on making sure that Efstratia knew what she wanted to do and understood the implications of her decision.

As far as Pamela is aware, the hospital did not need a written expression of her mother's decision to stop eating and drinking, and she thinks that Efstratia's oral statement was enough. As Pamela says, patients can't be force-fed against their will. Even when Efstratia was eating it had been almost impossible to get a suitable diet for her. She would tick the boxes on the menu form, indicating what she wanted, and when the food was delivered it was mostly incorrect. Pamela observes that nobody seemed to be concerned about whether or not her mother ate any or all of the food she was given.

Once Efstratia decided to stop eating and drinking her wishes were respected and the staff no longer brought her food. Pamela believes that they stopped offering her water, too.

Pamela found that the many tasks she had to undertake had an unbearable impact on the amount of time she could spend with her dying mother.

'The only thing you want is to be with the person who is dying. You don't want to spend time with matron or the nurses repeatedly correcting their mistakes and reminding them verbally not to lift my mother by her damaged shoulder before resorting to putting up handwritten notices around the room to remind them. You don't want to spend time chasing the maintenance man to mend a banging door that shook the medical equipment inside my mother's room. You don't want to chase the staff or to be made to wait forty minutes for moisturizing mouth swabs while my mother cried out, "Die! Die! Die!" You don't want to be challenged by a nurse saying, "Well, she wanted to stop drinking." You don't want to spend time finding her doctor or looking things up on the internet or phoning Switzerland. You just want to be with the person.

'I seemed to be organizing everything. It was energy-draining and made me very angry and frustrated. I had to do all this while hobbling along with a collapsed hip. That's my mother's stoicism in me coming out. I know she would have done the same for me.'

It took only five days for Efstratia to die after she stopped eating and drinking. Her doctor told Pamela that it normally takes longer than that. He thought that it was due to her strength of will to end her life.

'My mother's appetite was waning – she was eating less because the pressure of the mucus on her stomach made her feel full. She didn't go from three big meals a day to nothing. That must have made it easier for her to stop eating. She was weary, but she was also very lucid. My mother always had a good brain, and she knew exactly what was going on.'

For Pamela those five days went quite quickly. Efstratia was conscious most of the time, sometimes sleeping, but when Pamela was with her she was mostly awake. She was able to speak almost to the end of her life because Pamela and the nursing staff continually moistened her mouth with swabs.

Pamela is certain that her mother would have died before 25 January 2009 if she had been given the choice of an assisted death. She had expressed her wish to have help to die long before the two of them went on their second cruise of 2008.

The last night Efstratia was alive was very distressing, because she was coughing up a lot of phlegm. The medical team treating her used apparatus that was hideously noisy to suck up the choking mucus, a process Pamela describes as extremely exhausting, even traumatic, for the patient. Pamela herself was experiencing great pain and difficulty moving, standing and sitting as the result of her hip, although she tried at all times not to let her mother see how much she was suffering. She asked for a suitable chair, but one could not be found anywhere. The hospital declined to give Pamela a bed in her mother's room because they said it might pose a risk if Efstratia needed urgent attention. Pamela's reaction was to point out that there was no risk involved because her mother just wanted to die. Pamela wanted to stay with her mother during that last night, but she was forced to go home because suitable seating could not be provided: sitting on the available chair would have resulted in intolerable pain. As a result, Pamela was deprived of the opportunity to spend her mother's last night with her. She says that the memory and the loss will remain with her for the rest of her life.

When Pamela returned to the hospital the next day she found that her mother had been prescribed morphine during the latter part of the night. Pamela thinks it was Efstratia's sudden deterioration that influenced the doctors' judgement. They could now record the fact that she was in pain and distress, and they could justify giving her pain relief. Pamela sees this solely as the medical team protecting themselves.

On that final morning, as Pamela walked into the room with the doctor and the sister, her mother said, 'Oh, there's my daughter Pamela!'

'She was completely *compos mentis*, and she said those words as if she was proud that I was her daughter and pleased that I was there.' The dose of morphine was increased, and the staff suggested that Pamela should let her brothers know. When she asked how long it would be, the staff said to ask them to come immediately. Efstratia died a few hours later. Pamela is not sure whether or not her mother was conscious during those final few hours. 'I wanted to make sure that she wasn't disturbed, that she was peaceful, and I just wanted to be there with her.'

Pamela thinks that there are a lot of nurses who agree with the idea of assisted dying but cannot say so for fear of losing their jobs. She knows that one particular nurse agreed with what her mother was doing and that she saw the pointlessness of forcing terminally ill patients to suffer before they die. 'The ward sister was given the job of preparing my mother's body. She asked me to leave the room, but

I said, "No. I want to be here." I sat on a chair adjacent to the bed so that I could continue to be with her. I wanted to ensure that she was treated respectfully. I didn't want to talk, I just wanted to be there.

'The way the ward sister treated my mother after her death was absolutely wonderful. She washed my mother's body very gently and with great care before putting her in a pure white swaddling bag. She closed the zip very gradually until finally I could see nothing more of my dear mother. And all this time she was talking to her. She used the most lovely affectionate terms and words, saying things like "Sweetheart, I'm just going to roll you over now" or "Darling, I'm going to move your arm." There was something very beautiful, pure, simple, peaceful and loving about that experience. I am really pleased that I made sure I stayed in the room during the ritual and watched over how my mother was handled. I was able to watch as the nurse held and touched my mother with great gentleness.'

It is a tragedy that Efstratia's repeated pleas for help to die could not be met with that same loving compassion.

8
A NURSE'S PERSPECTIVE ON END-OF-LIFE CARE
by Andrew Heenan

In J.K. Rowling's *Harry Potter and the Deathly Hallows* Professor Dumbledore asks his friend for a last favour as he knows death is approaching. He tells him that he would infinitely prefer a fast and painless end to his life to a long-drawn-out and messy one but emphasizes that his friend needs to consider his position as he alone will know whether his soul will be harmed if he helps an old man avoid pain and humiliation.

A children's book featuring a man asking for assistance in dying in an entirely matter-of-fact way? Rowling did not feel a need to explore the ethical issues. She left that entirely to the reader.

This passage really made me stop and think how much things have changed where assisted dying is concerned. The topic used to be almost taboo, yet assisted dying is now legal in four of the United States of America and UK residents can go to Switzerland. That is hardly ideal, but it represents enormous progress and reflects a major shift in people's attitudes.

When I first started work in the National Health Service over forty years ago the debate – where it existed – was not even about assisted dying. It was about euthanasia, and that isn't merely a semantic difference; the debate effectively bypassed those most affected.

Even the issue of disease prognosis was rarely discussed beyond a frequently inaccurate guess. Indeed it used to be routine for doctors to be over-optimistic about prognosis, even with conditions such as polio where after the initial stages the outcome could be predicted with remarkable accuracy. In the 1970s I witnessed downright lies on more than one occasion. Whether this was a doctor's need to avoid delivering bad news or simply a paternalistic belief that it was 'kinder' is a matter for debate, and it was probably a combination of both. There is no doubt that doctors tended to the paternalistic, and delivering bad news might be seen as an admission of failure. My experience certainly supports the theory that physicians find it easier to break bad news than surgeons as there is no way they could blame themselves.

> One consultant surgeon would avoid speaking to patients if their operation was deemed 'unsuccessful'. He would face them once and explain the situation, but on subsequent ward rounds he would simply walk straight past them.[1]

As students we knew that challenging a doctor would achieve nothing; the patient or relative would be more upset, while our careers would be over. But I remember discussions with colleagues where we agreed that we would never lie in response to a direct question, although we were acutely aware that our silence was condoning dishonesty on other occasions. In practice few patients asked for more information than the consultant gave them, although – often – they appeared to know that there was more that they could be told, and they very often guessed the truth.

Even in the late 1970s many patients were still kept in the dark about their prognosis and the doctor's plan for treatment – or a decision *not* to treat. The words 'No Resuscitation' were often written in patients' notes without them or their families being aware of it let alone consulted. Some hospitals preferred the euphemism 'No Mayday' or a coloured label to ensure that only the 'right' people knew of the decision.

I never heard euthanasia discussed in relation to specific patients, although I did hear variations on 'You wouldn't let an animal suffer like that' and more targeted comments in relation to striving officiously to keep alive.

> The registrar, responding to his emergency call, came into the room where we were attempting to resuscitate a man in his eighties who was in the late stages of terminal cancer. He looked at each of us in turn, shaking his head, before asking rhetorically, 'What are we doing here?'

Already there were signs of pressure for patients to know more and to be told the truth. However, during my first ten years – in several different hospitals and in different specialities – I never saw a professional decision challenged. Back then I could never have imagined the level of assertion I saw ten years ago.

A patient's mother, who felt that her views were not being heard, removed the 'Do not resuscitate' order from her daughter's file. When challenged she calmly threatened to go to the newspapers. After renewed consideration the order was cancelled. At this stage the patient – aged twenty-two – had not been involved in the discussions at all, although she was later.

In the 1980s what should be said, when and by whom was more often a matter for discussion. Bad news was still the privilege of the doctor, but, although they hated to delegate this task, many doctors were loath to actually deliver bad news. On several occasions, when a colleague or I voiced concern over the delay – and the distress it was causing (or would cause) – we were ordered not to divulge the truth. It was at this time that I first used the mantra 'But if I am asked I shall not lie.' I do not now recall where I first heard it, but I know I was not alone in using it. And it was not just a mantra. I did tell the truth when asked, and I knew then, as I know now, that everyone gained by that honesty.

Part of the problem was that few doctors had had any education in breaking bad news, and they were aware of their limitations.

Following the failure of his second bone-marrow transplant it was apparent that a patient would not be able to survive a third. The patient did not even know that the second transplant had failed, and, despite being weakened by a chest infection, he was optimistic. The registrar had been delegated the task of explaining, but for four days he had made excuses. On the fifth day, after pressure from the nursing staff, he agreed to speak to the patient. He walked towards the patient's room, then turned and ran off the ward.

Some doctors, of course, were blithely unaware of their limitations.

The consultant specifically asked that a patient's wife be present on the Friday-morning ward round. The man had seen his GP with an abdominal ache that would not go away; he thought it might be constipation. He was thirty-five and had never had a serious health issue in his life. Blood tests, followed by ultrasound and a scan, revealed advanced liver metastases secondary to lung cancer. The consultant swept in, said, 'I'm sorry, Mr X, you have advanced cancer, and there's nothing we can do for you.' The patient cried, his wife fainted, the consultant moved on to the next patient and one of my colleagues ceased to be a smoker.

Communication was a problem in both directions, although I suspect that patients and their families were following the medical example.

A patient's wife was told that her husband had little time left. Her response was, 'Please don't tell him.' Within a couple of days the patient realized what was happening and asked for the truth. His response was, 'Please don't tell my wife.' Watching them sitting together in fearful silence was a strain for all until we managed to persuade them both to be more open. That couple merely reflected the prevailing medical opinion of the time: 'It's best if the patient doesn't know.'

It was not until 1983, in a London teaching hospital, that I saw a direct and open challenge to the medical hegemony.

On the weekly ward round a man who had come to realize that he was dying shouted at the ranks of junior doctors between him and the consultant. 'Where is he? He's happy to talk to me when I'm responding to the treatment, but where is he when it all goes wrong?' The consultant approached the bed, gave a full and honest explanation, answered the man's questions and the challenge was over. The man was not seeking control of the situation – he just wanted the truth.

In those days few doctors I met could have had a conversation with a patient about assisted dying, and few patients would have been well enough informed about their illness to raise the question.

I strongly believe that it is not just information that people want now; they want *control*. I am sure there are many factors involved here. We can put a man on the moon, we can transplant hearts, and people increasingly reject 'traditional' religious beliefs if not faith in its entirety. People are less likely to trust to God or fate, while the traditional assumption that 'Doctor knows best' is no longer acceptable.

We live in a consumer society in which we know the price of healthcare but not necessarily its value. In view of these and other factors I do not find it surprising that, faced with irreversible disease, people should seek more control over their own lives and deaths.

These major cultural changes have been mirrored within the health service and the professions, but healthcare has seen major changes of its own over the past forty years. There are several key 'health service' issues that have informed and influenced wider debates on death and assisted dying.

For example, chronic or increasing pain is a feature of many progressive neurological disorders as well as terminal cancer. Poorly managed pain will inevitably lead to a wretched life, and the expression 'poor quality of life' is weasel words for the appalling reality experienced by many.

Opioids (morphine, diamorphine and their derivatives) have long been – and still are – at the centre of pain control. But the way they are used has changed markedly. The oral form used to be a 'Brompton cocktail' – a concoction of diamorphine, spirits (usually whisky, gin or brandy) plus cocaine and chlorpromazine, a mixture designed to provide pain relief without inducing excessive drowsiness. While some people received it regularly, it was often given 'when necessary' (although a double dose at night was usual), with the hour-by-hour decisions being taken by nurses in a hospital setting.

In my experience, the effect of Brompton's varied greatly from person to person, some being heavily sedated while others got little benefit. Prescriptions rarely seemed to get the balance right between pain and drowsiness.

Research – primarily in cancer care – has led to analgesics being given on a regular basis. Overall, much less analgesia is required when the medicines are taken that way, and fewer side-effects are seen. The principle is to prevent pain rather than chase it.

One reason why pain control was so often inadequate was the widespread fear of addiction. This influenced prescribing on occasion and was frequently cited as the reason patients were denied painkillers when they asked for them. Leaving aside the obvious point (asked of me by more than one dying patient) 'Does it really matter?' we now know that, if the drugs are prescribed appropriately, the risk of addiction is negligible. The principle is that, where the drug is 'used up' by the pain, there is none available to become addicted to. And here, too, getting on top of the pain – rather than chasing it – usually allows for effective pain control. This was, of course, impossible when pethidine injections were usually prescribed four-hourly (it is largely ineffective after about three hours) and morphine was often prescribed six-hourly (benefits fade rapidly after about four hours).

There is now a much wider variety of methods whereby painkillers can be administered; rather than oral liquid or injection into muscle or just under the skin, the development of long-acting forms has helped many patients to avoid the peaks and troughs of pain control that once were a feature of chronic and terminal illness. These include twelve/twenty-four-hour tablets or capsules, long-acting liquids (using freeze-dried ingredients), sublingual forms, adhesive patches and sophisticated intravenous or subcutaneous pumps delivering a steady dose, safely and consistently, or allowing the patient to control the amount given (with safe-guards against overdose).

Indeed the pharmaceutical possibilities are so many and varied that most district general hospitals have a specialist pharmacist to advise.

Local and regional anaesthetics have also advanced significantly, both in the range of agents available and the skills and tools needed to use them. Many hospitals use transcutaneous electrical nerve stimulation (TENS), and some offer complementary approaches such as acupuncture, aromatherapy and relaxation (among others).

Far fewer people these days have pain that cannot be managed, and for many the control is good enough to allow them reasonable activity with few or no side-effects. 'I'm still aware of the pain,' said one patient, 'but it doesn't feel like my pain. It feels like it's someone else's!'

Possibly one of the biggest changes in pain control, affecting the largest number of people, has been the acceptance of Elisabeth Kübler-Ross's dictum 'Pain is what the patient says it is.' Kübler-Ross, an American, was a psychiatrist who chose to specialize in death and dying, at one point 'forcing medical students to face people who were dying'. She published her seminal work on the five stages of grief in 1970, and it proved highly influential on both sides of the Atlantic, especially among nurses. 'Pain is what the patient says it is' became a powerful tool for nurses, who saw pain much more than the average doctor. I saw one doctor splutter, 'But that's meaningless' with barely restrained fury, and on one level he was right, but the phrase does contain an undeniable truth. It was a major step in changing the focus of pain control from 'We'll do what we can' to 'What would you like us to do?' This approach works well with patient-controlled analgesia, the pump that gives the patient total control.

Kübler-Ross was a great supporter of the hospice care movement, believing that 'euthanasia prevents people from completing their "unfinished business"'. She had a series of strokes in 1995 when she was in her early seventies. In an interview in 2002 she said that she was 'ready for death', and she died in 2004.

Other distressing symptoms of chronic and progressive diseases have seen similar revolutions, if not so dramatic as pain control. Nausea, fits, tremor and even breathing difficulties can be managed more effectively with the army of pharmaceuticals now available.

The quality of life of someone diagnosed with a progressive neurological condition today is likely to be much better than someone in a similar situation forty years ago. The risk of recurrent infections can be reduced, incontinence can be managed and physiotherapy and occupational therapy have matured to become the leading professions in rehabilitation and maintaining function as long as possible. Technology has produced miracles in communication – Stephen Hawking's early insistence on speaking for himself has led the way in making speech synthesis acceptable, even familiar, to the world.

The movement to provide genuinely equal opportunities for people with disability has a long way to go, but accessibility and other problems are being considered as never before.

At the heart of many of these changes has been the hospice movement. Forty years ago the movement was in its infancy in the UK: St Christopher's, probably Britain's first modern hospice, opened in 1967. Led by Dame Cicely Saunders, the hospice movement has grown and developed. Saunders was a nurse and later trained as a social worker before becoming a doctor. With a deep interest in palliative medicine, she was uniquely qualified to lead by example as well as to campaign for change and growth.

It would be difficult to overestimate the magnitude of the changes improved palliative medicine has brought about for the many individuals who have benefited, as well as the changes it has forced on the medical and nursing professions. Palliative medicine was a small and unloved branch of medicine, specialist palliative care nurses did not exist (the first Macmillan nurse was not appointed until 1975) and research into palliation was sparse. The hospice movement challenged low expectations, encouraged research into symptom control, offered specialist education and dragged the NHS in its wake.

The movement is now an extensive network of care. Initially focusing almost entirely on people with cancer, its remit has widened to include many debilitating diseases, and it now offers research-based care and holistic support both within its buildings and in the home. I have no doubt that the development and growth of hospice services in the UK has led to major changes in the care of people with cancer and progressive neurological disease, particularly towards the end of life.

One consequence of these advances in healthcare has been a significantly extended life expectancy for people with incurable progressive diseases. This has occurred in parallel with the general extension of life expectancy. Other factors – such as a better understanding of the disease process, improved symptom control, improved management of concurrent illness and better ways of communicating with people who once were often cut off from those around them – have contributed to extended life expectancy. In part, this is also due to earlier diagnosis of many conditions, and with a greater understanding of genetics and disease processes this trend will continue and probably accelerate.

The development of living wills (now known as advance decisions) is another milestone in changing attitudes, among professionals as well as patients. This device was proposed in 1969 by Louis Kutner, a lawyer, as a way of allowing patients to decline life-sustaining treatment even if they were too ill to communicate.

In the UK this device is enshrined in law by the 2005 Mental Capacity Act, which provides a statutory framework. The Act, designed to empower and protect vulnerable people who cannot make their own decisions, makes it clear who can take decisions and in what circumstances, and it sets out how they should go about this.

The Act enables people to plan for a time when they may lose mental capacity, allowing them to limit, for example, the use of intravenous fluids and nutrition as well as deciding whether or not cardiopulmonary resuscitation would be appropriate.

The provisions of the Mental Capacity Act can be used by anyone living with a condition that involves, or may lead to, an incapacity to make decisions (such as progressive neurological disease, cancer, dementia). Its provisions could be used by others such as, for example, Jehovah's Witnesses who need to be sure that they are not subjected to a blood transfusion while anaesthetized.

In practice, the Act is not a perfect solution and has on occasion led to disputes and distress. But, considering it has gone from conception to law in less than forty years, it has been remarkably successful. Most of all, it has focused attention on the wishes of the individual. This, in turn, has led to a discussion about the competency of the individual at the time they wrote their advance decision. This is highly significant, for example, for people with Alzheimer's disease, and it raises issues of respite and lucidity when, for many, assumptions of a continuous and steady decline had been the norm.

Even more than that, the advance decision has further tipped the scale of control from healthcare professionals to the individual and is intended to ensure that decisions are based on need not diagnosis and are taken in the best interests of the individual. Furthermore, the individual's mental capacity at the time of signing the decision is the important factor, not his or her mental capacity at the time of any later dispute.

As well as the assumption that someone is capable of making decisions unless proved otherwise, the law even recognizes the possible validity of decisions that many would see as eccentric or unwise.

The advance decision allows someone with a progressive disease to specify, to a significant degree, how he or she wants the disease managed when that individual is no longer able to take part in the discussion.

The Mental Capacity Act is truly progressive, but, while it gives a measure of control and independence previously denied to people with progressive disease, it stops short of granting any control over the time or circumstances of dying. This is, arguably, an illogical omission in such a ground-breaking law and a source of frustration.

In outlining some of the advances in technology, science and care it is easy to give the impression that it is all good news: hospitals and hospices can do so much more, pharmacology and technology have come so far and professional education has progressed with more emphasis given to ethics, the patient's experience and communication. The professions have changed in many other ways, too, with higher standards expected, better monitoring and a higher bar to entry.

But have the professions changed with respect to assisted dying? While it would be unfair and impossible to generalize, I would suggest that some things *have* changed if only to reflect wider cultural changes.

Medicine is a profession that for many decades was controlled by the product of public schools – upper-middle-class white men. Doctors existed in a closed culture imbued with an expectation of power and control, albeit with great responsibility. While I suspect that few daughters of agricultural labourers have entered the profession, women have achieved numerical parity with men. Even in surgery, the last bastion of male medical power, women now have real career prospects, as do candidates from ethnic minorities.

> When a London medical school was shown to have racist selection procedures they were able to argue that, despite that, they were still the second largest in terms of ethnic-minority intake.

All that is in the past and is relevant only because it illustrates the depth of change forced on to the medical profession, with a modernized profession probably more prone to empathy and acceptance of new ideas.

Nursing has also been turned upside down, arguably replacing a profession built on a practice-based apprenticeship and somewhat lacking in theory with a profession built on academic education and somewhat lacking in experience. University-based recruiters no longer seek dedicated vocational trainees but prefer degree-level candidates who are schooled in managing a team of healthcare assistants rather than caring for vulnerable individuals. While this has given us a workforce willing and able to argue the ethics of assisted dying in the classroom, it has not necessarily given us nurses with the confidence or understanding to discuss these issues with real patients.

Nursing has also become less reliant on individuals driven by a religious calling, although, of course, many still are. Many nurses are drawn to work with people who are dying – or living with progressive disease – but the modern nurse, I believe, is much more likely to choose a career path based on other criteria.

In so far as it is possible to generalize, healthcare professionals broadly reflect the views of the wider population and are just as much in favour of changing the law on assisted dying. But my experience also suggests that hospice staff might hold a more polarized set of views. This is an area where much more research into attitudes is required.

So what do all these changes mean in practice? The likelihood of a sympathetic hearing from healthcare professionals is probably much higher, but the likelihood of assistance to die, pending a change in the law, is no higher at all.

The past forty years have seen unbridled progress within healthcare, limited only by ever-tightening purse strings, and many would argue that it is all good. However, every advance brings its own problems – for some people at least.

The hospice movement has brought many beneficial changes, but it is not the complete answer for every dying person. It is important to stress that each of the 220 or so UK hospices is unique, offering different services in different ways and run by different people with different outlooks. They also have different problems and different ways of dealing with them.

Arguably, hospices have become victims of their own success; as their reputation has grown, so has the number of referrals. As their skills and services have expanded, the NHS has taken advantage of this and happily passed over to the hospices work that was traditionally the job of the district general hospital. This is not bad in itself, but it has led to some hospices struggling to cope and has led to many rationing their services. In the early days of the modern hospice during the 1970s they were places where people went to die in peace; referrals were few and waiting lists were virtually unheard of.

Now, following referral, the patient may have to wait some time for a home visit. After an assessment they will be offered some kind of home-care package. Successive governments of all persuasions tell us that we all want to die at home. Opinion polls confirm this, and in an ideal world it is undeniably true. But this is not an ideal world, and the answer you get depends on the question you ask.

An elderly, severely debilitated person with uncontrolled pain, nausea and frequent falls (or other equally distressing problems) who has only an equally elderly, perhaps incapacitated, spouse to support him or her would probably prefer in-patient care. The realistic alternative may be a couple of home visits a week from a healthcare assistant, following a plan devised by a palliative care nurse after a one-hour first (and last) visit.

But, in many cases, no one is offering even that choice. The government is mindful of the cost, the opinion pollsters do not have the imagination to ask different questions and the hospices do not have the capacity. I do not know how common this scenario is, but I do know that it happens, and if the hospice movement cannot provide certainty then it has already failed some people.

Most of the early hospices were set up to help people with cancer. Even now not all of them can provide the breadth of skills required by the many and varied challenges of progressive neurological disease – although, without doubt, they can provide an infinitely better service than most non-specialist nursing homes and many geriatric wards.

One of the most serious criticisms of certain hospices has been their religious focus. In some cases this was a conscious policy, in others the unintended consequence of employing a majority of staff from a particular background.

In the words of one nurse, 'We were taken on a tour of the building. It started and finished in the chapel. I asked if it mattered what our beliefs were. "Oh no," said the Sister. "We say prayers for everyone."'

On occasion people have declined a place at a particular hospice because of its reputation. As one patient said to me, 'When you're dying, you don't need God rammed down your throat.'

Certain hospices have been 'too middle class', with decisions reflecting the paternalistic attitudes and experiences of senior staff.

> Two women were discussed at the meeting. One was an audibly working-class woman whose always untidy bed was surrounded by noisy, happy grandchildren almost every day, often so many that she was exhausted after playing with them. The other was a woman of low mood who hardly spoke unless spoken to, had one visitor each weekend but was always impeccably dressed and always wore her make-up for the doctors' round. The meeting concluded that the second woman had a better quality of life.

The reputation of being a service geared towards white middle-class Christian patients is simply unjustified in most cases – and almost certainly overstated in others – but it lingers on and continues to be an insurmountable barrier for some people.

Hospices are great facilities for the last stages of life; they exist for that, and they have the appropriate skills and resources. But for many people with progressive neurological conditions the disease progression is not a straight line and the end is rarely predictable. Death is more likely to be from an infection or other secondary process rather than the neurological condition itself. In practice, this often means that the hospice can help with respite care and crises but may not be the appropriate long-term solution.

Stephen Hawking, the world-renowned physicist (now aged seventy-one), was given a diagnosis of motor neurone disease when he was twenty-one with a life expectancy of two years. His is an exceptional case, but it is true to say that the amazing changes in survival rates and longevity in people with progressive neurological diseases have not been matched by advances in the rate of cure, and many of the more common cancers still have low cure rates.

This means an increasing number of people are living with incurable degenerative disease. While many – such as those with Alzheimer's disease – will experience a deterioration of their thinking abilities, many patients' cognitive functions remain intact. To a much greater extent than was the case for previous generations patients are able to articulate their feelings, fears and frustrations.

Traditionally, an assessment of society's healthcare needs has been dominated by mortality rates. This is changing as it has become apparent that both the economic and the human costs of chronic and progressive disease have been underestimated. It is now recognized that neurological diseases account for a much higher burden than digestive diseases, respiratory diseases and cancer.

The increase in the number of people affected has meant their voices are more likely to be heard. This in turn means that their experience is more likely to be listened to by a society that is just beginning to recognize the needs of people with disabilities and progressive diseases.

For many people the rapid progress in hospice care may well have completely removed any need for assisted dying. Hospices have an excellent service, built on honesty and trust, and patients can live out their final days or weeks in reasonable comfort and security.

But not everyone has an entirely positive hospice experience. For some people, the progress in providing care may have other effects. It may mean the extension of a life that, for the person living it, no longer has a purpose. Having come to terms with their situation, some dying patients may not wish to wait for their death to arrive:

they know there can be no guarantee that it will be pain-free and symptom-free. Nor, in some cases, is there a guarantee that there will be no further deterioration in bodily functions and their ability to communicate before the end of their life.

For some the simple fact of increasing dependence on others – however willingly offered – can be a source of distress. However good the hospice and however well-intentioned the staff, they simply cannot provide dying patients with what some of them need: control over their lives. Often it's the little things that hurt: needing increasing help with simple tasks; having to wait – even a short while – to achieve some mundane task that wouldn't have required even a moment's thought in better times.

As a nurse I dreaded the words 'Let me do it' or 'Don't help me' as they meant that I had misjudged how much help a person required or the amount of time he or she needed to achieve something. Every time I heard it I had to ask myself how many other times I had got it wrong, but the patient had not complained. I was also aware that every time I heard those phrases the patient had been reminded of his or her dependency. In many cases this would be an increasing dependency as the disease progressed, inevitably focusing the individual's mind on the end of his or her life.

The NHS is a different world from the one I entered some forty years ago. In many ways I have no doubt at all that it is much better. But, for people with progressive and ultimately terminal diseases, the challenges are much the same.

A large number will find effective pain control, while a small number will suffer distress owing to constipation, incontinence, pressure sores and difficulties with communication.

A much larger number will discuss their disease and their treatment options with their doctors, but their ability to control their destiny is little different from what was available forty years ago.

And too many people with terminal diseases will face problems too great to bear and challenges that are unfair to them, their families and their friends.

9
GOOD CARE BUT A BAD DEATH
Colin Marriage: 'Another week? I can't do another week!'

Colin Marriage was thirty-nine and in a relationship when he was diagnosed with cancer. He was forty and newly married when he died in 2012. He went to his GP in the summer of 2011 because the indigestion he had been suffering from was getting worse. The doctor diagnosed heartburn and prescribed antacids. When Colin returned a month later with the same symptoms the GP doubled the dose. After another month Colin went back to the surgery and told his GP that the pain had been so bad that he had considered calling an ambulance. That gave the doctor cause for concern.

A few days later his sister Kelley got a phone call from their mother saying that Colin had been admitted to hospital. She told Kelley, 'He was going to ring you, but his phone went flat. He thinks he's got gallstones. They've found some shadows on his liver, but nobody seems very concerned about them.'

Kelley was two when Colin was born. The siblings had what she describes as 'a pretty normal' upbringing. She says that Colin was 'a real boy' and that she was 'a good girl', meaning that he was into rough and tumble and she was into reading and writing.

Their father had died of lung cancer in 1999, living for only ten days between diagnosis and death. Kelley says that he and his family knew there was something seriously wrong with him, but repeated scans showed nothing because the tumours were hidden behind his heart and could not be seen. He died suddenly when the radiotherapy treatment he was having dislodged a blood clot which travelled to his heart and killed him.

When Kelley's mum told her that Colin had shadows on his liver Kelley was concerned because 'you immediately think the worst'. Her mother told her not to worry, saying that she would keep Kelley informed. Colin was in the West Suffolk Hospital in Bury St Edmunds, and Kelley asked her mother whether she should go and visit him that night. She replied, 'No. We don't know when he's going to be discharged or what's going on.' Kelley says that nobody apart from her seemed too concerned about the shadows, and she thought: Well, Mum's been to the hospital and she's spoken to him, so it must be fine.

Kelley's phone rang as she arrived home, and, when she saw that it was Colin she thought: Great – he's been discharged from hospital. But as soon as she heard his voice she knew something was seriously wrong. He said, 'I've been diagnosed with testicular cancer. I've been discharged from Bury hospital, and I'm going to Addenbrooke's on Sunday to start chemotherapy.' He told Kelley several times that there was a 90–98 per cent chance that everything was going to be OK. 'My prognosis is very good,' he said. Treatment for testicular cancer can be extremely gruelling, with chemotherapy administered daily for five days then repeated after a short break. A course of treatment usually lasts five months, but it is generally extremely effective. As Kelley says, 'Colin's friends and I have been known to refer to the time when it was *only* testicular cancer.'

Colin's diagnosis resulted because the hospital ran two pregnancy tests that were positive. Men start to produce blood markers similar to pregnancy hormones when they have testicular cancer.[1] 'The news was devastating,' says Kelley. 'I'd seen his name come up on the phone and thought everything must be fine, but now he was using the c-word and that's always hard to deal with, especially after what happened to our father.' When Colin continued, 'It's been hard enough telling you and my girlfriend. I don't know how I'm going to tell Mum,' Kelley offered to help, but he replied, 'No, it's my problem, and it's my job to tell her.' He drove to their mother's the next morning – she later told Kelley that when she saw Colin's car she knew it was serious. Colin wasn't the kind of person who would turn up unannounced. 'He was quite a spontaneous person, but if he was going to visit you he'd let you know in case you were going to be out.'

Colin was admitted to Addenbrooke's on the Sunday, and Kelley, their mother and Colin's girlfriend accompanied him. When the doctor saw the three women he told Colin, 'You've already won your battle because you've got so much support.' Kelley says that Colin was asked 'loads and loads of questions' and that they all thought the chemotherapy would start straight away because that's what Colin had been told at Bury hospital. When Addenbrooke's said that they were going to do more tests Colin asked whether that was because they hadn't been able to find tumours in his testicles. They kept scanning him, and he was still producing the tell-tale hormone, but they couldn't find a tumour. He spent the whole of the next week in Addenbrooke's undergoing tests. Their mother was growing very anxious, as she had known a cancer patient whose primary tumour couldn't be found. There was talk of the tumour starting in Colin's testicles before being dislodged and moving to another part of his body.

Kelley says, 'Apart from the pregnancy marker for testicular cancer and his liver – they'd found quite a few secondary tumours there – his test results came back normal. They were trying to find the primary site, so they did lots more blood tests. After a week his consultant said, "I think we should do an endoscopy." We thought that was a bit odd, given that his problems had been associated with his stomach and indigestion. You'd think he would have had an endoscopy sooner than that. But his GP said that it is very rare for anyone under the age of fifty to have anything wrong with their stomach that would require them to have an endoscopy, and they have been advised not to send anyone under forty for one. When they did the endoscopy they found lots of primary tumours in his oesophagus. Lots and lots . . .'

Colin had not been a drinker, but he had smoked. Despite that, he was very fit – he dived and played football as well as badminton.

After a week of tests he was discharged from Addenbrooke's. The hospital said that they would be in touch with the test results, but when they didn't contact him quickly Kelley and her mother told Colin he must ring the hospital. He spoke to a clinical nurse specialist on the ward in which he had stayed. It turned out that the hospital hadn't been in touch because his test results had only just come through. The nurse told Colin that he had something called adenocarcinoma,[2] but when he asked what that meant she said that she did not know. She said it was not her speciality, that she worked with the germ-cell cancer team.[3] She told Colin that he had been given an appointment to see a specialist in his type of cancer.

Kelley cannot now remember the exact date of Colin's diagnosis with testicular cancer. As she says, 'It's almost like it doesn't matter.' She describes the news that he had testicular cancer as devastating but says that it was wonderful to be told that most men make a full recovery. She remembers clearly that Colin's appointment with the adenocarcinoma specialist took place on 26 October 2011. Her brother phoned her immediately afterwards and told her that he been diagnosed with primary adenocarcinoma of the oesophagus and secondaries in his liver. Kelley describes this as the 'catastrophic diagnosis', coming so soon after Colin thought he had treatable testicular cancer, and says it was really hard for everyone when their optimism was crushed by the devastating news. 'It was a horrible phone call because I didn't know what to say.'

Kelley's partner, who was one of Colin's good friends, hired a car to take her and their two-year-old son Will to see him. Colin opened the front door as he saw the car pull up, and, when Kelley's partner saw him standing there he immediately said to her, 'A guy down our road who died of bowel cancer – that's what he looked like just before he died.' Kelley says that even Will seems to have known there was something wrong. 'He and Colin always shook hands when they parted. My brother would say, "Come on. You're a big boy. Let's shake hands." But as we left that day Will refused to shake his hand and gave him a kiss instead.'

Through all this Colin was trying to protect Kelley and his family. He told them that the consultant had said that it was possible that he might live for three years, adding, 'It all depends how one responds to the chemotherapy.' It was only a couple of weeks later that they discovered that his prognosis was really poor and that he had been given between a month and a year to live. Kelley says that Colin 'put a bit of a gloss on it. Once again, he was being really brave.'

Her brother was booked in for chemotherapy, and he saw a dietitian who told him to put on as much weight as possible – he had already lost about two stone because he was having trouble swallowing, but he had underplayed that problem with his family. They knew about Colin's indigestion but not about his swallowing difficulties, and it was a race to get him to put on as much weight as possible before he started chemotherapy. Colin loved eating. 'He kept on saying, "All I want is a cheese-and-pickle sandwich", but that was quite dry so he couldn't swallow it.'

Kelley and her brother had lots of friends in common because they were very close in age, and they went to music festivals and on holiday together. Many of their mutual friends started baking for Colin. He opened his front door one day and someone had left a tin of cakes on the doorstep – he never found out who that kind person was. On the day after his catastrophic diagnosis one of Kelley's friends turned up at her home with boxes of cakes and a trifle for him.

Colin didn't have the problems that many people experience on chemotherapy. He wasn't sick, although he had some tingling in this hands and feet. According to Kelley he felt really tired for about three days after each session, but he would bounce back again. When receiving chemotherapy treatment Colin was on a drip all day. Kelley went with him to the first session, and Colin said he could almost feel it working. He had seven cycles of chemotherapy at three weeks per cycle, and he had to take tablets between infusions. After about three months (four cycles) he started to get quite bad pain in his liver, and when his consultant examined him he said, 'You've got to lay off the fatty foods now. You're developing a condition called fatty liver.'

Colin responded well to chemotherapy – all the tumours in his oesophagus and liver shrank, and all the tumour markers in his blood went right down. Kelley learnt a lot about treatment for his condition during this time when Colin was so ill, but it was all secondhand knowledge because Colin wouldn't let Kelley or their mother attend any of the appointments with him. He just passed on the positive news and said that he felt a lot better.

He even went back to work part-time. Kelley says that his company was terrifically supportive. He worked at a waste-disposal site in Bury St Edmunds where half the waste was composted and the other half went to landfill.

In October, when Colin first got the catastrophic diagnosis, Kelley and her mother decided to organize a series of celebrations involving him. Following their mother's birthday the following week they celebrated Will's birthday in late November, Christmas and Kelley's birthday in early January. Colin was forty on 1 February 2012, and Kelley made a beef Wellington for the first time. 'Colin and I loved to cook, and we'd always wanted to make it together. It was great, and Colin was able to enjoy it. By then he was eating cheese-and-pickle sandwiches, and he appeared to be absolutely fine.'

Colin's consultant told the family that he had responded very well to the chemotherapy. He was hopeful that if Colin remained well for six months to a year he would be able to have a second round of treatment. The consultant also said that they had had some really exciting results from clinical trials and that his aim was to keep Colin well for as long as possible so that he would be fit to participate in one. The doctor's attitude was very positive.

Kelley says the family knew that it wasn't all good news, but everything was looking positive. In April 2012 Colin, his girlfriend, Kelley and Will went on holiday for a week. They stayed in a hotel near the Eden Project in Cornwall and had what Kelley calls 'the loveliest time. It was a really good holiday, and the weather was glorious.'

Then in June, when Kelley had arranged to go to the Algarve for a week with her partner and their son, Colin told them that he had started to feel poorly again. He said he felt very tired, his indigestion had returned and he didn't feel quite right. The hospital immediately conducted more tests that indicated the cancer had returned, although the specialists didn't know where it was. Even then Kelley says the family was thinking that he could have more chemotherapy and be enrolled in a clinical trial.

She asked Colin if he wanted them to cancel their holiday, and he said no. His appointment with the consultant was booked for the Wednesday after they were due back. While they were away Colin was at home and not working, so she kept on texting him, enquiring, 'How are you feeling?' and so on. Kelley told him that they would see him on the Sunday, the day after they returned, but her mother rang on the Saturday and said, 'I just want to warn you that Colin looks pregnant. I don't want you to be shocked when you see him.' Kelley hadn't seen him for a couple of weeks before they went on holiday. 'He really did look pregnant. He looked very grey and very, very tired.'

Colin saw the consultant the following Wednesday. He had promised to ring Kelley after the appointment, but the call didn't come. She phoned him many times, but there was no answer. She kept on ringing, and because she had the day off work she was in the park with Will when Colin finally called. He told her that his appointment with the consultant had only just finished and that they had been talking for a very long time. He said, 'They're admitting me to Bury St Edmunds hospital. It's really serious.'

Colin and his girlfriend had arranged to get married on 24 August 2012. He told his sister, 'They're going to start giving me chemotherapy tomorrow. They've said they'll get me to the 24th, and I'll be well enough for the wedding.' The doctors drained nine litres of fluid off his stomach. The cancer had returned in his liver, and he had some tumours in his lungs as well. Colin's consultant seemed to think that the cancer had come back as soon as they stopped the chemotherapy, but he said that if they had given him any more chemotherapy it would have killed him. The cancer was very aggressive.

Colin was admitted to Bury St Edmunds hospital to start chemotherapy straight away; he had to stay in because he wasn't well enough to go home. Kelley told him, 'I'm coming to see you today', and he replied, 'No. I don't want you to come now. I want a bit of time on my own.' He needed to adjust to the news.

The next morning Kelley went to work, but her boss kept telling her that she should go home. She went to see Colin that Thursday afternoon, and he was obviously very, very sick, and he had deteriorated a lot since she had seen him the previous Sunday. The nursing team was preparing for the new chemotherapy regime. There are two ways of administering chemotherapy. One is through a drip in the hand and other is a line in the neck that goes straight to the heart. Colin was adamant that he didn't want a line – he had heard that lines could get infected. But now he had to accept that a line was the only way to administer the drugs. Kelley says, 'Putting that line in was a real turning point, and there was no way back from it. Adjusting to that, accepting the finality of it, was really hard for him.'

On the Friday Kelley did a couple of hours' work early in the morning, so she could have a little bit of a normal life before she went to see her brother. Her mother was going into hospital every day. The Wednesday he had got the diagnosis he had asked Kelley if she could tell their mother. Kelley phoned her, and they had a very hard conversation. That Friday when she was at King's Cross Station on her way to Bury St Edmunds she got a call from Colin. He told her, 'I'm too poorly for chemotherapy.' Kelley asked, 'How long do you have?' and he replied, 'Up to a week. Please, can you tell Mum.'

Their mother had been planning to go to the hospital after work that day – the journey took her an hour by car – and Kelley couldn't remember what time she was leaving home, so she told Colin that she would go straight round there instead of to the hospital. She didn't want to pass on such devastating news over the phone, so she kept ringing her mother, but she didn't answer.

Before Kelley had the chance to speak to their mother Colin rang her again saying, 'I'm getting married tomorrow.' Kelley didn't know how to break all this news to their mother, so when she finally got hold of her and she said that she wasn't going to work that day Kelley asked her to meet the train at King's Lynn Station.

The first thing Kelley said when she saw her mother was, 'We've got a wedding to organize!' explaining, 'I thought I'd deliver the good news first.' The two of them went shopping for clothes for Will. He was to be a page boy, and he needed something nice to wear. They were in a shop when her mother asked, 'How long?' Kelley told her that Colin could live up to a week and says that her mother seemed to take the news very calmly. Telling her in public meant they both had to keep their emotions in check.

Kelley's mother found a pair of really nice grey trousers for Will. She had already bought her dress, hat and shoes, but Kelley hadn't yet bought an outfit for the wedding. She had a nice dress in her wardrobe that was black with tiny white flowers on it, so she told her mother that she needed to buy something to liven it up. 'Tomorrow is not going to be a black day. It will be one of our celebrations.' She bought a white cardigan and a pair of red shoes, and she found a shirt for Will she didn't really like which her mother loved, thinking: So what? The situation they were in brought everything into perspective.

Kelley stayed with her mother that Friday night, and she arranged for friends who were attending the wedding to collect Will and her partner – and her dress – and bring them to the hospital.

Meanwhile Will had developed chickenpox. Fortunately Kelley had a good friend nearby whose son had chickenpox at the same time. The other mother was very happy to look after both boys, so they could play together safely. Kelley had been exposed to Will's chickenpox, so her route to Colin's room was through a back entrance. She was worried because the wedding was going to take place in one of the waiting-rooms of the cancer wards in the hospital, and many patients with cancer have compromised immune systems. But when she suggested that she shouldn't bring Will to the hospital because of his condition the staff very helpfully told her to bring him to the waiting-room via the back route instead of through the ward.

On the Friday Colin was told that he couldn't have any more chemotherapy he had been moved to what Kelley calls 'a lovely room' on the ground floor. It had a door to a beautiful garden with a pond and ducks and water features. Soon after his diagnosis he decided that he did not want to go to a hospice, even though his consultant had suggested that he should visit one. The hospice at Bury St Edmunds had open wards – not individual rooms – and Colin told Kelley that he did not want to lie there surrounded by others who were dying. His GP had offered to care for him at home – to visit twice a day to check up on him and to give him whatever he needed – but Colin didn't want that because he said his fiancée would have to live in the house after he died, and he didn't want her to have unpleasant memories of his last days.

Quite soon after Colin's diagnosis his doctors told him that because of the nature of his cancer he would develop cirrhosis of the liver. Cirrhosis is irreversible and can lead to liver failure. The doctors warned Colin that one of the first signs of cirrhosis was shaky hands, and Kelley remembers her brother repeatedly holding out his hands to check for signs of tremor, knowing that liver failure would lead to his death. She remembers the look of disappointment that appeared in his big blue eyes every time he held out his hands and they were steady.

On the day of the wedding Colin's doses of morphine were timed so that he would be able to participate fully in the ceremony. Kelley describes the speed of his decline as astonishing, utterly devastating, and remembers that he could still just about stand but only with great difficulty. He told her that he could almost feel the cancer rampaging through his body. He used a wheelchair to get to the ceremony because, although he was able to walk the short distance to the garden, he couldn't make it to the waiting-room where the wedding was to be held. Kelley says the nurses were incredibly helpful and supportive that day. The wedding was organized, with the hospital staff and chaplain's help, by Kelley, her mother and Colin's girlfriend with her parents.

On the drive to the hospital with her mother for the ceremony Kelley got a text from Colin's fiancée saying, 'We'd like you to do a reading.' They suggested 'The Owl and the Pussy Cat', and she rehearsed it around fifty times on the one-hour journey. She felt it was vital that she could read it aloud without crying. In the event the reading went well, as the words that made her cry earlier had lost their power. Will stood with her when it was time for the reading and behaved immaculately.

Colin's bride wore the dress she had planned to wear in August. Colin's best friend was the best man. The two of them had organized the suit hire, and they had already had fittings. Colin's prospective father-in-law brought the suits to the hospital, but by then Colin had lost a lot of weight, and one could see how bony his shoulders had become. Kelley remembers that because he had grown so thin his enormous blue eyes looked even bigger and more expressive than usual that day.

The wedding was held in the afternoon. 'Sitting in the hospital waiting for the wedding to take place felt surreal. The wedding in August was going to be held in a beautiful barn in Suffolk, and Colin and his girlfriend had wanted it to be rustic. Because we both really loved cooking my brother and I were going to make big bowls of chilli and things like that. I'd planned to take the time off work to get the preparations done. And now we were having this other wedding . . .'

The reception was held in the waiting-room, too. It was big enough to hold the thirty guests who attended – everyone who was there had been invited to the August wedding, but a lot of people hadn't been able to make it at such short notice. Kelley met some of her brother's friends who she hadn't seen for years. For some of his friends – even those who had seen him fairly recently – Colin's physical state must have come as a shock.

'Colin came to the reception every now and again, but he had to keep going to his room. He was sitting in a wheelchair, and he'd say, "I need to go and lie down", but apart from that he wasn't showing any real signs of being ill. But he was sweating a lot, and you could see that the fluid was building up again – his stomach had started to swell.' Colin's new wife divided her time between staying with the guests and going to his room with him. She had been given a bed there from the start of his admission.

In a few days Colin had gone from being in little or no pain, which allowed him to stay at home, to being in such bad pain that he was prescribed oral morphine, which was provided almost immediately every time he asked for it. Kelley sees that as a measure of how dramatic his deterioration was.

When the reception was over Kelley's partner and Will returned to London in their friend's car. She decided to go home with her mother, and she went to see Colin before they left the hospital. When she promised him that she would look after their mother and his new wife, he said, 'I don't think it's going to be very long – and thank goodness for that.' Kelley told him that she wouldn't visit him the next day, Sunday, as it was his honeymoon and the last person he would want on his honeymoon was his sister! She spent the night with her mother, going home by train on the Sunday.

Colin's wife was with her husband all the time, and Kelley decided to work in the mornings and come into the hospital in the afternoons. On the Monday his stomach was badly swollen, so it was drained again. He was taking lots of oral morphine and was asleep more or less all the time when Kelley was there on the last Wednesday. As she left that day she told her mother, 'I'm not going to disturb him because he needs his sleep, so give him a kiss from me when he wakes up.' At that point Colin opened one eye and said, 'I've been great entertainment, haven't I?' Kelley joked, 'Yeah! Keep this up and I'm going to stop visiting!'

She recalls, 'Colin's stomach had started to swell again, despite being drained on the Monday. The doctors said they couldn't drain it again, that doing so would kill him, and he said, "Do it. Why are you keeping me hanging around? Just do it." And the doctor replied, "You know we can't do that." Colin wanted to know why not, and that's how I feel now – why not?'

By this time Colin was constantly vomiting, and the doctors kept trying different combinations of drugs to stop it, but nothing worked. 'All he was doing was sleeping and being sick. He couldn't eat or drink anything.' He was on a drip to keep him hydrated until the doctor told him that they weren't going to stop him drinking but they were going take the drip away. That day Colin said to Kelley, 'It's not right, treating people like this.'

She says, 'The end result was always going to be the same. Why did he have to suffer like that? There was never going to be a miracle cure for Colin. He was suffering really badly. He was in dreadful pain.

'When I last spoke to Colin, all he would say was, "I want this to be over. I want to die. What's the point?" He was quite clear about that – he wanted to die. He didn't want to suffer any more. While his mind was still quite clear he asked the doctors, "Why are you doing this to me?"'

Kelley says that, in a sense, he gave his doctors permission to end his life, and she has no doubt that her brother would have asked for an assisted death if that choice had been available to him.

Kelley didn't see Colin on the Thursday. She was exhausted, and he had got to the stage where he was saying, 'Stop coming to see me – you can't keep this up.' When she arrived at the hospital on the Friday she was told that Colin had said he didn't want to see anybody except his mother, his sister and his wife. Lots of his friends wanted to see him, but he said, 'I really don't want them to see me like this.'

She says, 'Mum and Colin's wife had been with him when the consultant came round earlier that day. Colin had asked him, "How long? How long now?" and the consultant replied, "Up to a week." Colin was horrified. He said, "Another week? Another week? I can't do another week!" and the registrar who was with the consultant started to cry. Colin kept on saying, "Why are you doing this to me?"'

Colin was taking oral morphine and paracetamol as well as other medication. On the Friday the doctor suggested administering morphine through the line in his neck. Although that was the quickest and most efficient way to get the pain relief into his system, it still took a couple of hours to obtain Colin's consent. Kelley thinks he knew that the line would take matters out of his control compared to the oral morphine and that there would be no way back. He just wanted to die – he didn't want any more treatment. He wanted his suffering to be over.

Kelley's mother told her that Colin had 'gone', mentally, that he wasn't really there any more. The morphine had taken over, and he was having absolutely everything done for him. He couldn't get out of bed to go to the toilet or into the garden. He was just lying there.

Kelley last saw her brother alive on Saturday 14 July 2011, and she says, 'He was just not there at all.' After the wedding he was in bed all the time and was asleep most of the time. She says that there was a gradual but unstoppable decline in his health. 'He just deteriorated.' On the last day she saw him he started to get really agitated and angry – a couple of times he had tried to rip out all of his tubes and drips, so he was sedated.

While Kelley was travelling to Bury St Edmunds on the Tuesday her mother was already at the hospital. She was sitting with Colin when a nurse came in and asked her, 'Is he more agitated now than he was recently?' She replied, 'I'm not sure. I don't know.' The doctor gave him more sedatives and told Kelley's mother that anyone who wanted to see Colin needed to get to the hospital as soon as possible, but it was too late. Colin's wife had picked Kelley up from the station, and they were still on the way to the hospital when Kelley's mother rang, saying, 'You've got to get here right now, as soon as you can.' By the time they arrived Colin was dead.

Colin died on 17 July 2011. He had lived for ten days after being admitted to hospital, three days longer than the doctors had originally estimated. Kelley says that she didn't want him to live for those last three days because 'It's not about the quantity of time you have with someone but the quality of that time.'

She says the medical staff could not have treated Colin better. She did not meet his consultant because Colin wouldn't let her, but Colin spoke very fondly of him. She adds that it is hard to say whether anything could have been done differently except for the fact that Colin wanted help to die. She praises the hospital, saying the staff team was brilliant, even down to not making him go to the hospice. He might have been taking up a bed that someone else could have used, but they didn't send him home because that wasn't what he wanted. They listened to his wishes, but Kelley says that towards the end they did not hear what he really wanted or, if they did, they could not act on it. As far as the NHS was concerned, they did everything they could, but in those last days it was not enough. The care was excellent, but, for Kelley, caring goes beyond trying to make someone comfortable. She says that Colin wasn't part of the world – and he no longer wanted to be – from the day before he got married.

She has a good friend who is a vicar. The two of them have discussed the issue of assisted dying. He told her, 'We can't have assisted dying because of the families who might say, "Oh, Grandma's gone a bit loopy. Let's get rid of her."' Kelley told him, 'That's not what this is about. It's about terminally ill people making a choice for themselves.'

'You can't *not* make something the law just because someone might break it. That's farcical, because what is the point of the law? You can't not have a law against murder just because some people might commit murder. You can't say, "Stealing is wrong, so let's not have a law against it because some people might steal." If we permitted assisted dying some people might break the law, but they are doing that already. Surely it's better to have a proper procedure and policy and have it out in the open.'

Kelley is quite sure that nothing but death could have helped Colin. He was in intolerable pain and was not capable of doing anything for himself. He hated his life because 'he had no independence and no dignity whatsoever'. For her the big contrast with her father's death was that her father wanted to continue to fight his cancer. He was undergoing radiotherapy to give him more time when the blood clot went to his heart and killed him. Kelley would support anyone who wants to live just as passionately as she would support someone's wish to die. It's about choice, and her father had a choice because he wanted to carry on living. Kelley points out that we help people to fight cancer if they want to, but there's a point where we fail people who want to die because we can't help them any more. Stopping someone having an assisted death doesn't make them live for ever. It's just the difference between prolonging their death and shortening their suffering, making the end of a person's life tolerable. Of course she would want Colin to be here now but not at any cost. What he lost, his life, was something he wanted to give away. She says that it was horrible and it wasn't actually a life any longer.

When her father died Kelley did not make it to the hospital in Southend. She was working in London when her mother rang and asked her to get there as soon as possible. She arrived in time to see her father's body, and he looked angry, probably because he hadn't wanted to die. At that point Kelley swore she never wanted to see another dead body again, but she had to see her brother because her mother had been alone with Colin at the time of his death. She was waiting, with his body, at the hospital for Kelley and Colin's widow to arrive. Kelley says that her brother looked as though the weight of the world had been taken off his shoulders. 'His skin was yellow because his liver had failed at the end. He didn't look well, but he looked peaceful at last.'

Colin and his fiancée made their wedding plans only after he had sorted out his funeral. He decided what music and readings he wanted to have, so the funeral started with the Madness song 'One Step Beyond' because he thought it would be funny. He had started planning the event very early on when he wrote his will. He was clear that he didn't want any religious readings, and he wanted his friends to carry him into the crematorium. Kelley remembers that the one awkward thing was that he had spoken to his fiancée about having 'Always Look on the Bright Side of Life' played at the end of the service. Kelley thought it a great idea. She felt it was the perfect song to end the ceremony, but Colin's widow looked appalled. Kelley couldn't understand. 'What's wrong? Colin and I loved *Monty Python* . . .' His widow said that Colin wanted it, but he was worried that it might upset their mother, but Kelley's mother said, 'I'm already upset. What difference is it going to make?' So that's what they listened to as they left the crematorium. Kelley did a reading, and later Colin's ashes were scattered at sea.

This is the anonymous poem that Kelley read at her brother's funeral:

Feel no guilt in laughter, he'd know how much you care.
Feel no sorrow in a smile that he is not here to share.
You cannot grieve for ever; he would not want you to.
He'd hope that you could carry on the way you always do.
So, talk about the good times and the way you showed you cared,
The days you spent together, all the happiness you shared.
Let memories surround you, a word someone may say
Will suddenly recapture a time, an hour, a day,
That brings him back as clearly as though he were still here,
And fills you with the feeling that he is always near.
For if you keep those moments, you will never be apart
And he will live for ever locked safely within your heart.

Colin's story was included in the Dignity in Dying booklet *Four Reasons to Change the Law*. Kelley's description of her brother's last days stands in stark contrast to the photograph of him taken on a sea-fishing trip. Colin's broad smile appears alongside her moving words:

> We reassured him that pain relief and care is so good these days that he would be able to die peacefully and in comfort . . . Colin asked his doctor how long he had left. When the doctor told him he expected him to live for about another week he cried – the first time I had seen him cry since he was a child – not because he had so little time left but because he was in such pain, unable to eat or sleep properly, and he could not stop being sick.

She is full of praise for the care the hospital gave Colin but critical of the doctors' inability to give him the help he really wanted – help to die.

Kelley had thought about assisted dying before Colin was diagnosed with cancer but not a great deal. When she and her partner talked about the case of Dan James, the paralysed ex-rugby player who died with Dignitas's help at the age of twenty-three, Kelley had said, 'Good on his parents. They must have really loved him!' but her partner had responded, 'I think it's appalling.' She feels he may hold this attitude partly because he is a lawyer.

Kelley doesn't want her mother or anyone she loves to endure what Colin experienced at the end of his life. She got in touch with Dignity in Dying about a month after he died because there was a nagging thought at the back of her mind, almost as though his death would be worthless if she didn't act. She says that telling Colin's story seemed to give his death some point. 'I knew a bit about Dignity in Dying, and I had some sympathy with its goals because of my grand-dad's stroke.'

Kelley's partner has said to her on a few occasions, 'I know why you are doing this, but couldn't you use your time more wisely? What about helping the poor?' She thinks that the way we treat people when they are born and when they die says a lot about society, especially when we don't get it right. To her the beginning and the end of life are vitally important. She feels that we don't deal well with death in our society although it is something that happens to all of us and it cannot be stopped.

Kelley works for the NHS, and she says that, as an employer, the service was fantastic throughout her brother's illness. Her manager was terrific, telling her that if she needed to take time off work she should just take it. Since Colin died she has spoken to people at work about his death. One person said that what she was doing in speaking up about Colin's difficult death was 'brilliant', and Kelley's manager was supportive of her aims. Kelley says that bad deaths happen to a lot of people, but we don't talk about them. At any rate, it's good to know she has the support of some of the people who work for the health service.

'I knew what palliative care meant, so when Colin said, "It's palliative care for me", his words were more powerful than when he told me how long he'd got left. If people want palliative care fine, but . . . I understand the problem the medical professional has with assisted dying, but couldn't it be a medical specialism? It's preserving life at any cost that is so wrong. Sometimes care can mean looking after the patient's best interests, and prolonging life isn't necessarily the best thing for someone who is dying. I don't think it's complicated. I believe you should be able to have a choice at the end of life.'

10
THE FUTURE FOR ASSISTED DYING IN ENGLAND AND WALES
by Sir Graeme Catto

Before considering what the future of assisted dying in England and Wales might look like it is worth taking a moment to examine the current position. The reality is that assisting someone to die remains illegal in the UK, but prosecutions are uncommon. In February 2010, following the Debbie Purdy case, the Director of Public Prosecutions (DPP) set out the circumstances under which someone would be likely to face prosecution for helping another person to die in England and Wales. The policy makes a clear distinction between 'compassionate' and 'malicious' acts, with the former being unlikely to be prosecuted. This, however, does not safeguard either those who are assisted to die or those who assist them, as the investigation occurs only after the person has died. There are no safeguards in advance of that irrevocable act.

The 1961 Suicide Act decriminalized suicide and introduced the crime of assisting someone to end their life, which carries a sentence of up to fourteen years in prison. The Act explicitly gives the DPP discretion over whether or not to prosecute cases of encouraging or assisting in a suicide. The guidelines introduced in 2010 effectively decriminalized amateur assistance in dying. That said, the accounts that run through this book, illustrating the problems with the present law, show that the current situation is far from acceptable. Those opposed to change claim that the law has 'a stern face and a kind heart' and is therefore satisfactory as it is. A law that forces people into the desperate decisions we encounter in this book cannot be described as kind. It is, in the words of the Commission on Assisted Dying, 'inadequate and incoherent'.

I approach this issue from a number of different perspectives. I remember my father going out most evenings, at around ten o'clock, to provide the pain relief and compassionate care in which he as a GP passionately believed and which was highly valued by his patients and their relatives. I have never succeeded in providing the same quality of care that he delivered over his many years in practice. As a consultant physician for more than thirty years I have seen patients decline life-saving treatment and cause their own deaths, sometimes prematurely in my opinion. I have also seen terminally ill patients who wanted to die with dignity in their own homes admitted to hospital because there was inadequate help for them where they really wanted to be. I witnessed my parents' deaths, and my mother's lingering death was particularly important in helping to shape my views on this issue. As one of the eleven members of the Commission on Assisted Dying (COAD) I was influenced by the views of colleagues and experts; our report was produced after a year-long investigation that included public evidence sessions, consultations, international research and externally commissioned papers. Finally, I am the present Chair of the campaigning organization Dignity in Dying. Founded in 1935, Dignity in Dying has been campaigning in one way or other for almost eighty years to increase choice at the end of life. All of these perspectives link to persuade me that terminally ill, mentally competent adults should be allowed an assisted death if that is their settled wish. They should be allowed to die with dignity at a time and place of their choosing. I believe that the law will change and that it will change more quickly if we make our views better known to our legislators.

We are undoubtedly at a turning point in the history of assisted dying and the campaign for greater choice at the end of life in the UK. COAD found that 'the current legal status of assisted suicide is inadequate and incoherent'. This conclusion is all too often supported by the press coverage which regularly surrounds this issue. Week after week we read of terminally ill fellow citizens, frail and disabled, making the difficult and expensive journey to Switzerland where they are able to determine the time and manner of their deaths. I simply do not understand why we deny them the right to die with dignity at a time and place of their choosing in their own country.

In this book we read about Ron Clinch and John Close and their decisions to travel to Switzerland. John's story movingly describes the practical difficulties he encountered and the emotional demands that the planning and the journey placed on his family. John would not have encountered those problems if he had been able to choose to end his life in the comfort of his own home.

There has also been increased reporting in the media of people approaching the end of their lives and choosing to stop eating and drinking in order to bring about a swifter death. We read about Pamela Tuson's mother Efstratia's decision to do just that after all other options were exhausted. The option she really wanted was an assisted death.

We read of individuals taking the decision to attempt to end their lives at home, often alone, to avoid putting their loved ones at risk of prosecution. Liz Smith's parents, Barbara and Don, both tried and failed to end their lives in secret, and Neil Love took carefully planned actions under cover of night while his wife slept in the next room. We hear, all too often, of people whose deaths caused great distress to their family and friends and who would have sought different, more dignified ways to end their lives had that choice been available to them.

The case for a change in the law is movingly and persuasively argued in the account of Colin Marriage's death. When told he had one more week to live Colin wept, not because he wanted more time but because he simply wanted the suffering to end. For anyone to be in such a situation is just unacceptable. In all compassion we must work together to ensure greater choice at the end of life.

COAD recommended that, subject to a number of important safeguards, the law should be changed to allow terminally ill, mentally competent adults to have an assisted death if that was their wish. That view is supported not only by all of the authors in this book but by many accounts in the media. The vast majority of the public also want this option to be available to them and to their loved ones. Public opinion polls have consistently shown steady and unwavering support for assisted dying for terminally ill, mentally competent adults.

The 2010 and 2007 British Social Attitudes (BSA) surveys found that the majority of the British public support assisted dying. In the 2010 BSA survey 82 per cent of the general public agreed that a doctor should probably or definitely be allowed to end the life of a patient with a painful, incurable disease at the patient's request.[1] The 2007 BSA survey found that 80 per cent agreed that a person with a terminal and painful illness from which they will die should be allowed an assisted death.[2] The 2007 BSA survey explored in detail whether assistance in dying should be extended to people who are not terminally ill (assisted *suicide* rather than assisted *dying*) and found that support dropped significantly for this. Only 43 per cent agreed that a doctor should be allowed to end the life of somebody with an incurable and painful illness from which they would *not* die, and support fell further (to 41 per cent) when this question was considered for someone who is 'not in much pain nor in danger of death but becomes permanently and completely dependent on relatives for all their needs'.

Research shows us that a small majority of doctors are opposed to assisted dying. Their religious beliefs and medical specialities influence their views. A survey in 2009 found that 64 per cent of doctors agreed and 34 per cent disagreed with the notion that 'a person with an incurable and painful disease, from which they will die, should not be allowed by law to be assisted to end their life'.[3] Doctors who work in palliative medicine or hold a religious belief are more likely to be opposed to assisted dying. A different survey from the same year found that 49 per cent of GPs and consultants were opposed to – and 39 per cent were in favour of – a change in the law to permit assisted dying.[4] With regard to nurses, following a consultation of its members the Royal College of Nursing moved from opposition to a position of neutrality on assisted dying in July 2009.

Analysis of the 2010 BSA survey revealed that the majority of the general public with a religious belief support assisted dying; 71 per cent of religious people and 92 per cent of non-religious people agreed that a doctor should probably or definitely be allowed to end the life of a patient with a painful incurable disease at the patient's request.[5]

The 2007 BSA survey found that the majority of disabled people are supportive of assisted dying; 75 per cent of people with a disability believed that a person with a terminal and painful illness from which they will die should be allowed an assisted death.[6] Some opponents, including certain organizations that represent disabled people, are concerned that assisted dying legislation would lead to a 'slippery slope' and the devaluation of disabled people's lives. Research, including the 2007 BSA, shows that the majority of disabled people disagree with this view, perhaps because choice is the principle at the heart of both the disability rights movement and the campaign for assisted dying.

The public were polled in April 2013 on their support for Lord Falconer's Assisted Dying Bill which would give terminally ill adults with a prognosis of six months or less the option to control the time and manner of their deaths. More than two-thirds said that they would like to see Lord Falconer's Bill pass through Parliament and made law.[7]

Doctors are widely perceived as being more inclined to oppose a change in this aspect of the law than the general population. In order to challenge the prevalent but incorrect view that *all* doctors are opposed, an organization called Healthcare Professionals for Assisted Dying (HPAD) was founded by the late Dr Ann McPherson, CBE. HPAD represents those doctors, nurses and other healthcare professionals who believe that dying patients should not have to suffer against their wishes, nor should they be forced to take desperate decisions in order to be in control of their deaths. Alongside access to good-quality end-of-life care HPAD supports a change in the law to allow terminally ill, mentally competent adults the choice of an assisted death within clear safeguards.

As well as campaigning to change the law, HPAD campaigns for medical Royal colleges and representative bodies to become neutral on the issue of assisted dying, believing that this is primarily a matter for Parliament and not for the medical profession. Some colleges *are* neutral. As noted above, following a lengthy consultation and based on a variety of views from its members, the Royal College of Nursing adopted a neutral stance in 2009. The Royal College of Psychiatrists is also neutral on the issue, as is the Royal College of Paediatricians; other colleges simply choose not to take a position at all.

Some churches and religious organizations have also expressed opposition to a change in the law on assisted dying. While opinion polls find that the vast majority of people with faith support a change in the law on assisted dying, the views expressed by the leaders of some religious organizations are quite different. The Catholic Church is one of the most active opponents, but other denominations of Christianity approach the issue differently. In April 2013 the General Assembly of the Unitarian Church voted in favour of supporting the legalization of assisted dying.

Other religious groups take a range of views on assisted dying. For example, the teachings of Buddha don't deal directly with the subject, and there is therefore no unanimous view on it. Similarly, there is no single Hindu view, with some thinking it would amount to 'doing harm' (which is forbidden) and others believing that helping to alleviate another person's suffering is a compassionate, permissible act. The general Islamic approach to assisted dying is that human life is sacred, given by Allah, and that he alone should end life. The Jewish tradition is to preserve life and therefore – broadly – the Jewish view would oppose assisted dying. Sikh teachings suggest that life is a gift from God and should be left in his hands, but this is not absolute. Any summary of the views of religious leaders on assisted dying is contradicted by opinion polls showing that many people of faith disagree with their leaders and choose to come to an independent interpretation of how we should approach choice at the end of life.

Following the success of HPAD, several faith leaders have spoken out in favour of greater choice at the end of life. Rabbi Jonathan Romain created a group called Inter-Faith Leaders for Dignity in Dying (IFDiD). Still in its infancy, IFDiD hosted its first highly successful seminar exploring faith issues and assisted dying in May 2013.

During the seminar a number of faith leaders, including the Most Reverend Lazar Puhalo, retired Archbishop of Ottawa, Canon Rosie Harper of the Church of England, Rabbi Dr Jonathan Romain, Reverend Professor Paul Badham and Methodist Minister the Reverend Baroness Kathleen Richardson expressed their support for Lord Falconer's Assisted Dying Bill.

The Most Reverend Lazar Puhalo said:

Assisted dying is different to assisted suicide because assisted suicide implies killing people who have the choice to live, whereas assisted dying will help those who are going to die anyway but would otherwise have to go through lots of pain and suffering to get there . . . When a dying person is suffering intolerably then everything must be done to help.

Professor Paul Badham stated:

Jesus taught that the whole of religious law could be summed up by saying that we should love our neighbour as ourselves. His golden rule was that we should always treat others as we would like to be treated ourselves.

IFDiD coordinator Rabbi Dr Jonathan Romain described the seminar as a landmark event. It was the first time that those from a religious background had entered the debate on assisted dying in a positive way. He said:

I have been incredibly encouraged by today's debate. This seminar provided an important opportunity for people with faith to explore the issues of assisted dying in a safe and non-judgemental environment. I am confident that IFDiD can usefully support the progress of Lord Falconer's Bill through the House of Lords and continue to explore and develop the crucial role of faith leaders in a country which allows the choice of assisted dying.

It is often suggested that disabled people do not support a change in the law on assisted dying. While it is true that many representative groups for the disabled oppose a change in the law, that view is not reflective of the general disabled population. Research shows that around 75 per cent of disabled people support the legalization of assisted dying for terminally ill, mentally competent adults. Indeed, there are a number of disabled people trying to make their voices heard in favour of assisted dying in the current debate.

End-of-life issues are now more widely discussed than ever. Increasing life expectancy and the increased numbers of elderly and very elderly individuals in the population may be part of the reason. Perhaps ageing baby boomers, well accustomed to making decisions about their own lifestyle over the years, are both observing the sometimes distressing ways that their parents' lives end and are seeking greater control over the time and place of their own deaths. Whatever the reason, more of us are making our wishes clear to family and friends. Most of us wish to die at home. The proportion of the population in favour of assisted dying has not changed over the last few years, but people who support that choice are now more active in making their views known. We are less willing to accept as anomalies distressing memories of loved ones dying without dignity. We recognize that these problems are, unfortunately, far from uncommon.

More people are now willing to report their experiences, and the impact of such reports cannot be underestimated. We are more aware of the unnecessary suffering ordinary people experience simply by coming to the end of their lives. Some people die sooner than is necessary so that they are physically able to travel to Switzerland, some die alone and some cause even greater suffering and distress by botching their attempts to end their lives. We know that assisted dying legislation has worked well in Oregon for more than a decade. The evidence from that state and from other places which permit assisted dying indicates that only a small and stable proportion of dying patients choose an assisted death. (Just 0.2 per cent of all deaths in Oregon are as a result of the state's Death with Dignity Act.) Many more terminally ill patients derive great comfort from knowing that such an option exists if their suffering becomes unbearable, as evidenced by the fact that around 40 per cent of patients who receive a prescription for life-ending medication in Oregon do not to take it. The law in the UK will change but not, I fear, before many more will die without dignity, regardless of their wishes and at a time and place they did not choose.

It is right that we should focus on the factual aspects of assisted dying, on opinion polls, experiences from other countries and ethical considerations. Inevitably, however, we are influenced by our own experiences of death. In my case, the most important influence comes not from the many patients I have seen at the end of their lives but from my mother's death. In September 1977, having returned from the USA, I was interviewed for a post as senior lecturer in medicine and honorary consultant physician with an interest in renal medicine. To celebrate my appointment I went that evening with my father to a football match. Just after half-time my father was called out, not – as often happened – to attend to an injured player or a spectator who had become unwell but because my mother had experienced a fit and had been taken to the local hospital. As chance would have it, she was admitted to my own ward where my colleague was the receiving physician. Investigations were negative, and my mother was discharged home only to have a second fit a few weeks later.

On this occasion the brain scan showed a tumour in an inoperable site. The consultant neurologist, with whom I shared the ward, could not be sure if the lesion was a primary brain tumour or a secondary deposit from an unknown primary. He told my father and me that my mother would be dead within nine months. While no treatment was likely to be effective, he suggested that radio-therapy might slow the progression of the cancer.

My mother, at sixty-one years old, was an active individual who managed a large group general practice, enjoyed golf and led a busy social life. My father was devastated by the prognosis and determined that my mother should be protected, as he saw it, from the truth; his view at the time was 'you must not take away all hope'. My mother was clearly anxious but faced up to the radiotherapy without complaint. Always impeccably groomed, her hair fell out, and she resorted to a headscarf rather than a standard-issue wig (which she did accept later). Within a few weeks she had difficulty finding the correct word, although initially she had alternative ways of expressing her thoughts. By Christmas her speech was clearly impaired and it was increasingly difficult to converse, her eyes revealing the depth of the feelings she could not describe. Early in 1978 she became bedridden at home, and, before Easter, she was admitted to hospital, once again to my ward although not under my care. There she languished until her death in June. She could not speak or express her wishes in any way. She did not appear to recognize anyone. She had to be fed and required full nursing care, which in a busy acute ward was frequently inadequate. Her wig was often askew, creating a bizarre appearance, and she would have been appalled at how she looked had she been aware of it. Seeing her several times every day was distressing, and I longed for her life to end without further indignity.

I do not know what my mother suffered. The legacy of her death, however, was a lasting memory, not of a bright alert wife, mother and grandmother whom we all loved but of a wasted body we scarcely recognized. Only as the years passed were we able to put this image of her final months into perspective and remember the person that she had been and the full life she had lived. Given her forthright views, I have no doubt that she would have sought an assisted death and would now support the campaign to change the law.

We in the UK are not alone in considering legalizing assisted dying. COAD took evidence from several of the jurisdictions that permit some form of assisted dying. This evidence influenced not only COAD's recommendations but also the Assisted Dying Bill, which Lord Falconer tabled as a Private Member's Bill in the House of Lords on 13 May 2013.

Lord Falconer's Bill provides what I believe to be a robust and appropriate assisted dying law for the UK. His Bill allows for a person who is terminally ill, mentally competent and who has six months or less to live to seek and lawfully be provided with assistance to end his or her life. The terminally ill person must make the request and no other person – including the patient's doctor, family or partner – would be able to initiate the process of requesting an assisted death. In order to be eligible the person must be a terminally ill adult who is aged eighteen or over, and that individual must have a clear and settled intention to end his or her life. The Bill extends only to England and Wales, and the person must have been ordinarily resident in England or Wales for at least a year when he or she makes the initial request for help to die. This Bill would not permit people to travel to England and Wales to have an assisted death.

The person asking for assistance to die would sign a declaration in the presence of an independent witness who is neither a relative nor involved in the person's care or treatment. The declaration would then be countersigned by two doctors. The attending doctor would usually be the person's GP or specialist consultant, and the second doctor would be an independent doctor from a different practice or clinical team. Both doctors, acting independently of each other, would examine the person and his or her medical records. They would need to agree on the person's diagnosis and prognosis, that the individual had the capacity to make the decision to end his or her life and was making a voluntary and fully informed decision. Both doctors would explore the individual's motivation for requesting an assisted death and would ensure that the patient was informed of all the available end-of-life options.

If both doctors sign the declaration, the attending doctor would write a prescription for the necessary medication. The prescription would only be delivered after a fourteen-day 'cooling off' period (or six days if both doctors agreed that the person was likely to die within one month). The attending doctor (or another doctor or nurse authorized by the attending doctor) would, when the cooling off period had passed, deliver the medicine at the patient's request. The doctor would check that the person had not revoked his or her declaration and establish whether or not he or she wished to revoke it. The doctor would remain with the person until either the life-ending medication had been taken and the person died or the individual decided against taking the medicine at that time. Regulations would provide that the medicine could only be delivered immediately before it was to be self-administered, and, if the person chose not to take it, the medication must immediately be removed before being returned to the pharmacy from which it was dispensed as soon as reasonably practicable.

The patient would have to self-administer the medication. In most cases this would mean swallowing it. However, when necessary, the patient could use a feeding tube, syringe driver or other mechanism to take the medication. The assisting healthcare professional could lawfully put the medication into a tube or syringe driver, but the dying person would need to carry out the final act to end life, for example, by activating the syringe driver. The Bill would not permit voluntary euthanasia when life-ending medication is administered to a patient at their request (for example, by injection).

Crucially, the Bill enables healthcare professionals and others who are involved in caring for individuals who are terminally ill to refrain, on the ground of conscientious objection, from assisting a person to die in accordance with the Bill. At the time of writing, Lord Falconer's Private Member's Bill is scheduled to be debated in summer 2014, and it is worth taking some time to look at the parliamentary procedure this will involve.

A Private Member's Bill is a public Bill introduced by a Member of either the House of Lords or the House of Commons. Lord Falconer's Bill will be introduced into the House of Lords.

Once a Bill is approved by the parliamentary authorities as being in the correct format it can be introduced. In this case, Lord Falconer introduced his Assisted Dying Bill on 13 May 2013. When a Bill is introduced it receives its first reading, which consists of the person tabling the bill reading out a short summary of the Bill's intentions. The introduction and first reading of a Bill are formalities, and there is no debate at this stage.

A new procedure in the House of Lords dictates that second reading debates will take place in the order in which the Bills were tabled in that parliamentary year. There is no set time for taking Private Members' Bills (although traditionally the second reading takes place on a Friday); when and if they are heard is dependent on how much time remains once all government business is completed.

At the second reading the principles of a Bill are debated. The peer who tabled the Bill opens the second reading debate and has a right of reply after the Minister has responded to sum up the debate. If a peer wishes to oppose the second reading of a Bill (and thereby defeat the Bill for that session) this is normally done through an amendment that 'this House declines to give the Bill a second reading'. If the amendment is won the Bill is defeated. If a vote is not called, or if it is called and passed, the Bill progresses to the committee stage.

The committee stage ensures greater scrutiny of a Bill. Each part is considered in detail, and amendments may be proposed to improve or change aspects of the legislation. This can typically take several days of debate. Once a Bill has been considered in committee it proceeds to the report stage where the amended Bill is considered and further amendments can be proposed. Finally, there is a third reading debate where the final version of the Bill is considered. Like the second reading, the third reading debate can allow for a vote on a Bill if an opponent tables an amendment declining to give the Bill a third reading.

After passing the third reading a Bill is then introduced into the House of Commons where it must pass through the same stages (first reading, second reading, committee, report and third reading). If a Bill is amended it must be passed back to the House of Lords, which decides whether or not to accept the Commons' amendments. This stage is known colloquially as 'ping pong' – the Bill is passed from one House of Parliament to the other until both Houses agree on the final version of the Bill.

Once a Bill has the approval of both Houses it must be granted Royal Assent. This role was traditionally undertaken by the King or Queen signing the Bill into law, although in modern times it is done by an official nominated by the monarch.

For people currently facing the end of their lives this description of the long and arduous process a change in the law takes will bring little comfort. There are, however, some steps they can take now to have some control over the time and manner of their deaths. Under the current law we all have the right to refuse treatment, including artificial hydration and nutrition, and we have the legal right to state our desire to refuse such treatment in advance in case we are unable to make such decisions at the time of our final illness. This can be done either through an advance decision to refuse treatment or, by proxy, through a lasting power of attorney (LPA) or both.

An advance decision is a great help for the patient and their loved ones as well as for the healthcare team looking after the patient. It allows healthcare professionals to follow the patient's wishes for treatment, even when communication with the patient becomes difficult either because of physical disability or because the patient has lost the capacity to make decisions. Many people wrongly believe that the next of kin can, when necessary, make these decisions on a patient's behalf. Unless the patient has made a specific LPA or an advance decision, any treatment or non-treatment decisions ultimately lie with the doctor whose views and values may differ from those of the patient.

Treatment refusal in an advance decision is legally binding. A patient can refuse any treatment, including life-sustaining treatment such as artificial nutrition and hydration, resuscitation or breathing machines. An advance decision can also be used to ask for specific treatment, although such requests are *not* legally binding. An advance decision can be amended at any time if the individual changes his or her mind about what he or she wants. A patient with mental capacity can also override the advance decision verbally at any time.

The onus is on the patient to ensure that the medical professionals are aware that they have signed an advance decision form. It is therefore important that the whole issue of what an individual would want to happen at the end of life is discussed with relatives and with any regular treating healthcare professional, such as the GP.

Appointing an LPA is another way of ensuring that the individual's wishes are followed when the person is no longer able to make his or her own decisions. There are two types of LPA, one for property and financial affairs and one for health and personal welfare. The health and personal welfare LPA would help to ensure that the patient had the end-of-life care and treatment desired.

Whether or not to combine a health and welfare LPA with an advance decision requires some consideration. An advance decision comes into effect as soon as it has been signed and witnessed correctly, while an LPA takes time to register – currently at least six weeks. An LPA is valid only once it has been registered with the Office of the Public Guardian. An advance decision is in the patient's own words and represents his or her decisions; it doesn't rely on another person to make choices for him or her. Advance decisions work well if they apply to a patient's specific circumstances at the end of life, whereas an LPA can apply to a wider range of healthcare situations. The patient's attorney will be able to make any health and welfare decision on the individual's behalf, including decisions about life-sustaining treatment if given that power. Once created, an attorney has considerable power and responsibility.

Cost is another factor to take into consideration: advance decisions are free, whereas an LPA currently costs £130 to register. Both advance decisions and LPAs are legally binding. If both the LPA and the advance decision deal with refusing or consenting to the same treatment, the more recent will take precedence. For example, a health and welfare LPA that specifically grants someone the authority to make decisions about life-sustaining treatment will invalidate any previously signed advance decision. However if a person appoints a health and welfare LPA first (regardless of whether or not it provides authority to give or refuse consent to life-sustaining treatment) and subsequently makes an advance decision which is valid and applicable in the circumstances, the advance decision takes priority.

We have more choice over how we can die under the current law than many realize. While the majority of people would want just comfort care at the end of their lives, only 3 per cent of us have made our wishes clear in an advance decision. That said, none of the individuals featured in the moving cases we have encountered in this book could have chosen the death they would have wanted under the current law. If we are to provide the compassionate care and choices so many wish for at the end of their lives the law must be changed to allow terminally ill, mentally competent adults to have assisted deaths (if that is their settled view). The real-life stories told in this volume demonstrate why, with the necessary safeguards in place, we should be able to choose the time and place of our deaths. The guidelines from the DPP are helpful in clarifying who is unlikely to be prosecuted for helping a terminally ill individual to die with dignity, but enabling professional involvement in the UK would require a change in the law.

COAD concluded that it would be possible to devise a legal framework with necessary safeguards to allow terminally ill people the option of an assisted death. Such a framework, supported by appropriately trained healthcare professionals, would reduce the risk of abuse and better protect individuals – such as John Close and Liz Smith's father Don – who find themselves faced with invidious choices.

The evidence that informed COAD's work and information gathered from places with assisted dying legislation in place, demonstrated that the potential risks to those considered vulnerable are minimized effectively with robust safeguards. In fact, there was no evidence in those jurisdictions that legalizing assisted dying had caused vulnerable people to be put at risk of being helped to die against their wishes. Indeed those opting for an assisted death may well be physically frail but are invariably feisty individuals well able to make their views clear. Moreover, where assisted dying legislation has been enacted, palliative care services are also excellent, and assisted dying is regarded as just one option for those who are terminally ill. Furthermore, enabling unrestricted discussion of all the options available resulted in greater openness and a clearer understanding of end-of-life choices between professionals, patients and their families.

The legislative programme that most closely resembles Lord Falconer's Bill has been in place in Oregon for more than a decade. Not only is there no evidence of patients being coerced into an assisted death against their wishes but there has also been no attempt to widen the eligibility criteria to include patients who are not terminally ill. The 'slippery slope' argument, frequently raised by opponents of legislative change, has no basis in fact.

The future for assisted dying in the UK is greater choice at the end of life. I have no doubt that the public in the UK want that outcome and will increasingly insist that it becomes a reality for terminally ill, mentally competent adults. The change we want to see will happen more quickly if we make our views known to our legislators in both Houses of Parliament. We can do that best by ensuring that the media, local and national, are made aware of concerns with the present law and by supporting the continued efforts of individuals such as Lord Falconer and organizations such as Dignity in Dying. Only when we have succeeded in changing the present law will we know for sure that we will be able to die with dignity at a time and place of our choosing.

That does not seem to be an unreasonable request.

11

A RECENT DEATH AT DIGNITAS
Ron Clinch: 'Want to share this one, Brian?'

Ron Clinch died with help from Dignitas at the age of seventy-four on 2 February 2012. He was a strong-minded and independent man who hated the idea of being completely helpless and dependent on other people. He wanted to achieve a dignified and peaceful death after intolerable suffering.

He was happily married to Kay for over fifty years. Their only child, Julie, was born in 1968, and in 1970 the family decided to live abroad. They moved to the island of Ibiza where Ron and Kay earned a living by renovating houses. Although they had intended to return to the UK before Julie started school, they stayed for over thirty years, and Julie was educated in Spain.

Ron, Kay and Julie were always very close, supportive of one another and openly loving. Ron's devotion to Kay and Julie underpinned his life. That devotion is typified by the fact that he would not let them travel to Dignitas with him – he didn't want them to risk prosecution on his behalf, nor did he want their final memories of him to be set so far away from their home.

Ron's thoughtfulness meant that the last time Julie and Kay saw him he was in the ambulance as he started his overland journey to Dignitas. His brother Brian was by his side.

Their journey was complicated by Ron's dependence on oxygen, which was a feature of his illness, idiopathic pulmonary fibrosis (IPF). He was diagnosed with the condition in October 2009, at which time he was given a life expectancy of two to five years. He lived for another two years and four months, and his ability to breathe deteriorated steadily over that time as the fibroids, after which the condition is named, began to obstruct his lung capacity. Ron had a lung biopsy at the Royal Brompton Hospital, but the cause of his IPF could not be found. In other words, his illness was idiopathic. A doctor suggested that something Ron had inhaled, which remained in one of his lungs, had been attacked by his strong and resilient immune system. This had led to the formation of a fibroid (or scar tissue) which, in turn, led to the unstoppable formation of more fibroids. In the UK 50 per cent of IPF patients die within three years of diagnosis, and with about five thousand deaths from the condition every year it kills more British people than leukaemia or ovarian cancer.

There were two oxygen concentrators in Ron's bedroom at home in Milton Keynes, and by the time of his departure for Dignitas he was using them both at the same time, day and night, with each of them running at full capacity. Kay would set them up to provide a flow rate of seven and a half litres a minute on each machine. He also had oxygen cylinders to get him through the brief but frequent times he needed extra help to get his breath back after exerting himself to walk across the room or go to the toilet. Ron, Kay and Julie were very concerned to make sure that enough oxygen was available for the journey to Dignitas. They were also worried about the supply that would be provided after Ron arrived in Switzerland. Their fears were allayed when the ambulance technician said, in response to Julie's last-minute question about how much they were carrying, 'We have enough oxygen to get to the moon and back.' Julie says she had never been so relieved in her life.

Dignitas clearly took those concerns about the oxygen situation seriously because they changed their practice of recent years. Ron was helped to die within a few hours of arriving in Switzerland, whereas most people are obliged to wait one full day between meeting the doctor and taking the life-ending medication. Ron and Brian slept in Dignitas's premises in Pfäffikon near Zurich that night to ensure his medical needs could be adequately met. This came as a huge relief to Brian who, not having seen his brother in the latter stages of his illness, had not anticipated how potentially serious and very alarming Ron's oxygen deficiency could be both for Ron himself and for anyone trying to help him.

During the night Brian woke up in the room he was sharing with Ron and realized that the constant hiss from the cylinder had stopped. He was able to switch the feed to the other tank before Ron woke up. There's an unmistakable irony in this: Brian almost certainly saved his brother's life so that he could die the following day.

Brian's action in reconnecting Ron's oxygen supply prevented the acute panic that would have overwhelmed Ron if he had woken up to find that his lifeline had been cut off. This was a very real fear, especially after Ron's discharge from hospital in January 2012. By that time he had become totally reliant on oxygen as he needed a very high level twenty-four hours a day. After being discharged from hospital he did not leave his home and its reliable oxygen supply again until the day he started his journey to Dignitas.

Ron, Kay and Julie had discussed the possibility of flying to Zurich, but as Ron's reliance on supplementary oxygen increased they realized that he would not be allowed on a scheduled flight. They looked into the cost and possibility of chartering a plane privately, but there were so many restrictions on carrying cylinders that they did not feel able to make the necessary arrangements. Julie considered the possibility of driving her father to Zurich, but they wouldn't have been able to take enough oxygen in the car. An overland route with paramedic assistance was their only option, and Kay found an ambulance company that was willing to undertake the mission. When she discussed the requirements for the journey with the man who ran the company – without being specific about the reason for the trip – Kay said, 'It's to go to Switzerland.' He replied, 'I understand. We've done this before', words that brought utter relief and joy to Kay, Ron and Julie.

Julie saw her father every day toward the end of his life. 'The only day I didn't see him was the Monday before he died because he was asleep all afternoon. But in one way I didn't want to, because it was horrible seeing him like that. I don't know how my mum coped with it, because living with someone who is so ill, seeing their deterioration . . . It's scary to be with someone who is out of breath all the time.'

Just before Christmas 2011 Ron's breathing deteriorated, and he was taken to the A&E department of Milton Keynes General Hospital. Julie accompanied him, and they asked the A&E doctor what was going to happen in the course of Ron's illness, explaining that they didn't know because nobody would tell them what the next stages might be. Ron had asked Professor Wells at the Royal Brompton Hospital what he could expect as his IPF progressed, and the Professor informed Ron that IPF was one of the cruellest ways to die. Ron desperately wanted to know what that meant, what would happen to him. He and Julie had already worked out that fifteen litres of oxygen a minute was the maximum he could be given by the concentrator he had at home. Ron was approaching that level when he was admitted to hospital.

The A&E doctor whom Ron and Julie quizzed about IPF said that, as the illness progressed, Ron's ability to breathe would be increasingly impaired. She told them that he would start to lose weight because he wouldn't be able to eat and breathe at the same time, that he would probably become panicky and scared and that eventually he would be put on morphine because he wouldn't be able to breathe.

Ron asked the A&E doctor, 'Do you agree with assisted dying in Switzerland?' The A&E doctor's reply was intriguing. She said, 'I would put my dog down.' Julie was relieved that fundamentally the doctor appeared to agree with the idea of assisted dying.

Ron was diagnosed with a lung infection, which the hospital got under control, and his oxygen use was reduced to ten litres a minute. Julie and Kay believe that Ron thought he would get his reliance down to six or seven litres a minute, meaning he would live with IPF for a few more years. His hopes were dashed when the antibiotics were stopped and his oxygen use started to creep up again.

Ron also wanted to enjoy one last Christmas, although he would rather not have spent it in hospital. On Christmas Day 2011 Julie, Kay, her partner Neil and her son David visited Ron in hospital after having lunch together at Julie's home. It was only because Ron was an in-patient that Brian found out how ill his brother was: when Brian rang to wish the family a Happy Christmas he was told that Ron wasn't there. Naturally Brian asked why, and the details of Ron's illness emerged. Ron's inclination for privacy meant that up to that time he had kept information about his illness to himself and his immediate family. When he was released from hospital Ron spoke to Brian about his plans to go to Dignitas.

While Ron was in hospital he told one of the nurses that he was going to Dignitas, saying, 'My name is already on the list.' She replied, 'I don't blame you. That's where I'd go.' And Julie described how her father lay in his hospital bed as one of the nurses cleaned up after an elderly man one day. Ron called out, 'You look after him – it could be you one day', and the nurse replied, 'No way. I'll be off to Switzerland first!'

Ron wanted to go home from hospital as soon as possible. Kay was seventy the day after he was discharged, and Julie says that Ron had wanted to celebrate his beloved wife's birthday with her one last time.

When Ron came home, getting him dressed was taking Kay a very long time – he could hardly move and even simply turning over in bed took all his breath. If he didn't move he could get by on fifteen litres of oxygen a minute, but if he moved he was immediately exhausted. He found eating and talking very difficult and tiring, and Julie says he was like a heroin addict anguishing about his oxygen supply, always asking, 'Where is it? How much have I got left?'

Dignitas had offered to book a hotel for two nights but when Kay rang the ambulance company to book the transport they said that Ron should not be in a hotel but a hospital bed. Kay realized that Dignitas had not grasped the seriousness of Ron's condition. Wanting to know whether they could help Ron die the day he arrived in Switzerland Kay kept on dialling Dignitas until finally someone answered the phone. She was very relieved to hear a voice at the end of the line and asked the person if it might be possible for Ron to be helped to die as soon as possible after he arrived.

Julie is angry that, because of people whose goal is to prevent the law changing to permit assisted dying in the UK, she had to wave goodbye to her father from the driveway of his house and was not able to be with him when he died. She admits that her father had initially told his family that he did not want any of them to accompany him, but she would have defied his wish had she felt safe in doing so. Julie also acknowledges that Ron made it clear that her role was to stay at home to look after Kay; it had already been agreed that she would not go to Switzerland. But Julie's fundamental motivation to stay at home was that she was afraid of losing her job if her actions came to her employer's attention.

Despite her fears, Julie was still in two minds about whether or not to accompany her father. When she went to her parents' house the night before he left for Switzerland she took her passport with her. It was only when her uncle, who had driven up from Devon, arrived that she felt able to stay in the UK. Julie was also very worried about the effect Ron's death would have on her son David, who was twelve when his grandfather died. Julie and Kay had originally decided not to tell him, but a couple of days before Ron was due to leave for Zurich Julie changed her mind and agreed with her father that it would be better to be honest with David. Julie is now very glad that they did tell him the truth. David has since said that he would have been angry if he had found out only later how his grandfather had died, if everyone else had known in advance what was going to happen but he had not been told.

It was very hard for David to say goodbye to his grandfather for the last time. David was on a sleepover the previous Saturday night, and after collecting him late Sunday morning Julie sat him down in their home and told him what was going on. At that point David became hysterical, so Julie calmed him down, comforted him and explained the situation as best she could. Later that afternoon she took him to see his grandfather, and David and Ron sat on the couch talking while Julie and Kay stayed in the kitchen.

On the day before Ron left for Dignitas Julie and David were in the house when Brian arrived. The presence of the man whose role was to escort Ron to his death brought matters into sharp focus for everyone. Ron asked David to go upstairs to get some of his clothes. David collected the items, and when he was downstairs again Julie saw that he was in tears. He dropped the clothes to the floor, blurting out to Julie, 'I can't do this. I can't do this.' Her reaction was understandable. She said, 'Let's go home. Go and say goodbye to Dadda.' David emerged after three or four minutes, and Julie has since learnt that Ron told his grandson to be good and to make his mother proud of him.

David was very upset after saying goodbye, and Ron suggested that the two of them leave straight away. Kay went to see Ron, and Julie took David to the car. As they reached the car they were approached by the husband of a neighbour who, earlier that afternoon, Julie had asked to witness Ron's signature on a disclaimer he had written about his impending journey. It was another indication of how concerned Ron was to protect his family that the day before he left the UK he was still worried about Kay and Julie getting into trouble.

Apart from those neighbours hardly anybody outside the family knew what was going on. Kay told nobody except Brian and his wife, while Julie confided in her best friend and one person at the school where she works. She let out a huge sigh of relief when her father and uncle reached France because only then did she know for sure that none of the people who knew about her father's decision had prevented him attaining his goal.

Julie now thinks that if someone told her that they wanted to live with a terrible illness through to the end she would sit through it with them, but she feels that everyone should have the right to end their suffering. And she says that she would go through the experience again, that she would help someone else to die. She says she would have gone to prison for any length of time to help her father achieve a peaceful and dignified death.

Once Ron had decided to accept Dignitas's provisional green light he pushed very hard to get the earliest date he could for his assisted death. He had left it as late as he possibly could before asking for the go-ahead, and by then he was on fifteen litres of oxygen a minute and the possibility of his being put on to a ventilator was getting very real. Julie feels that nobody should have go through what he experienced at the end of his life.

Julie's partner Neil was available to take care of David during her father's last night in Milton Keynes, so she was able to return to her parents' home and spend the night with them. Ron, Kay, Julie and Brian watched television until quite late, when Brian announced that he was going for a lie-down in Ron's old bed upstairs. After he left, Julie and her dad watched more television, and she sat beside him stroking his leg gently.

When Kay and Julie helped Ron get to bed for the final time they couldn't get his oxygen supply adjusted properly. Kay had sorted out some things for Ron to take to Zurich, and it dawned on her that she must have already packed a vital component of the system, a connector they now needed. When they found it, it wouldn't go on to the concentrator, and then they discovered that the cylinder by the bed was empty. Through all of this Ron just lay there. 'It was horrific because he was so out of breath. He was a very strong-willed, independent man, and I'll never forget him just lying there looking at me totally helpless as he couldn't communicate. He was probably thinking, Calm down, or Hurry up, but we were just panicking,' says Julie.

In the end Julie and Kay connected both of the concentrators as well as a small oxygen cylinder, and after a long time they got Ron comfortable. Kay went upstairs to bed, and Julie lay down on the sofa. At one point she thought she heard her father call out, and when she stuck her head round the door she saw him playing patience on his notepad computer. She spent the rest of the night sitting with him until the transport arrived at four o'clock.

The ambulance crew tried to get their trolley into the dining-room where Ron had been sleeping since returning from hospital, but it wouldn't fit. Ron had been loaned a commode at the same time as his hospital-type bed. Julie knew that he had never used it and that it moved on wheels, so she suggested that Ron could sit on it and be wheeled into the lounge where the trolley was waiting for him. The crew was very patient and let him get his breath back at every stage of the process. He needed to breathe as deeply as possible after pulling his legs up, after sitting up, after getting his legs over the bed and after every other movement. Once he was on the trolley they raised it up, and Julie thought it was going to hit the ceiling. She remembers thinking: If this doesn't give him a heart attack nothing will!

Julie and Kay are quite open about the fact that they had hoped Ron would have a heart attack or die in his sleep. Julie says their biggest fear had been that Ron would have a stroke and be unable to travel to Switzerland, and the two of them are very aware that you have to be very brave to go through with a death at Dignitas.

Julie says her father looked really smart on the bed in the back of the ambulance. Despite the effort it took when he was ill, he always shaved and made sure he was well turned out. Against his preference he had started wearing T-shirts and tracksuit bottoms while in hospital to make the caring tasks easier, and he carried on dressing that way after being sent home. The day he left for Dignitas 'His hair was combed, and he was wearing a smart brown fleece.' Ron even took a pair of shoes with him to Switzerland, but he didn't get the opportunity to wear them.

Kay went into the ambulance to say goodbye privately. When they were ready to leave Ron said, for everyone to hear, 'Kay, you've been a fantastic wife, and you've really looked after me.'

Ron's wife and daughter waved goodbye to him as the ambulance drove off. Brian sent regular texts keeping Kay and Julie informed, so they knew that the ambulance got to Pfäffikon at around seven o'clock on Wednesday evening.

When Ron and Brian arrived they found (to their huge relief) that Dignitas had provided two big cylinders of oxygen. After Kay told Dignitas how much oxygen Ron would need they clearly decided that putting him in the hotel down the road overnight with two or more cylinders before transferring him to their premises the following morning wasn't a viable option.

They arrived at the Dignitas apartment an hour late, and the person designated to connect up the oxygen had left. The cylinders were ready, but there didn't appear to be a connection that would allow both of them to work at the same time. With only one source, Ron wouldn't be able to get enough oxygen to allow him to regain control of his breathing. There was what Brian described as 'a bit of a cock-up and a feeling of panic', and Ron spent the first two hours after he arrived in Pfäffikon searching through the pot of connectors he had brought with him to try to get the supply to work properly. It is sad that Ron wasted valuable time that evening cutting tubes and trying to get enough oxygen flowing to keep him alive until he died.

After talking to Ron, the volunteer doctor agreed with the provisional green light he had earlier been given. Her agreement meant that Ron could be given an assisted death. Realizing just how ill Ron was, the doctor decided to stay in the Pfäffikon building overnight with him. She had brought her big husky dog, and Ron was not sure at first if he wanted the animal in the room with him. The doctor told Ron that she would put her pet on a blanket outside, but he said, 'No, no. Bring it inside.' The dog was very friendly, and Ron, despite his initial reservations, loved it being there.

When Brian rang Julie the next morning she had the opportunity to speak to her father for half an hour. Ron told her that after his death he didn't want them to sit around crying. He wanted them to celebrate his life and his release from intolerable suffering. He also mentioned that he had had a bad time in the night with his oxygen supply, despite the assistance of the doctor.

In the morning the Dignitas assistant arrived to supervise the medication. He made up an anti-emetic and offered it to Ron before they did the paperwork. Ron agreed to take it, and they completed the forms. According to the schedule the woman with the video camera was supposed to arrive thirty minutes after Ron took the first drug, but she was delayed by heavy snow and an hour elapsed. The assistant told Ron not to worry. He said, 'Your stomach will still be fine if it's in there for an hour.'

One of Ron's favourite groups was Queen. He gave Kay the song 'You're My Best Friend' for their wedding anniversary, and he had wanted to listen to that track as he died. He thought Kay or Julie had packed the CD in his bag, but for some reason it wasn't there. When Ron and Julie talked that last morning he told her that the doctor had gone out the previous night to look for a recording of 'You're My Best Friend'. She had failed, despite asking everyone and looking everywhere. Ron asked the doctor if she would stay with him as he died, but she explained that she couldn't. She had already missed two parts of a five-part course, and she would fail the course if she missed another part.

The woman with the video camera finally arrived, and the Dignitas assistant asked Ron, 'Do you want me to make up the second drug?' Ron answered, 'Yes, yes', and the assistant told him, 'When I come back I will have to ask you again if this is what you want.' Ron said, 'Oh all right', and the assistant joked, 'Well, don't mess around!' When he came back with the second dose Ron asked Brian, 'Want to share this one, Brian?' and Brian replied, 'No, not this one. Cheers, Ron.'

By this time Brian had managed to download 'You're My Best Friend' to his phone, and he played it as Ron drank his final drink and ate some chocolate to take away the taste of the life-ending medication. Brian told Kay and Julie that Ron was 'fast asleep' only four minutes after taking the drink. At that point Brian asked the assistant if he could take the oxygen mask off Ron's face but was told, 'No, not at the moment. He is comfortable. Leave it on for fifteen minutes, as he is now in a coma.' He was almost certainly reasoning that Ron still needed a good supply of oxygen at that point and that removing the mask might have caused him distress. Julie feels that it might even have hastened his death through oxygen deprivation.

A trace of the chocolate was in Ron's saliva which was dribbling, just slightly, from the corner of his mouth. Brian wiped it away but left the mask in place. The assistant told Brian that within half an hour Ron would be dead. As is always the case the police and the undertaker came later to deal with the death.

Brian flew back from Zurich to Luton the day Ron died. When Julie met him as he came out of the terminal he told her about the difficult night he and Ron had experienced. He broke down when he told her about his brother's death. Brian's son and daughter-in-law had recently lost a newborn baby, and he said that till then that had been the worst experience of his life. Doing what he did for Ron was far worse, he told Julie.

The night Brian got back he sat up with Kay and Julie until 2.30 in the morning talking and laughing and crying while he told stories about Ron's last day.

Julie has been surprised by the different reactions of people she has spoken to about her father's death, and she tells more and more people as time goes by. She feels proud of what Ron did, as does Kay. Julie says, 'He did it. It was his choice – and good for him.' They know that their views on assisted dying are increasingly accepted, but they feel the subject is not sufficiently discussed. They also think that those who are opposed to assisted dying must be unaware of the reality of the situation, perhaps because they have not spent time with people who are terminally ill.

Kay poses a question that so many people who are in favour of assisted dying have asked: 'Why is it that the people who don't want anything to do with assisted dying don't want anybody else to have that choice?' She adds, 'If you don't want to do it, you don't have to.'

Julie is very forceful when she says, 'I want that option. If Ron had had that option in England, he would not have had to spend the last few months of his life worrying about Dignitas. When to go? How to get there? Would he be able to get enough oxygen during the journey? If he hadn't had to go to Switzerland to achieve a good death we might have had him for one more day. I couldn't see him going on for more than two days.'

Kay adds that if Ron hadn't been married and didn't have family she didn't think he would have had the strength to deal with the emails and communications by himself, and he would almost certainly have had to go to Dignitas much sooner. 'He needed to get all these original documents, and we had to pay a notary public to come to the house to certify the one Ron needed to confirm that he was resident in England.'

Kay is aware that some people in Switzerland are trying to stop Dignitas's work, proposing a tax which would mean that anyone coming into the country for their help to die would have to pay £30,000 on top of the fees that Dignitas charges. 'What do people get out of trying to stop people doing this? It's not affecting anybody else in any way. If you don't have the money you can't do this. In Belgium, in Holland, the doctor will come round to you at home. We are so far behind.'

She talks about the inequity of having to be able to afford to travel to Switzerland especially if, like Ron, you are too ill to travel on a scheduled flight and need to use a private plane or an ambulance. Kay feels that the price they paid for the ambulance was very reasonable. If they had chartered a private plane it would have cost £35,000, but the ambulance only cost £2,600. 'I thought it was fantastic.' She contacted the company afterwards to thank them for what they did. 'Their service was absolutely wonderful.'

Ron wasn't bothered about having his ashes returned to England. It was Julie who wanted them back. When Ron's ashes arrived at Kay's home she rang Julie saying, 'Your dad's turned up with Parcelforce.' Julie remembered that Kay had previously expressed her reservations about having the urn in the house, so she suggested putting it in the garage. Kay wasn't prepared to do that, and Julie knew she was upset, so she suggested that her mother strap the package in the front passenger seat of the car and drive the urn round to Julie's house.

She told Neil and promptly burst into tears. He asked what she wanted to do with the ashes, and she said she didn't know but was excited that her father was back. When she saw her mother's car arrive she rushed outside. On the front seat was a box with wax seals and string. Julie and Kay were very emotional while opening the box, but their sorrow soon evaporated. To their amazement, even in death, people couldn't get Ron's name right, and it tickled them that he had returned home as Roland and not Ronald. They laughed, and it undoubtedly raised their spirits at what would otherwise have been a very sad moment.

Kay is concerned about who will take over running Dignitas after Ludwig Minelli dies as he is in now in his eighties. She understands why, after the law changes, some people will be excluded from the assisted dying process because they do not meet the necessary safeguarding criteria. If someone is not an adult, not terminally ill or not mentally competent they will be ineligible. She is also bewildered by the fact that so many people criticize those countries that have introduced legislation to permit assisted dying, and she is appalled by the fury and fire of the opposition.

Julie admits that she is a very emotional person who cries easily, but going through what their family has experienced makes her certain that one should be able to talk to one's doctor about assisted dying. Julie says that if she needed an assisted death, even if it took five doctors to say that you qualified, she would go through the process. Ron actually discussed alternatives to Dignitas, such as gassing himself in a car with carbon monoxide, but Julie wouldn't let him dwell on such options. And he could simply have turned off his oxygen supply, but this would have been so distressing for him and anyone with him at the time that it is unlikely that he ever gave it serious consideration. The relevance of this speculation is that some seriously ill people who are suffering intolerably do have an alternative to travelling to Switzerland or committing suicide at home: while everyone has the option of refusing treatment, even if that refusal can lead to death, someone who is reliant on dialysis, for instance, has the option of turning off the machine that is keeping them alive.

On their last afternoon together Julie talked to her father and recorded the interview on video. She asked Ron lots of questions, 'the kind you wouldn't normally ask', and although she hasn't yet watched the film she can watch it whenever she wants to – or feels able to – in the future. During the evening of that last day, while they were watching television together, Julie realized that very soon she wouldn't be able to ask him any more questions, so she asked what she called 'the big one'. His immediate answer to the question 'Are you scared of dying, Dad?' was 'Nope! I'm not scared.' It was the fact that Ron was about to have an assisted death that enabled him to answer so swiftly and positively. The prospect of being given competent and compassionate help to die removed his anxieties about dying badly, and he had nothing left to fear.

12

THE RIGHT TO AN ASSISTED DEATH

by Ray Tallis

Dedicated to the memory of Dr Ann McPherson

I have been preoccupied for nearly a decade by the need for a change in the law to legalize the choice of assisted dying for mentally competent people with terminal illness who have expressed a settled wish to die. In summer 2011 I was elected Chair of a new group, Healthcare Professionals for Assisted Dying (HPAD), whose immediate aim is to represent the views of doctors, nurses and other healthcare professionals who favour a change in the law. I took over this role from Dr Ann McPherson.

I was privileged to know Ann, sadly only for a short time, before she died in June 2011. By a bitter irony she had a hideous death, which her daughter – a consultant dermatologist – described in harrowing detail in the *British Medical Journal*.[1] Despite her unbearable symptoms, which had resisted the best possible palliative care, any physician assisting her to die (by, for example, writing a prescription for life-ending medication) would have been prosecuted for manslaughter and been liable to a fourteen-year gaol sentence.

That anyone could oppose such a humane ambition as decriminalization of assisted dying may seem astonishing. But there has been highly organized opposition to a change in the law. Some opponents have appealed to religious principles such as 'the sanctity of life', but more often than not wrap up their opposition in a cloak of pragmatic concerns intended to instil fear. They frequently talk of 'the slippery slope', arguing that if Ann had been allowed her wish people with disabilities would be pressurized to choose death against their wishes and 'burdensome' older people would be advised that they were surplus to requirement.

*

Unfortunately, most of the energy in winning the argument will have to be directed at countering the bad and sometimes dishonest arguments that are already in play. And it is these false arguments – and making a case *against* the case against rather than the positive case *for* – that I will focus on. It would, however, be remiss of me not to remind you of the core of the positive case. And here it is.

First, unbearable suffering, prolonged by medical care and inflicted on a dying patient who wishes to die, is unequivocally a bad thing. From this it follows that not doing (or, worse still, prohibiting) what has to be done to prevent this is unacceptable cruelty. I add this because I believe it is not those who support assisted dying but those who oppose it who have the moral case to answer and who should be on the defensive. And, second, respect for individual autonomy – the right to have one's choices supported by others, to determine one's own best interest, when one is of sound mind – is a sovereign principle.

And that's it.

So much for the positive case. Irrefutable, one would think. But, of course, it has been answered, and I want to devote the remainder of this chapter to dealing with the objections that have been raised by opponents of assisted dying. If I am something of an expert on these objections, it is because, to my shame, in the past I subscribed to them myself. The reason I changed my mind was that, prompted by Lord Joffe, I examined the arguments more critically and acquainted myself more fully with the relevant facts. There is, of course, nothing dishonourable about being persuaded by facts and arguments. But for some people they are irrelevant. For many opponents of a change in the law conceal what really lies behind their views: religious belief.

And so one should welcome the rare, exemplary candour of the speech given by Baroness Richardson of Calow when the House of Lords gave Lord Joffe's Assisted Dying for the Terminally Ill Bill its second reading: 'There is no doubt that the [Joffe] Bill has shocked the religious communities . . . It has undermined the security some of us have felt that God is to be in control of life and death.'[2]

Most of those who are religiously opposed to assisted dying are less honest. They are sufficiently savvy to know that references to God would cut little ice in a present-day British society even among those who profess religious beliefs, the majority of whom support assisted dying. The data from the most recent British Social Attitudes Survey – consistent with findings over many years – reveal that religious belief seems hardly to reduce the tendency to be in favour of assisted dying, with 82 per cent of the general population and 71 per cent of those who designate themselves as having religious belief supportive of assisted dying.[3] And indeed for many people religious belief is a key factor in their support for assistance to die on the grounds of compassion.

Mary Warnock, in her book *Dishonest to God: On Keeping Religion Out of Politics*,[4] has described how religiously motivated opponents will duck and weave between absolutist arguments based on faith and pragmatic or consequentialist arguments that appeal to empirical 'evidence' about anticipated adverse consequences for society.

When the bishops switch from their impregnable argument that God is the giver of the sacred gift of life (impregnable in the sense that it is theological and not supported by evidence or capable of proof), it is to the vulnerability of the terminally ill or otherwise suffering that they turn.[5]

This is what we might call the 'belt and braces' or, better perhaps, 'belt and gaiters' approach, slithering between arguments from principle and arguments based on what are presented as facts. It is reminiscent of the Groucho Marx quip: 'These are my principles, and if you don't like them . . . Well, I have others.' What applies here is 'These are my (inviolable) principles, but if you don't like them I have some facts that will bring you round to the same conclusion as me.' The facts, however, are not as convenient as opponents of assisted dying would wish. So they resort to principle-warped factoids; and we must examine these head on.

In dealing with the religiously motivated case against assisted dying I shall also examine a couple of principles that enshrine fundamental values, one religious and one secular. The religious principle will be that of the sanctity of life, and I shall recall how it has never been regarded as unassailable in any society – it has always been applied inconsistently – so it is irrelevant to the case for or against assisted dying. Most importantly, it has no relevance to the question of the value of life as invoked in this context. The secular principle I shall look at will be that of the right to have decisions that affect only one's own welfare respected – the principle of autonomy – and I shall show that while there are problems with this, which have been pointed out by religious opponents, such problems as it has are common to all ethical principles when applied in real life.

I am not an epidemiologist of error, but it seems to me that the most common objection to changing the law is that assisted dying is actually unnecessary or would be unnecessary if optimal palliative care were universally available. This is not true, as my experience as a doctor for over thirty-five years made clear, when I was responsible for patients whose symptoms were uncontrolled even when they had first-rate palliative care. The harrowing stories in this book show just how untrue this is. It is a reminder not only of how palliative care may ultimately fail in some patients – in some cases catastrophically – but also how important it is sometimes to be reminded of the terrible human reality behind the sometimes abstract facts.

And Ann's own death – typical of so many others (including those of my mother and father) – is eloquent, if terrible, testimony. The description of her protracted end by her daughter is compelling in its awfulness:

My mother was diagnosed with pancreatic cancer in 2007. For at least three years her life with cancer was worth living. She put up with many 'new normals' as she called them. A new normal to take regular morphine to control pain . . . a new normal to have a chest drain *in situ* which she herself drained daily; a new normal to eat only baby food. She put up with these and other trials and was grateful always for the medical support and interventions that made her life possible. To continue her work, to spend time with friends and family, to enjoy the days she knew were so precious.

On 3 May 2011 Mum had had enough. A scan had confirmed that the cancer had spread to around the gastric outlet so that she could no longer eat anything solid, and even fluids were difficult. Her chest drain had started to leak and was pouring out fluid to drench dressings. She had lost a huge amount of weight. She was getting pressure sores.

She wanted to die, she needed to die. Her GP was wonderful and set up a morphine drip to control the now uncontrollable pain and discomfort. Mum said that she hoped to drift away that night. But there was no drifting away. What followed were three weeks of unbearable agony. She had become highly tolerant to morphine.

We would try to dress and move her but it became increasingly difficult. By now she had two morphine drips, one in each wasted leg which needed re-siting often. Her drain site poured fluid, her bedclothes were drenched. Her last spoken words to me three days before dying (while I was trying to change her nightdress with a lovely carer) were 'HOLD . . . MY . . . HEAD.' There was no dignity. There was no Mum; just a wounded animal who needed drips changed.

Night after night we would expect that she would not wake up. She could not receive the medicines that would relax her tiny gasping frame. My brother and sister were up and down from their homes and families. They were not coming to say goodbye: that had been done weeks earlier, just to sit hopelessly. It is an honour to care for someone you love, but it no longer felt honourable to try to care for someone who wants to be dead.[6]

Her body hung on to the (very) bitter end:

Even as she died her body seemed furious with its final fight, gasping to the end, and in a desperate haunting shudder I found myself sitting in pools of expelled fluid. That was not what she wanted. Mum had seen this happen before and wanted to avoid it, for future patients and their families.[7]

Thus the testimony of a loving daughter. So much for palliative care as a panacea. And Ann's case was not unusual. We have seen from the stories in this book just how bad deaths can be, even where the medical teams have done their best. Whereas pain can usually be controlled and even nausea and breathlessness – although this may be more difficult – the sense of utter helplessness as one is disintegrating lies beyond the reach of palliation. Many patients still have bad deaths, the 560 suicides by seriously ill Britons in 2010[8] and the nearly 220 Britons who have undertaken dreadful journeys to Dignitas in Switzerland[9] to end their suffering in the past decade represent just the tip of the iceberg.

International experience also confirms that palliative care fails some patients. To take one example, for the past ten years assisted dying has been legal in Oregon under the Death with Dignity Act. Oregon has among the best palliative care of the fifty states in the USA, and yet nearly 90 per cent of those seeking assisted dying are in receipt of hospice care.[10] This is not to diminish the huge benefits of palliative care which can help a great many dying patients achieve a dignified death but to acknowledge honestly that it, like other modes of healthcare, has its limitations. The eminent palliative care physician and opponent of assisted dying Baroness Finlay has admitted in the House of Lords that 'palliative care is not a blanket panacea in all cases'.

There are those who state that the availability of assisted dying as an 'easy' option has inhibited investment in palliative care. I have heard it claimed by an eminent opponent of a change in the law on several occasions that palliative care does not exist in countries where there is legislation in favour of assisted dying. International experience, of course, does not support this. The usual pattern is that liberalization of the law (in some countries, such as the Netherlands, far beyond anything I would support) has been accompanied by increasing investment in palliative care services. In Oregon the proportion of people dying in hospice care – a marker of the availability of palliative care – has more than doubled since the Death with Dignity Act was introduced. A recent authoritative report by the European Association of Palliative Care (2011) came to this conclusion:

> The idea that legislation of euthanasia and/or assisted suicide might obstruct or halt palliative care development thus seems unwarranted and is only expressed in commentaries rather than demonstrated by empirical evidence . . . There is scant evidence of the supposed underdevelopment of palliative care.[11]

It is also dogmatically asserted by those who oppose it that liberalizing the law will break down trust between doctor and patient. This is not borne out by the evidence. A Europe-wide survey put levels of trust between doctors and patients in nine European countries highest in the Netherlands,[12] and 97 per cent of patients were confident in their GP. More recently it has been noted that the present law permitting euthanasia and assisted dying is supported by 92 per cent of the population in the Netherlands ten years after the law was introduced.[13] None of this should come as any surprise: in countries with assisted dying, discussion of end-of-life care is open, transparent, honest and mature, not conducted in a cloud of ambiguity as it is in the UK. And the knowledge that your doctor will not abandon the therapeutic alliance with you at your hour of greatest need will foster, not undermine, trust.

If these factoids don't deliver the results that are desired, then the antis up the antes: more quasi-facts, rumours and urban myths are mobilized. Legalization of assisted dying, opponents assert, will set us on a road that leads inevitably to assisted dying for people who are not dying but who have a non-terminal chronic illness or disability; and then to such people who do not wish to die and/or cannot express their wishes either way. In addition, the slippery-slopers tell us, the law will create or legitimize a culture in which when you are frail, infirm and judged to be a burden to others you will be expected out of decency to seek assistance to die. And it is implied that this is what is already happening somewhere or other.

The first step in dealing with such claims is to reiterate certain distinctions. A law to permit mentally competent, terminally ill adults who are suffering unbearably to receive assistance to die at their considered and persistent request would not at the same time legalize assisting people with non-terminal illnesses to commit suicide or legalize voluntary euthanasia, in which people can have their lives ended by someone else. Assisted dying would not apply to people with disabilities who are not terminally ill; elderly people who are not terminally ill; people with non-terminal illness; or people who are not mentally competent, including those who have dementia or depression. These distinctions are not vague or ambiguous, and they are clear to the general public; for example, while a consistent 80 per cent or more people support assisted dying, the support for assisted suicide for the non-terminally ill runs at only 40 per cent.[14] Society would not somnambulate towards mass euthanasia for people who have no wish to die.

What is more, there is international experience to which we may refer to settle the argument about the inevitability of the slippery slope. The most relevant is the experience in Oregon. It is most relevant because the Death with Dignity Act, which was introduced over a decade ago, is very close to the laws that have been considered in England, although the Bill proposed by Lord Falconer (due to receive its Second Reading in the House of Lords in 2014) has more safeguards. In Oregon the proportion of deaths that are assisted has never risen above 0.2 per cent.[15] The average age of those who have assisted dying is lower than the average age of deaths, so elderly people are not disproportionately represented when you take into account the fact that the overwhelming majority of deaths take place in old age. The typical profile of a person who avails himself or herself of assisted dying is a strong-willed middle-class person used to getting his or her way – hardly representative of groups traditionally depicted as 'vulnerable'.[16] What is more, there is no evidence in Oregon of extension of assisted dying to assisted suicide for people with non-terminal illnesses, nor is there any public appetite for this.

Needless to say, the Oregon experience, being so inconvenient for opponents of assisted dying, has been misrepresented. In a debate Mary Warnock and I had with him on BBC Radio 4's *Start the Week*, Lord Gummer reported that the rate of assisted dying in Oregon had increased by 300 per cent in the first few years of legislation. This was true, but it was meant to suggest that this was something out of control. The full picture was that the number of assisted deaths increased over a few years as the law began to be implemented in practice, from a minute figure of 16 to 64 and that since then the percentage has remained, as I mentioned, low at 0.2 per cent.

I am going to come back to the slippery slope when I talk about principles and values, but I want to make a couple more points on this issue. If there is a slippery slope, legislation – with all the safeguards envisaged in a Bill such as the one proposed by Lord Falconer – would, to borrow the ethicist John Harris's metaphor, 'apply crampons rather than skis'.

The Dutch experience, frequently misrepresented by those against assisted dying, illustrates this. Rates of non-voluntary euthanasia (that is, doctors actively ending patients' lives without having been asked by them to do so) decreased from 0.8 per cent of all deaths in 1991 (approximately 1,000 deaths) to 0.4 per cent in 2005 (approximately 550 deaths).[17] In the UK a study published in *Palliative Medicine* in 2009 found that in 0.21 per cent of deaths attended by a doctor life was ended with an explicit request from the patient (in other words, voluntary euthanasia) and in 0.3 per cent of cases life was ended without an explicit request from the patient (in other words, non-voluntary euthanasia).[18] This means that approximately 2,600 people in the UK are being given direct help to die, with or without their explicit request, outside any relevant legal framework.

We may treat the claim made repeatedly by the *Daily Mail* in the latter half of 2012 that 130,000 elderly people were being killed each year as a result of being placed on an end-of-life care pathway (the Liverpool Care Pathway)[19] – in order that hospital trusts will be financially rewarded and managers and doctors can work together to clear beds and improve turnover – as, well, the *Daily Mail*. Even so, we may still maintain that the present clinical, ethical and legal fudge, in which ploys such as continuous sedation and starvation and dehydration are in some cases used to get round the prohibition on assisted dying, is unacceptable. Those who are concerned for the safety of patients, far from opposing a change in the law, should support legalizing assisted dying in view of the scrutiny it would bring to bear on medical practice. Not only is it possible to devise a law with sufficient safeguards against abuse, but a law regulating assisted dying would itself be a mighty safeguard.

Let me wind up my tour of factoids with a final group that are generated by the fear that mistakes would be made: mistakes that are of particular concern since, in the case of assisted dying, they are irreversible. Opponents often treat their audiences to tales of individuals who asked to be assisted to die and then who, after talking to an understanding physician, one who is (to appropriate the catchy name of a campaign group) into 'Care not Killing', change their minds and subsequently live long, happy, contented lives. The caring not killing physician (quite unlike a homicidal character like me) will receive a postcard from his or her patient announcing that she has just climbed the north face of the Eiger single-handed without ropes ten years after requesting assistance to die. I exaggerate, of course, but some of the stories beggar belief. However, they carry huge potential weight and lead people to draw very large conclusions. As Bertrand Russell said, 'Popular induction depends upon the emotional interest of the instances, not upon their number.'

How shall we address the concern that physicians may not read the patient's mind correctly and/or his or her ability to make a rational decision? Well, it is easy to build in time for reflection in any law: it should include ample opportunity to change one's mind. Lord Falconer's Bill has a minimum period of fourteen days between prescribing and administering life-ending medicine, reduced to six days if the patient is expected to die within a month.

And people do change their minds. The experience in Oregon is compelling: only a tiny minority of those people who discussed assisted dying with their doctors actually received, cashed and took the prescription. This is the principle of emotional assurance. Many people will have taken comfort from having banked a prescription and many more from knowing that this option is available. Where there is doubt about the patient's mental competence or about the absence of a treatable depression, psychiatric advice can be sought. None of these safeguards is available for people going to Switzerland to have their life ended in a Dignitas clinic or where patients commit unassisted suicide. As the law stands at present, patients cannot even discuss assisted dying with their doctors. I suspect that once you have embarked on a journey to Switzerland it is very difficult to change your mind. You have boarded a train you cannot get off. And as for the rationality of a decision, there are ways of testing competence and the presence or absence of reversible depression. Patients experiencing a horrible death may well be depressed, but this does not mean that they are not competent to make a decision. What is more, in every other area of medicine there is a presumption of competence: the patient is presumed to be of sound mind and able to make a rational decision unless there is clear evidence to the contrary.

What about the other worry, that the medical diagnosis could be wrong? In most cases, this seems highly unlikely. A candidate for assisted dying will have widespread advanced illness, clear objective reasons for suffering, in which palliation has failed, and the ultimate outcome will not be in doubt. Rejecting legalization of assisted dying will not, of course, save the occasional misdiagnosed patient from unnecessary death from medical error; it will simply ensure that that avoidable death – as well as that of all those correctly diagnosed – will be more prolonged. What is more, raising the possibility of an assisted death will prompt review of the case, and this may turn up the very rare example where clear-cut, advanced disease turns out to be nothing of the sort. In short, it is possible to envisage circumstances in which the request for assistance to die may be life-saving.

Much attention has been paid to errors doctors make in prognosis. In fact, again, the likelihood of the prognosis being seriously wrong will be considerably less in very advanced disease. Most studies have shown that doctors greatly overestimate the prognosis, expecting patients to live longer than they do. What is more, doctors already rely on estimates of prognosis when they move to management plans that will shorten life, such as withdrawing life-supporting medical care (insulin, artificial ventilation), exploiting the so-called 'double effect' (of which more presently), colluding in the patient's death by starvation and dehydration or initiating continuous deep sedation.

The truth is that medicine is a probabilistic art. This is evident when we look at the outcomes for elective or non-emergency surgery in patients who may, in many cases, be reasonably fit. One very large study showed a significant mortality – up to 5 per cent – in very elderly patients receiving elective surgery to prevent future problems. We accept that as an occasional consequence of trying to alter the natural history of disease. So why do we set impossibly high standards of certainty and clinical accuracy in the case of patients who wish to die when we settle for much lower standards for patients who do not wish to die? Why do we raise the bar above the balance of probabilities, above 'beyond reasonable doubt', to 'beyond, beyond reasonable doubt'?

Why, in this context, do we believe, as we do not elsewhere in medicine, that it is better that thousands should suffer unnecessarily than that a very rare mistake might be made? Why cannot the fully informed competent patient make the decision in full awareness of any residual uncertainties? Why is it better that nature should take its cruel course than that a doctor should hasten the death of a patient? A cynic would say that doctors oppose assisted dying because they are trained to hasten death only by accident. Or accidentally on purpose – the so-called 'double effect'. I shall return to this, and the medical profession, in due course.

Life, we are told by people who believe this kind of thing, is a gift of God. Consequently, we may not take away a life God has created, even at the request of the person whose life is at issue. This principle is absolute, non-negotiable. But is it? Can it be? In actual practice the history of those religions that explicitly profess the sanctity of life as an absolute basic principle – Christianity, Judaism, Islam –

shows that it is (to put it politely) inconsistently applied. The notion of the 'just war', where people will be killed in large numbers and against their will rather than individually at their request, is accepted; in many explicitly religious countries judicial execution is commonplace, and this may not only be for murder but for lesser crimes, or for non-crimes such as apostasy or blasphemy or being gay. And, to pre-empt the claim that this is evident only in distant countries about which we have only prejudices, let me give you two examples nearer home: the Anglican response to events in the Second World War and, more recently, the rhetoric around the recent Iraq War.

In 1944 George Bell, the Bishop of Chichester, condemned the area bombing of civilians in German cities; it was, he said, an unjust pursuit of a just war. He was opposed by his fellow bishops, including the Archbishop of York, who said, 'It is a lesser evil to bomb [that is, kill] the war-loving Germans than to sacrifice the lives of our fellow countrymen . . . or to delay the delivery of many now held in slavery.' It appears that it is better to kill others directly in order possibly to save others indirectly. There are circumstances, it would appear, under which orthodox opinion allows a utilitarian calculus to trump the 'inviolable' principle of the sanctity of life, illustrating Baroness Warnock's point about the slithering between absolutist principles and pragmatic considerations.

And let me take an example even nearer home. Rowan Williams, until recently Archbishop of Canterbury, has led the Anglican Church in its violent opposition to legalizing assisted dying. It goes against Christian values, he says. 'We are committed as Christians to the belief that every life in every imaginable circumstance is infinitely precious in the sight of God.' Assisted dying would be 'a major shift in the moral and spiritual life in which we live.'[20] Now, contrast that forthright response with his statement on the eve of the Iraq War. 'Doubts persist', he said, in his joint statement with the Archbishop of Westminster, 'about the moral legitimacy of a war with Iraq.'[21] This muted response to a war in which predictably large numbers of people were killed who had no wish to be – over six hundred thousand as it turned out[22] – was at a time when two million of his fellow citizens had taken to the streets to protest out loud against this clearly unjust and criminal war.

One could be forgiven for thinking that there are religious beliefs that see assisting the death of someone who is dying and wants to die as morally more hazardous than raining death on a city filled with people who want no such thing. One could be forgiven even for concluding that the sanctity-of-life principle, while supporting the position that it is always wrong to assist someone to die who is terminally ill and longs to die, will suggest that is less wrong to kill a perfectly healthy man, woman or child who does not wish to die.

But we need to dig a little deeper. Why do the opponents of assisted dying invoke a clearly vulnerable principle whose theological resonance would be rejected by most people, even although, as I mentioned at the beginning of this chapter, that they are usually less than candid and invoke the factoids we examined earlier? I think it is because it seems to them to be the only way of defending, standing up for or protecting something that we would all wish to defend, stand up for or protect: the fundamental ethic of valuing human lives – our own and those of others – as infinitely precious. This is reflected in the reason given in his presidential address to the General Synod by Rowan Williams for his rejecting legalization of assisted dying: 'It will create an ethical framework in which the worthwhileness of some lives is undermined by the legal expression of what feels like public impatience with protracted dying and "unproductive" lives.'

In other words, behind the appeal to the supposedly absolute (but in fact negotiable) principle, there is the implicit assumption or claim that the religious principle of the sanctity of life is the only source of the value we place upon life, as much in a secular as in a religious society; if we question it we shall devalue life; and we shall particularly devalue the lives of those who are powerless or are already likely to be devalued. Elderly people, people with disability, people who have mental illness will be at risk.

Most of us can see that this is nonsense, but it is none the less worthwhile spelling out the obvious. Let me personalize this to make it clear. My wife and I have been happily married for over forty years. We can imagine a time when one of us is terminally ill, nearing the end and in unbearable misery and wanting to die. We would both like there to be a law to make it possible for us to get the help one or other of us may need. Let us suppose that I become terminally ill first and I ask her to seek help from a physician to help me to die and she complies with my wish. This cannot imply that she is colluding in my devaluation of my own (and consequently our shared) life. If I am devaluing any part of my life, it is only the next few suffering-filled weeks – not the preceding seventy or (better) eighty years or (better still) ninety years. Even less is either of us devaluing human life in general or the irreplaceable preciousness of human beings. Neither she nor I is devaluing anyone else's life: the lives of old people, of people with disability, of people from minority groups. My wife is simply respecting my judgement of the value of the last few days of a life, days filled with unbearable suffering. Indeed, we are enhancing the value of life by doing our best to prevent our own lives being diminished by the sustained horror of unbearable and pointless suffering. We are respecting those things by which we judge our lives and our shared personal experiences. Those who truly love life want to honour it by dying well.

The assertion that legalizing assisted dying would erode the value we place on each other's lives – in particular those who are vulnerable and dependent on our good will – is, of course, an empirical claim. It may be tested by looking at social trends in places where the law has been liberalized. The evidence, such as it is, is in the opposite direction. The care for people with dementia in the Netherlands is superb, and places such as Hogeway are moral exemplars that put other countries, including the UK, to shame.[23]

The irrelevance of the sanctity-of-life doctrine to determining whether or not the law should be changed is evident to many religious opponents of assisted dying which is why so many factoids are mobilized to try to influence opinion by instilling fear. There are other ways of influencing opinion both directly by appealing to the public and indirectly through influencing bodies that carry considerable clout with those who are in a position to change the law, most notably the medical profession, where organizations such as Care Not Killing and the Christian Medical Fellowship are punching above their numerical weight.

The Catholic Church played a prominent role in the formation of the Care Not Killing Coalition via the Catholic Bishops' Conference of England and Wales. In the document 'Faith in the Future: 2006–2008' they state:

> The work of the Church supporting and promoting pro-life issues has been given a real boost through Faith in the Future. The Care Not Killing Alliance was established in 2005 to work with other faith groups, palliative care organisations and disability rights groups, forming a broad coalition of parties concerned with the legalisation of euthanasia . . .

Only four of the known thirty member organizations of Care Not Killing are non-religious. So much for 'a broad coalition'. Dr Peter Saunders, CEO of the Christian Medical Fellowship and Campaign Director of Care Not Killing, made the strategy clear:

> As Christian doctors we oppose euthanasia and assisted suicide because we believe in the sanctity of human life made in the image of God . . . But to win the debate on

assisted dying we need to be using arguments that will make sense to those who do not share our Christian beliefs . . . Christian doctors need to play a key role in this debate; and they will do so most effectively by learning to put what are essentially Christian arguments in secular language.

The muddling of euthanasia, assisted suicide and assisted dying is not accidental: it is an essential element in a strategy intended to further the idea that legalizing assisted dying has a built-in slippery slope.

In Parliament opponents of change are even more effective in cloaking a principled objection to change in the clothes of pragmatic concern. Resistance to change, specifically in the House of Lords, is organized by the supporters of Living and Dying Well, co-chaired by Lord Carlile, QC, and Baroness Finlay. Launched in 2010, they describe themselves as 'a public policy think tank' whose aim is to 'promote reasoned discussion and to publish evidence-based information on the laws relating to euthanasia and assisted suicide'.[24] A former part-time press officer of Living and Dying Well, and researcher to Baroness Finlay, now associate editor of the *Catholic Herald*, recently wrote about the need to separate pro-life campaigns:

> One key group would defend the rights of the unborn child and the other would focus on opposing the legalisation of assisted suicide and/or voluntary euthanasia.
>
> Both groups would take a strictly evidence-based approach to influencing and resisting future legislation. Religious sentiments or distracting arguments about sexuality would be kept out of the equation.[25]

We have already seen the 'strictly evidence-based approach' referred to by Living Well and Dying Well in action. But we have not touched on one aspect of this approach: namely, the occasional fabrication of the required evidence. Prompted by a poll in May 2012, which found that 62 per cent of doctors were in favour of the British Medical Association (currently opposed to assisted dying) adopting a stance of neutrality,[26] the *British Medical Journal* published a leader from the editor Fiona Godlee calling for this stance at their upcoming Annual Meeting where it was to be debated.[27] The *British Medical Journal* invited its readers to respond to the editorial by voting for or against neutrality. Astonishingly, over 80 per cent of those who voted were against neutrality, quite different from what had been found in the scientific poll. This surprising result prompted an analysis of voting patterns. In a two-day period there was a huge surge in votes. During this time there were many anomalies, the most striking being one individual, apparently located in Iceland, who voted against neutrality 168 times.

One could not have clearer evidence of how the debate against assisted dying is being hijacked. This was a rerun of what happened in 2006 when Lord Joffe's Assisted Dying for the Terminally Ill Bill was being debated in the House of Lords. The Euthanasia Prevention Coalition – an international body based in Canada – flooded two polls of British public opinion, one run by Bath University and one by the *Evening Standard*, with 'No' votes from Canada and the USA.

One might expect the leaders of the Church to be opposed to assisted dying (although they are at odds with the majority of their flocks). More surprising, and more shocking, is the seemingly strong opposition from the medical profession. The leading medical Royal Colleges, such as the Royal College of Physicians, the Royal College of Surgeons and the Royal College of General Practitioners, are currently against assisted dying, as is the British Medical Association, although Clare Gerada, Chair of the Council of the Royal College of General Practitioners, has called for her college to move to a position of neutrality.[28] It was this position of the (unrepresentative) 'representative medical bodies' that provoked Ann McPherson, along with her friend Professor Joe Collier, and supported by Dignity in Dying, to establish Healthcare Professionals for Assisted Dying (HPAD) in October 2010. The most modest of its aims was to send out a signal that the medical profession was not unanimous in its stance towards assisted dying.

This is, in fact, an understatement. Many resent how the debate has been hijacked by special-interest groups inside the profession as well as without. Recent polls have supported this view. For example, the most reliable information suggests that between 30 per cent and 40 per cent of doctors are in favour of liberalization of the law.[29, 30] What is more, only a third of 1,000 doctors in a survey in October 2011 were opposed to having assisted dying for themselves.[31] I have already referred to the study published in May 2012 of 1,000 GPs which found that 62 per cent of respondents felt that the representative medical bodies should adopt a stance of neutrality towards the issue: that is to say, should be actually representative. This study clearly worried opponents of assisted dying, to judge by the sharp practice it triggered which I mentioned earlier. No surprise, therefore, that the British Medical Association refused a request in 2013 (from Healthcare Professionals for Assisted Dying) for a survey of its members' views. It might deliver the 'wrong' answer.

It is important to question the legitimacy of the medical profession's extension of its authority to matters that are for society as a whole to decide. Individual doctors are, of course, entitled to express and campaign for their views on the ethical case for, and the potential social impact of, liberalizing the law. So long as no healthcare professionals are obliged, against their conscience, to help a dying patient achieve an assisted death the role of their representative bodies should be confined to speaking on those areas where they have special expertise: for example, the safeguards and codes of practice necessary should any law be implemented and more explicitly medical matters, such as determining prognosis and setting guidelines for optimal end-of-life care. For the profession to go beyond this is a gross example of paternalism or, given that a large proportion of the profession is female, 'parentalism'.

At this point it is important to set aside an objection to this argument that I have often encountered. Is it not sometimes the duty of the medical profession – and indeed Parliament – to be paternalistic and to ignore public opinion because it may be ill-informed and may have rather unsavoury views? After all, if there were a referendum on the death sentence today we would find that the majority of the British public would be in favour of bringing back hanging. The analogy is not valid because those who are seeking to restore the death penalty do not envisage themselves or their loved ones being strung up. Those in favour of assisted dying are advocating something they would want for themselves or for those they care for. This is why the paternalism argument is relevant.

Given that there are physicians of good will, deep religious convictions or none, and expertise in palliative care, with passionate views on both sides of the debate, the proper stance of medical bodies is one of neutrality. This does not mean indifference; rather, what the American physician Timothy Quill has called 'studied neutrality'. This is what the Royal College of Nursing has chosen, after a survey of its members that produced 49 per cent of responses in favour and 40 per cent against. The fact that the nurses are more in tune with the public on this issue is not entirely surprising. As Joyce Robins, co-director of Patient Concern, has written, 'Nurses . . . are likely to be at the bedside of the dying and hear and understand patients' and relatives' feelings. Doctors appear briefly so it is easier for them to stick to . . . the status quo.'[32] To put it bluntly, it is easier for the less imaginative among the medical profession to bear the sufferings of others heroically as they do not have to experience it minute by minute, hour by hour, day by day. Until the colleges and the British Medical Association adopt a position of neutrality there will be a serious obstacle to a full, open and honest debate on assisted dying.

So we are left with fudge – clinical, ethical and legal fudge. Doctors wishing to avoid assisted dying and yet humanely committed to achieving the same end already make liberal use of ploys such as: the double effect, where the primary intention is to control symptoms, although this may accidentally hasten death; withdrawing treatments such as artificial ventilation in someone who has lost their respiratory drive, which will ensure death with 100 per cent certainty; the institution of continuous sedation, which reduces a person to a breathing body; or, worst of all, standing idly by while a patient has an unassisted death by thirst or starvation. So what is behind this anomalous and, it seems to me, in some cases unacceptable behaviour, which exploits distinctions without real differences? After all, C. Everett Koop, the former US Surgeon General, described withdrawal of dialysis in terminally ill patients as 'euthanasia by omission'. Something is clearly at work here, making people think irrationally.

For some, it is the incorrect belief that assisting a terminally ill person to die would be contrary to the very ethos of medicine. The British Medical Association's opposition is defended by the argument that 'it is alien to the traditional ethos and moral focus of medicine'. Repeatedly one hears it said by doctors that they went into medicine 'to save lives not to end them'. Behind this kind of statement – which, as Marcia Angell said in a recent article,[33] focuses too much on the physician and not enough on the patient – is the feeling that to participate in assisted dying is to contravene, even to betray, the solemn undertakings of doctors entering the medical profession.

In its classical form, the Hippocratic Oath includes this promise: 'I will not give a lethal drug to anyone if I am asked, nor will I advise such a plan.' But it also adds (in the same paragraph) 'and similarly I will not give a woman a pessary to secure an abortion'. In other words, doctors involved in abortion would also be in breach of the oath, but this does not cause problems for the vast majority of the profession. It also enjoins doctors to be chaste and religious. Well, you may judge my chastity from the fact that I have two children and the fervour of my religious belief from the fact that I am a strong supporter of the British Humanist Association. In neither instance do I feel that I have betrayed my professional calling.

So the classical oath is an anachronism. The oath has been brought up to date in various ways. One widely used version, introduced in 1964, has this key paragraph:

> Most especially must I tread with care in matters of life and death. If it is given to me to save a life, all thanks. But it may also be within my power to take a life; this awesome responsibility must be faced with great humbleness and awareness of my frailty.

This seems to allow for assisted dying. And the Declaration of Geneva, adopted by the General Assembly of the World Medical Association at Geneva in 1948, and most recently amended in 2006, says only that 'I will maintain the utmost respect for human life.' This is consistent with supporting assisted dying under the circumstances we envisage. It does not say anything about not taking life. In short, the claim that support for assisted dying violates the fundamental ethos of the medical profession is unfounded.

Indeed, the opposite would appear to be the case. Charles Bulman, a retired surgeon, commented in his written evidence to the 2012 Commission on Assisted Dying: 'As a professional, I can recall numerous examples of patients who have requested assistance to die and in almost every case I have felt that I denied my professional duty of care by my refusal to help.' It may well be the case that medical opposition to assisted dying, far from originating in moral concerns, is due to moral laziness: the unavailability of assisted dying spares doctors from making decisions. Without a law in place the decision is already made: the doctor can truthfully say, 'I can't help you.' In the meantime a certain amount of life-shortening help is offered to patients outside of the safety of the law under the cover of darkness.

In making the case for legalizing assisted dying I invoked the patient's right to choose, behind which lies the principle of autonomy. This principle has been singled out for attack by opponents of legalization. Most of the reasons for attacking the appeal to autonomy may be set aside. Here are a couple. The first, that we do not belong to ourselves but are God's possessions, does not get much traction in a secular society. Most of us happen not to believe this. If it were true, however, it might lead us to deny ourselves the right to any autonomy. The second is an inescapable truth that autonomy always is and should be limited by the circumstances in which we are living and acting. It is possible, of course, to agree with this – the harm principle – without being committed to any particular position on assisted dying.

It is worth reflecting a little on this principle. It is difficult to improve on its first formulation by John Stuart Mill:

> That the only purpose for which power can rightfully be exercised over any member of a civilized community, against his will, is to prevent harm to others. His own good, either physical or moral, is not a sufficient warrant. He cannot rightfully be compelled

to do or forbear because it will be better for him to do so, because it will make him happier, because, in the opinion of others, to do so would be wise, or even right.[34]

And he spells this out clearly enough for everyone to understand:

The only part of the conduct of anyone, for which he is amenable to society, is that which concerns others. In the part which merely concerns himself, his independence is, of right, absolute. Over himself, over his own body and mind, the individual is sovereign.[35]

Opponents of assisted dying have argued that being assisted to die is not something that concerns only the individual who is directly affected. There will be effects on society as a whole through, they claim, the devaluation of human life. I have dealt with this supposed devaluation already.

But there is another challenge that I think requires more thought. It relates to the question of the consistency with which the principle is applied. If you argue for assisted dying on the basis of respect for autonomy, why do you restrict its availability simply to people who are terminally ill, who are deemed to be mentally competent and so on? Why do you oppose a law that would go beyond assisted dying and permit assisted suicide for people who are not terminally ill, even although they request it? Surely a human right is a human right? Doesn't consistency demand of us that we accede to the request of anyone of sound mind who seeks our assistance to die, even if the reason is something as nebulous as being 'tired of life'? It may not lead down to the involuntary slaughter of people who are seen as undesirable, surplus to requirement or merely unproductive, as Rowan Williams suggested. But it may take us to a place where none of us would like to be. Let me explore this.

Supposing you come across someone about to jump off a bridge. You establish that he is not being forced to do this at gunpoint. Do you then say 'Good luck' and let him get on with it? Of course not. Even less would you be willing to accede to his request for assistance in jumping off. There are several practical reasons why one would treat this case differently from that of a dying patient seeking assistance to die. We have no history of what has led up to his despair; we have no idea of the cause; he could well have an entirely solvable problem; we could save him for a happy life. To say 'Get on with it' would be a disgustingly callous indifference to human life.

And we don't have to look at such an extreme example to see that we do not simply accede to people's wishes, even over things that seem to affect directly only themselves. But this may seem to be a retreat from the assertion of the primacy of autonomy. Should the invocation of autonomy authorize the progressive extension of the cases in which dying could be assisted? If it did not lead to this slippery slope wasn't this because the principle of autonomy was being applied inconsistently? Haven't I joined the Groucho Club – 'These are my principles, and if you don't like them . . . Well, I have others' – along with my religious opponents?

I think it is possible to deal with this problem entirely honestly, as follows. In all cases the application of a non-religious ethical principle – as opposed to an absolutist religious one – has to be put in context; it is right to begin with the principle, but it may not always be right to apply it without limit; this applies to every aspect of human life. Assisted dying respects autonomy, and it has a clearly defined scope. Assisting anyone who wishes to jump off a bridge will, unlike assisted dying, have clear-cut adverse consequences, spreading an ethos of cruel indifference to what may be remediable suffering, precisely this devaluation of human life that opponents of assisted dying say they fear. So this presents us with a challenge: we have to judge the place where the gain in individual autonomy is offset by harms to society as a whole. To some extent this will be a calculus of benefits, harms and risk of harm.

This apparent retreat from the boundless application of the principle of autonomy is entirely different from the appeal to, and deviation from, the principle of sanctity of life for which I criticized some of the religiously motivated opponents. For their deviations are from a principle that is claimed to be absolute and inviolable; and their deviations are into killing in war and other modes of behaviour that require further justification; and the original principle sits ill with a utilitarian calculus of greater and less benefits that the Archbishop of York invoked in response to the Bishop of Chichester. The harm principle that limits autonomy, by contrast, is an intrinsically utilitarian principle that makes up part of a coherent picture that weighs autonomy and harm in the same scales.

The need to restrict the application of the principle that supports it is not a problem unique to assisted dying. It is present throughout our judgements of the correct thing to do. We have to do something that I have called 'dichotomizing over a continuum'.[36] Take, for example, free speech, which gives me the right to express my views without censorship. This sounds fine – an unquestionably Good Thing – but it may have unintended consequences that require us to mobilize a second principle to modify the first: the harm principle. If someone exploits the principle of free speech to indulge in hate speech – say, making anti-Semitic remarks designed to provoke a pogrom – the harm that is caused has to be reined in by invoking another principle banning the use of speech that causes harm. Anyone who is considered to cause such harm will have their claim to exercise their autonomy overridden and is justly charged with a criminal offence.

There will, however, be a continuum, rather than a natural break, between totally acceptable and totally unacceptable speech, and yet we have to draw a line at right angles to this at a point that will seem to some arbitrary: we have to divide a continuum in two. This side of the line is a legitimate exercise of free speech, we judge; and that side of the line is an illegitimate and criminal abuse of the principle of free speech.

And the same applies to considering the age of criminal responsibility; or (to come closer to our present concerns) where we judge a medical treatment to be futile and consider it appropriate to withdraw life-extending treatments such as kidney dialysis or artificial respiration; or, indeed, to decide what counts as a permissible application of the doctrine of double effect, in which treatments aimed at symptom relief are permitted to be used even if they shorten life – just as much as to the decision to assist dying. There is, in short, nothing uniquely flawed about limiting the application of the principle of autonomy when we use it to support the case for assisted dying.

The fundamental point is that the legalization of assisted dying is extending the application of the principle of autonomy, even although it is not rendering it boundless. There remains the fact that any good principle – such as that we should not hold immature human beings to the adult level of accountability for crimes – cannot determine from within itself the scope of its application and it could always be (ab)used to justify actions we do not wish. We have to decide on an age of criminal responsibility; the sharp cut-off is an artefact. In the case of assisted dying the continuum of the application of the principle of respecting autonomy has clear points at which it can be considered no longer to be sovereign. There are distinctions between terminal and non-terminal illness; between people who do and people who do not have a serious illness; between people who have and people who do not have mental competence; between assistance to die and euthanasia; and between voluntary and involuntary euthanasia. If there is a slope downwards from one to the other it has a high coefficient of friction.

Some of those who accept the facts and the arguments that I have presented may still oppose legislation on the grounds that only a small minority of dying people would seek assistance and an even smaller number would use the prescription. I think this was one of my own grounds for opposing legalization. Wouldn't it prove a sledgehammer to crack a nut, a leap in the dark that threatens all of us, for the sake of a few people? Even if it did not have the dangerous consequences our opponents claim, it would most certainly upset flocks (I think that is the collective term) of prelates (although not their congregations), something not to be lightly dismissed. Well, I happen to believe that even small numbers of people going through unbearable hell are important and there is something wrong in a society that cannot see that. What is more, the availability of assisted dying would bring much comfort to many more sufferers than actually use it because it brings an all-important sense of having some control, as we know from the Oregon data to which I referred.

It has been argued that, since the Director of Public Prosecutions has not, in the several years since he introduced his guidelines for prosecution of those who have assisted another to die, referred any cases sent to him for prosecution, things are fine at present. No law is needed. Let us muddle on in the usual British way. This will not do. First, assisting someone to die remains a criminal offence: the relative or friend is the 'suspect' and the patient the 'victim'. Since 'suspects' usually spend months under investigation before being told whether or not they are to be prosecuted, there is huge anxiety and stigma at an already intensely distressing time. Thus a *de facto* history of sensible decisions so far is not as good as a law that permits assisted dying within clear limits and safeguards. What is more, a future more hawkish Director of Public Prosecutions may have a quite different attitude and use the current sixteen tests of motivation – yes, sixteen tests – to draw different conclusions as to whether assistance has been compassionate or motivated by criminal intent.

Most importantly, it remains a criminal offence for any medical qualified practitioner or other healthcare professional to give advice. Assistance is therefore delegated to amateurs who have to assume a huge responsibility at a time when they are already greatly distressed and may well be incompetent to carry it out. This morally repugnant situation, imposing a final cruelty on those who have seen their loved ones suffer appallingly, is unacceptable. That cruelty will be compounded by the investigations that must currently take place after an assisted death. This is illustrated by this story from a grieving husband, former test cricketer Chris Broad, whose wife killed herself before motor neurone disease ended her life: 'Michelle had organised the end of her life remarkably well – left little gifts for her tennis club members and notes for me and the children . . . And [the police] just swooped up all those things and took them away.'[37]

We therefore need a change of the law – and soon. I am an optimist, and I believe that even if the Church and the representatives of the medical profession continue to disrespect the considered opinions of their respective memberships their views will eventually be discredited as unrepresentative. With this obstacle out of the way, Parliament may indeed come to support legislation in favour of assisted dying.

Indeed, my optimism extends to the belief that rational argument, rather than pre-rational opinions, will win the day and the law will be changed. For this to happen a small but vocal minority, prepared to tolerate other people's suffering heroically for the sake of their idea of God and of his will, must be challenged. Opponents of change make a lot of noise. It is time that the relatively silent majority made more, so that, as Ann McPherson hoped, 'Needless suffering at the end of life would become a thing of the past.'

Notes

CHAPTER 2

1. *The New York Times*, 1986.
2. HL Deb, 1 December 1936, Vol. 103, cc465–505.
3. HL Deb, 1 December 1936, Vol. 103, cc465–505.
4. HL Deb, 28 November 1950, Vol. 169, cc552–9.
5. Airedale NHS Trust v. Bland (1993), AC 789, HL.
6. Airedale Hospital Trustees v. Bland [1992], UKHL, 5 (4 February 1993), Lord Goff of Chieveley.
7. *British Medical Journal*, 1996; Vol. 313, No. 643, p. 1.
8. Ms B v An NHS Hospital Trust [2002] EWHC 429 (Fam) (22 March, 2002).
9. www.dignityindying.org.uk/patrons.
10. Judgements – The Queen on the Application of Mrs Dianne [sic] Pretty (Appellant) v. Director of Public Prosecutions (Respondent) and Secretary of State for the Home Department (Interested Party).
11. Case of Pretty v. The United Kingdom ECtHR judgement, April 2002, Application No. 2346/02.
12. Assisted Dying for the Terminally Ill Bill [HL], 12 May 2006, Hansard.
13. Mental Capacity Act 2005.
14. Mental Capacity Act 2005.
15. A legally binding advance decision, as well as advice about completing the form, is available from Compassion in Dying: http://www.compassionindying.org.uk/about-advance-decisions.
16. The language of the 1961 Suicide Act was changed in 2009 by the Coroner's and Justice Act from 'aid, abet, counsel, or procure the suicide of another' to 'encourage or assist a suicide'.
17. R on the application of Purdy v. DPP and others, Court of Appeal (Civil Division) judgement, Neutral Citation Number: [2009] EWCA Civ 92, Case No. C1/2008/2626.
18. [2009] 1 Cr App R 32, 106 BMLR 170, (2009) 106 BMLR 170, [2009] UKHRR 1005, [2009] EWCA Civ 92, [2009] 1 Cr App Rep 32.

19. R (on the application of Purdy) (Appellant) v. Director of Public Prosecutions (Respondent) [2009], UKHL 45, Lord Hope of Craighead.
20. *Policy for Prosecutors in Respect of Cases of Encouraging or Assisting Suicide*, issued by the Director of Public Prosecutions, February 2010.
21. *Policy for Prosecutors in Respect of Cases of Encouraging or Assisting Suicide*, issued by the Director of Public Prosecutions, February 2010.

CHAPTER 4

1. Under the chemical name diamorphine, diacetylmorphine is prescribed as a strong analgesic in the UK, where it is given via subcutaneous, intramuscular, intrathecal or intravenous route. Its use includes treatment for acute pain, such as in severe physical trauma, myocardial infarction, post-surgical pain and chronic pain, including end-stage cancer and other terminal illnesses: http://en.wikipedia.org/wiki/Diamorphine.
2. http://en.wikipedia.org/wiki/Principle_of_double_effect.

CHAPTER 6

1. Brief of Amicus Curiae Coalition of Mental Health Professionals at 17, Gonzales v. Oregon, 126 S. Ct. 904 (2006) (No. 4–623).
2. P. Lewis and I. Black, 'The Effectiveness of Legal Safeguards in Jurisdictions That Allow Assisted Dying'. Evidence submitted to the Commission on Assisted Dying (2012).
3. Oregon Health Authority (2013), Summary of Oregon's Death with Dignity Act (1998–2012).
4. Oregon Health Authority (2013), Summary of Oregon's Death with Dignity Act (1998–2012).
5. http://www.compassionandchoices.org/2013/07/16/end-of-life-law-the-oregon-experience.
6. L. Ganzini, T.A. Harvath, E.R. Jackson et al., 'Experiences of Oregon Nurses and Social Workers with Hospice Patients Who Requested Assistance with Suicide', *New England Journal of Medicine* (2002), Vol. 347, No. 8, pp. 582–8.
7. C. Campbell and J. Cox, 'Hospice and Physician-Assisted Death: Collaboration, Compliance, and Complicity', *Hastings Center Report* (2010), Vol. 40, No. 5, pp. 26–35.
8. M.P. Battin, A. van der Heide, L. Ganzini et al., 'Legal Physician-Assisted Dying in Oregon and the Netherlands: Evidence Concerning the Impact on Patients in "Vulnerable" Groups', *Journal of Medical Ethics* (2007), Vol. 33, pp. 591–7.

9. L. Ganzini, E.R. Goy, S.K. Dobscha and H. Prigerson, 'Mental Health Outcomes of Family Members of Oregonians Who Request Physician Aid in Dying', *Journal of Pain Management* (2009), Vol. 38, No. 6, pp. 807–15.

10. 2012 Death with Dignity Act (2013), Washington State Department of Health.

11. P. Lewis and I. Black, 'The Effectiveness of Legal Safeguards in Jurisdictions That Allow Assisted Dying'. Evidence submitted to the Commission on Assisted Dying, 2012.

12. H. Buiting, J. van Delden, B. Onwuteaka-Philpsen et al., 'Reporting of Euthanasia and Physician-Assisted Suicide in the Netherlands: Descriptive Study', *British Medical Council Medical Ethics* (2009), Vol. 10, p. 18.

13. M. de Boer, R.-M. Droes, C. Jonker et al., 'Advance Directives for Euthanasia in Dementia: Do Law-Based Opportunities Lead to More Euthanasia?' *Health Policy* (2010), Vol. 98, pp. 256–62.

14. M.K. Dees, M.J. Vernooij-Dassen, W.J. Dekkers et al., 'Perspectives of Decision-Making in Requests for Euthanasia: A Qualitative Research Among Patients, Relatives and Treating Physicians in the Netherlands', *Palliative Medicine* (2012), Vol. 27, No. 1, pp. 27–37.

15. B.D. Onwuteaka-Philipsen, 'Trends in End-of-Life Practices Before and After the Enactment of the Euthanasia Law in the Netherlands from 1990 to 2010: A Repeated Cross-Sectional Survey', *Lancet* (2012), Vol. 380, pp. 908–15.

16. M.L. Rurup, H.M. Buiting, H.R. Pasman et al., 'The Reporting Rate of Euthanasia and Physician-Assisted Suicide:. A Study of the Trends', *Medical Care* (2008), Vol. 46, No. 12, pp. 1198–1202.

17. M.L. Rurup, H.M. Buiting, H.R. Pasman et al., 'The Reporting Rate of Euthanasia and Physician-Assisted Suicide: A Study of the Trends', *Medical Care* (2008), Vol. 46, No. 12, pp. 1198–1202.

18. C. Seale, 'End-of-Life Decisions in the UK Involving Medical Practitioners', *Palliative Medicine* (2009), Vol. 23, No. 3, pp. 198–204.

19. M.C. Jansen-van der Weide, B.D. Onwuteaka-Philipsen BD, A. van der Heide and G. van der Wal, 'How Patients and Relatives Experience a Visit from a Consulting Physician in the Euthanasia Procedure: A Study Amongst Relatives and Physicians', *Death Studies* (2009), Vol. 33, pp. 199–219.

20. C. Centeno, D. Clark , T. Lynch et al., 'Facts and Indicators on Palliative Care Development in 52 Countries of the WHO European Region: Results of an EAPC Task Force', *Palliative Medicine* (2007), Vol. 21, pp. 463–71.

21. *The Quality of Death: Ranking End-of-Life Care Across the World; A Report from the Economist Intelligence Unit*, Economist Intelligence Unit, London, New York and Hong Kong, 2010.

22. K. Woitha, Y. Engels, J. Hasselaar and K. Vissers, 'The Organisation of Palliative Care in the Netherlands', in S. Ahmedzai, X. Gomez-Batiste, Y. Engels et al., *Assessing Organisations to Improve Palliative Care in Europe* (EU-funded book), European Association for Palliative Care, Milan, 2010, pp. 181–95.

23. K. Chambaere, C. Centeno, E.A. Hernandez et al., 'Palliative Care Development in Countries with a Euthanasia Law'. Evidence submitted to the Commission on Assisted Dying by the European Association for Palliative Care, 2011.

24. J. Bilsen, R. Vander, B. Stichele et al.,'Changes in Medical End-of-Life Practices During the Legalization Process of Euthanasia in Belgium', *Social Science and Medicine* (2007), Vol. 65, No. 4, pp. 803–8.

25. K. Chambaere, J. Bilsen, J. Cohen et al., 'Continuous Deep Sedation Until Death in Belgium: A Nationwide Study', *Archives of Internal Medicine* (2010), Vol. 170, p. 5.

26. T. Smets, J. Bilsen, J. Cohen et al., 'Legal Euthanasia in Belgium: Characteristics of All Reported Euthanasia Cases', *Medical Care* (2010), Vol. 42, No. 2, 187–92.

27. K.V. Beek and J. Menten, 'The Organisation of Palliative Care in Belgium', in S. Ahmedzai et al., *Assessing Organisations to Improve Palliative Care in Europe*, 2010, pp. 117–36.

28. T. Smets, J. Cohen, J. Bilsen, et al., 'Attitudes and Experiences of Belgian Physicians Regarding Euthanasia Practice and the Euthanasia Law', *Journal of Pain and Symptom Management* (2011), Vol. 41, No. 3, pp. 580–93.

29. J. Bilsen, R. Vander, B. Stichele et al., 'Changes in Medical End-of-Life Practices During the Legalization Process of Euthanasia in Belgium', *Social Science and Medicine* (2007), Vol. 65, No. 4, pp. 803–8.

30. http://www.telegraph.co.uk/news/worldnews/europe/switzerland/9170059/ Almost-300-assisted-suicides-in-Switzerland-per-year.html.

31. Dignitas official figures: http://www.dignitas.ch/images/stories/pdf/statistik-ftb-jahr-wohnsitz-1998-2012.pdf.

32. Assisted Dying for the Terminally Ill Bill (2005).

33. Regional Euthanasia Review Committees: 2009 Annual Report.

34. Suicide Act 1961 updated by the Coroners and Justice Act 2009.

35. Crown Prosecution Service, *Policy for Prosecutors in Respect of Cases of Encouraging or Assisting Suicide*, 2010.

36. L. Bazalgette, W. Bradley and J. Ousbey, *The Truth About Suicide*, Demos, London, 2011.

37. For example, George Martin (2013): www.bbc.co.uk/news/uk-england-nottinghamshire-21782052, and Barbara Grainger (2012): www.belfasttelegraph.co.uk/news/local-national/northern-ireland/now-mlas-must-act-on-helping-loved-ones-to-die-with-dignity-28869969.html.

38. General Medical Council, *When a Patient Seeks Advice or Information About Assistance to Die*, General Medical Council, London, 2013.

39. General Medical Council, *Guidance for the Investigation Committee and Case Examiners When Considering Allegations About a Doctor's Involvement in Encouraging or Assisting Suicide*, General Medical Council, London, 2013.

40. A. Van der Heide, D. Bregje, B. Onwuteaka-Philipsen et al., 'End-of-Life Practices in the Netherlands Under the Euthanasia Act', *New England Journal of Medicine* (2007), Vol. 356, No. 19, pp. 1957–65.

41. J. Bilsen, J. Cohen, K. Chambaere and G. Pousset, 'Medical End-of-Life Practices Under the Euthanasia Law in Belgium', *New England Journal of Medicine* (2009), Vol. 361, No. 11, 1119–21.

42. C. Seale, 'End-of-Life Decisions in the UK Involving Medical Practitioners', *Palliative Medicine* (2009), Vol. 23, No. 3, pp. 198–204.

43. A. Chapple, S. Ziebland, A. McPherson and A. Herxheimer, 'What People Close to Death Say About Euthanasia and Assisted Suicide: A Qualitative Study', *Journal of Medical Ethics* (2006), Vol. 32, No. 12, pp. 706–10.

44. G. Cooney, G. Lewando Hundt, G. Goodall and J. Weaver, *Choices and Control When You Have a Life-Shortening Illness: Researching the Views of People with Motor Neurone Disease*, Picker Institute Europe, Oxford, 2012.

CHAPTER 8

1. These unattributed comments and quotes come from Andrew's own experience and from conversations with patients.

CHAPTER 9

1. Blood tests are used to identify and measure tumour markers (usually proteins present in the bloodstream) that are specific to testicular cancer. The typical markers used to identify testicular cancer are AFP alpha1 feto protein, Beta-HCG and LDH, and a pregnancy test may be used to identify high levels of Beta-HCG. Adapted from http://en.wikipedia.org/wiki/Testicular_cancer.

2. Adenocarcinoma is a cancer of an epithelium that originates in glandular tissue. Epithelial tissue includes, but is not limited to, the surface layer of skin, glands and a variety of other tissues that line the cavities and organs of the body. Malignant adenocarcinomas invade other tissues and often metastasize given enough time to do so. Adapted from http://en.wikipedia.org/wiki/Adenocarcinoma.

3. Germ-cell tumours can be cancerous or non-cancerous, and the germ cells after which they are named normally occur inside the gonads (ovaries and testicles). Adapted from http://en.wikipedia.org/wiki/Germ_cell_tumours.

CHAPTER 10

1. S. McAndrew, 'Religious Faith and Contemporary Attitudes', in A. Park, J. Curtice, K. Thomson et al. (eds), *British Social Attitudes: 2009–2010: The 26th Report* (2010), Sage, London, pp. 87–113.
2. E. Clery, S. McLean and M. Phillips, 'Quickening Death: The Euthanasia Debate', in A. Park, J. Curtice, K. Thomson et al. (eds), *British Social Attitudes: The 23rd Report – Perspectives on a Changing Society* (2007), Sage, London, 2007, pp. 35–54.
3. C. Seale, 'Legalisation of Euthanasia or Physician-Assisted Suicide: Survey of Doctors' Attitudes', *Palliative Medicine* (2009), Vol. 23, No. 3, pp. 205–12.
4. W. Lee, A. Price, L. Rayner and M. Hotopf, 'Survey of Doctors' Opinions of the Legalisation of Physician Assisted Suicide', *British Medical Council Medical Ethics* (2009), Vol. 10, No. 1, p. 2.
5. S. McAndrew, 'Religious Faith and Contemporary Attitudes', in *British Social Attitudes: 2009–2010: The 26th Report*, pp. 87–113.
6. E. Clery, S. McLean and M. Phillips, 'Quickening Death: The Euthanasia Debate', in *British Social Attitudes: The 23rd Report – Perspectives on a Changing Society*, pp. 35–54. Additional analysis of survey results supplied by E. Clery in correspondence with Dignity in Dying, March 2010.
7. YouGov survey for Dignity in Dying, 2013.

CHAPTER 12

1. T. McPherson, 'My Mum Wanted an Assisted Death But We Watched Her Die Slowly and in Pain', *British Medical Journal* (2012), Vol. 334, p. 4007.
2. Assisted Dying for the Terminally Ill Bill [HL], 2005.
3. S. McAndrew, 'Religious Faith and Contemporary Attitudes', in *British Social Attitudes: 2009–2010: The 26th Report*, pp. 87–113.
4. Mary Warnock, *Dishonest to God: On Keeping Religion out of Politics*, Continuum, London, 2010
5. Warnock, p. 63.
6. McPherson, p. 35.
7. McPherson, p. 35.

8. L. Bazalgette, W. Bradley, J. Ousbey, *The Truth About Suicide*, Demos, London, 2011.

9. Dignitas official figures: http://www.dignitas.ch/images/stories/pdf/statistik-ftb-jahr-wohnsitz-1998-2012.pdf.

10. Oregon Health Authority, Oregon's Death with Dignity Act, 2012.

11. K. Chambaere, C. Centeno, E.A. Hernandez et al., *Palliative Care Development in Countries with a Euthanasia Law*, European Association for Palliative Care, Milan, 2011.

12. Z. Kmietovicz, 'R.E.S.P.E.C.T: Why Doctors Are Still Getting Enough of It', *British Medical Journal* (2002), Vol. 324, No. 7328, pp. 11–14.

13. *The Report of the Commission on Assisted Dying*, Demos, London, 2012.

14. E. Clery, S. McLean, M. Phillips, 'Quickening Death: The Euthanasia Debate', in *British Social Attitudes: The 23rd Report – Perspectives on a Changing Society*, pp. 35–54.

15. Oregon Health Authority, Oregon's Death with Dignity Act, 2012.

16. M.P. Battin, A. van der Heide, L. Ganzini et al., 'Legal Physician-Assisted Dying in Oregon and the Netherlands: Evidence Concerning the Impact on Patients in 'Vulnerable' Groups', *Journal of Medical Ethics* (2007), Vol. 33, No. 10, pp. 591–7.

17. B.D. Onwuteaka-Philipsen, A. Brinkman-Stoppelenburg, C. Penning et al., 'Trends in End-of-life Practices Before and After the Enactment of the Euthanasia Law in the Netherlands from 1990 to 2010: A Repeated Cross-Sectional Survey', *The Lancet* (2012), Vol. 380, pp. 908–15.

18. C. Seale, 'End-of-Life Decisions in the UK Involving Medical Practitioners', *Palliative Medicine* (2007), Vol. 23, pp. 198–204.

19. *Daily Mail*, 26 October 2012.

20. Rowan Williams, Christian Institute, 2012.

21. BBC News, 2003, 'Archbishops Doubt Morality of Iraq War': http://news.bbc.co.uk/1/hi/uk/2781783.stm.

22. G. Burnham, R. Lafta, S. Doocey and L. Roberts, 'Mortality After 2003 Invasion of Iraq: A Cross-Sectional Cluster Sample Survey', *The Lancet* (2006), Vol. 368, No. 9545, pp. 421–8.

23. For a discussion of the Hogeway Village see 'On Caring and Not Caring', in Raymond Tallis, *Reflections of a Metaphysical Flaneur*, Acumen, Durham, 2013.

24. www.9-12bellyard.com/barristers/item/69-lord-alex-carlile-of-berriew-qc.

25. M. Teahan, 'The Pro-Life Movement Needs to Be Divided If It Is to Win Battles in Parliament', *Catholic Herald*, 3 July 2012.

26. Doctors.net.uk survey of GPs, 2011.

27. F. Godlee, 'Assisted Dying: Legalisation Is a Decision For Society Not Doctors', *British Medical Journal* (2012); p. 344: e4075.

28. C. Gerada, 'The Case for Neutrality on Assisted Dying – A Personal View', *British Journal of General Practice* (2012), Vol. 62, No. 605, p. 650.

29. W. Lee, A. Price, L. Rayner and M. Hotopf, 'Survey of Doctors' Opinions of the Legalisation of Physician Assisted Suicide', *British Medical Council Medical Ethics* (2009), Vol. 10, No. 2.

30. C. Seale, 'Legalisation of Euthanasia or Physician-Assisted Suicide: Survey of Doctor's Attitudes', *Palliative Medicine* (2009), Vol. 23, No. 3, pp. 205–12.

31. Doctors.net.uk survey of GPs, 2011.

32. Joyce Robbins, personal communication.

33. M. Angell, 'May Doctors Help You to Die?' *New York Review of Books*, 11 October 2012.

34. John Stuart Mill, *On Liberty*, John W. Parker and Sons, London, 1859, p. 22.

35. Mill, p. 22.

36. R.C. Tallis, 'My Bald Head: The Ethics of Hair-Splitting', in *In Defence of Wonder*, Acumen, Durham, 2012, pp. 132–8.

37. M. Chorley, 'Change "Unsafe" Law on Assisted Dying, Says Ex-Police Chief', *Independent*, 1 January 2012.

About the Contributors

JO CARTWRIGHT has worked for Dignity in Dying since 2006. She joined the organization as an intern while completing an MA in Human Rights. Her first degree, from the University of East Anglia, was in Bio-medicine. Now Dignity in Dying's Campaigns and Press Manager, her interest in end-of-life issues goes back to those days in Norwich. Part of her undergraduate studies involved working as a nursing assistant. In that role she witnessed first-hand the horror that can occur when an individual does not have the choice of an assisted death. She cared for Clare, a woman of twenty-seven who suffered from juvenile Huntington's disease (HD) and cancer. When the two women first met Clare made it clear that she didn't want to suffer as her father (who died of HD) had done. Tragically, without the option of an assisted death, Jo witnessed Clare suffering unimaginable pain, distress and anguish before she finally died, despite being given the best possible palliative care. During her time at Dignity in Dying Jo has worked closely with families affected by the same issues. She has learnt that her experience with Clare was, sadly, far from unique and has vowed to challenge the law in memory of Clare and the many others who have suffered and continue to suffer because the current law does not allow people to exercise choice and control at the end of life.

REVEREND JOHN CARTWRIGHT is a Congregational Minister who earns a living as a freelance tutor, mostly of philosophy. Believing that freedom to choose in all aspects of human life is an important constituent of believing in God has directed his attention to thinking about assisted dying, as has his experience of being with those close to death. Among his qualifications, he has an MA from Nottingham University, a PGCE from Cambridge and he completed his ministerial training at Mansfield College. He is also a longstanding member of Mensa.

SIR GRAEME CATTO is President of the College of Medicine and Chairman of Dignity in Dying. A former President of the General Medical Council, he was Vice-Principal at King's College London, Dean of the Guy's, King's College and St Thomas' Hospitals' Medical and Dental School and Pro Vice-Chancellor, University of London. After graduating in Medicine with honours from the University of Aberdeen, he obtained a Harkness Fellowship from the Commonwealth Fund of New York to study at Harvard University. He worked as a physician with an interest in renal medicine and has published widely on different aspects of nephrology and immunology. Formerly Chief Scientist at the Scottish Health Department, Dean and Vice-Principal at the University of Aberdeen and Governor of the Science Technology Park in Qatar, he is currently Emeritus Professor of Medicine at the University of Aberdeen.

LESLEY CLOSE was born in Oxford, the youngest of three children. Her life was changed completely by her brother John's assisted death at Dignitas on 26 May 2003. Subsequent media appearances, telling John's story and arguing the case for changing the law gave her the confidence to write a book about a good friend who is a talented textile artist and teacher. Having proved to her own satisfaction that she was up to the task she decided to write about the subject which has become her passion, assisted dying. Her e-biography of her brother, published on the tenth anniversary of his death, is available on Amazon, and she is working on another book. Lesley has been a spokesperson for Dignity in Dying since her brother's death, and was made a Patron of the organization in 2009.

ANDREW HEENAN started work at his local psychiatric hospital in 1970 with no intention of remaining longer than a brief work experience before university. Three years later he emerged as a registered mental nurse. He went on to take the registered general nurse course, intending to return to mental-health nursing. However, he then took three years out for university, returning to the NHS to study cancer nursing. This eventually led to commissioning a bone-marrow transplant unit, primarily for people with leukaemia, before leaving the NHS for several years to be a journalist. His first role was Clinical Editor of the *Nursing Times*. He then became launch Editor of the *Journal of Wound Care*. He went on to be relaunch Editor of *Professional Nurse* and launch Editor of NursingTimes.net. He returned to the NHS as a staff nurse, closing his career as a senior screening practitioner for the NHS bowel-cancer screening programme.

DAVINA HEHIR is responsible for developing Dignity in Dying's policies on end-of-life care and assisted dying and for developing the organization's legal work. She led the Dignity in Dying team that worked on the Debbie Purdy case. This resulted in the important recognition that, in certain circumstances, people should not be prosecuted for helping a loved one to die.

SIR TERRY PRATCHETT, OBE, is the acclaimed creator of the global bestselling *Discworld* series, the first of which, *The Colour of Magic*, was published in 1983. In all, he is the author of fifty bestselling books. His novels have been widely adapted for stage and screen, and he is the winner of multiple prizes, including the Carnegie Medal, as well as being awarded a knighthood for services to literature. Worldwide sales of his books now stand at eighty-five million, and they have been translated into thirty-seven languages. Sir Terry has been a Patron of Dignity in Dying for some years. He wrote the 2011 Dimbleby Lecture on the topic of assisted dying and fronted the BBC documentary *Choosing to Die*.

PHILIP SATHERLEY has a background in healthcare research. He was a researcher at Cardiff University in the School of Nursing for ten years and has worked for Dignity in Dying since 2009. His interest in evidence-based practice has strongly influenced his views on assisted dying, believing that the best quality research should inform the debate.

PROFESSOR RAYMOND TALLIS is a philosopher, poet, novelist and cultural critic and was until recently a physician and clinical scientist. Born in Liverpool in 1946, one of five children, he trained as a doctor at Oxford University and at St Thomas' in London before going on to become Professor of Geriatric Medicine at the University of Manchester and a consultant physician in the Healthcare of the Elderly in Salford. Professor Tallis retired from medicine in 2006 to become a full-time writer, although he remained Visiting Professor at St George's Hospital Medical School, University of London, until 2008. His national roles have included Consultant Advisor in Healthcare of the Elderly to the Chief Medical Officer; Chairmanship of the Royal College of Physicians Committee on Ethical Issues in Medicine; Chairman of the committee reviewing ethics support for front-line clinicians; and membership of the Working Party producing a seminal report *Doctors in Society: Medical Professionalism in a Changing World* (2005). In July 2011 he was elected Chair of Healthcare Professionals for Assisted Dying (HPAD). He is a patron of Dignity in Dying.

Useful Addresses

UK

Dignity in Dying (campaigning organization)
181 Oxford Street
London W1D 2JT
020 7479 7730
info@dignityindying.org.uk
www.dignityindying.org.uk

Compassion in Dying
(provides advance decisions)
181 Oxford Street
London W1D 2JT
020 7479 7731
info@compassionindying.org.uk
www.compassionindying.org.uk

Friends at the End (FATE)
11 Westbourne Gardens
Glasgow G12 9XD
0141 334 3287
info@friends-at-the-end.org.uk
www.friends-at-the-end.org.uk

Samaritans
(will listen while you talk 24 hours a day,
   365 days a year)
Freepost RSRB-KKBY-CYJK
Chris, PO Box 90 90
Stirling FK8 2SA
08457 909090
jo@samaritans.org
www.samaritans.org

Motor Neurone Disease Association
PO Box 246
Northampton NN1 2PR
01604 250505
enquiries@mndassociation.org
www.mndassociation.org

Huntington's Disease Association
Suite 24, Liverpool Science Park IC1
131 Mount Pleasant
Liverpool L3 5TF
0151 331 5444
info@hda.org.uk
www.hda.org.uk

Cancer Research UK
Angel Building
407 St John Street
London EC1V 4AD
020 7242 0200
www.cancerresearch.org

Dementia UK
Resource for London
Second Floor
356 Holloway Road
London N7 6PA
020 7697 4160
info@dementiauk.org
www.dementiauk.org

British Lung Foundation
73–75 Goswell Road
London EC1V 7ER
03000 030 55
helpline@blf.org.uk
www.blf.org.uk

AUSTRALIA

Christians Supporting Choice for Voluntary
   Euthanasia
Villa 1, Hampton Mews
4 Wills Place
Mittagong,
NSW 2575
iagree@christiansforve.org.au
www.christiansforve.org.au

Dying with Dignity ACT
PO Box 55
Waramanga
ACT 2611
secretary@dwdact.org.au
www.dwdact.org.au

Dying with Dignity NSW
PO Box 25
Broadway
NSW 2007
+61 2 9212 4782
dwd@dwdnsw.org.au
www.dwdnsw.org.au

Dying with Dignity Queensland
PO Box 432
Sherwood
QLD 4075
+61 1300 733 818
dwdq@dwdq.org.au
www.dwdq.org.au

Dying With Dignity Tasmania
P O Box 1022
Sandy Bay
Tasmania 7006
+61 450 545167
dwdtas@dwdtas.org.au
www.dwdtas.org.au

Dying With Dignity Victoria
5a/602 Whitehorse Road
Mitcham
VIC 3132
+61 3 9874 0503
office@dwdv.org.au
www.dwdv.org.au

BELGIUM
Association pour le Droit de Mourir dans la
   Dignité Belgique (ADMD-B)
Rue du Président 55
B-1050 Bruxelles
+32 2 502 0485
info@admd.be
www.admd.be

CANADA
Association Québécoise pour le Droit de
   Mourir dans la Dignité (AQDMD)
C.P. 404, Succursale Mont-Royal
Ville Mont-Royal
Québec, H3P 3G6
+1 514 341 4017
info@aqdmd.qc.ca
www.aqdmd.qc.ca

Dying with Dignity
#802, 55 Eglington Avenue East
Toronto
Ontario, M4P 1G8
+1 416 486 3998 or toll free +1 800 495 6156
info@dyingwithdignity.ca
www.dyingwithdignity.ca

Farewell Foundation
322–720 6th Street
New Westminster
BC, V3L 3C5
+1 604 521 1110
info@farewellfoundation.ca
www.farewellfoundation.ca

Right to Die Society of Canada
145 Macdonell Avenue,
Toronto
Ontario, M6R 2A4
+1 416 535 0690 or toll-free +1 866 535 0690
info@righttodie.ca
www.righttodie.ca

FRANCE
Association pour le Droit de Mourir dans la
   Dignité (ADMD)
50 rue de Chabrol
75010 Paris
+33 1 4800 0416
infos@admd.net
www.admd.net

GERMANY
Dignitas-Deutschland e.V.
Schmiedestrasse 39
30159 Hannover
+49 511 336 23 44
dignitate@t-online.de
www.dignitas.de

LUXEMBOURG
Association pour le Droit de Mourir dans la
  Dignité (ADMD-L)
1a, rue Christophe Plantin
L-2339, Gasperich
Luxembourg
+352 2659 0482
secretariat@admdl.lu
www.admdl.lu

NEW ZEALAND
End-of-Life Choice
PO Box 22346
Khandallah
Wellington 6441
+64 4 938 0317
membership@ves.org.nz
www.ves.org.nz

SOUTH AFRICA
Dignity
PO Box 927
Cape Town 8000
+27 79 037 2858
lee@dignitysa.org
www.dignitysa.org

SAVES – The Living Will Society
PO Box 1460
Wandsbeck 3631
KwaZulu-Natal
+27 31 266 8511
livingwill@3i.co.za
www.livingwill.co.za

SWITZERLAND
Dignitas
PO Box 17
8127 Forch
+41 43 366 1070
dignitas@dignitas.ch
www.dignitas.ch

EXIT-Deutsche Schweiz
Mühlezelgstrasse 45
Postfach 476
CH-8047 Zürich
+41 43 343 3838
info@exit.ch
www.exit-ch

EXIT Association pour le Droit de Mourir dans
  la Dignité (Suisse Romande)
Case Postale 110
CH 1211
Genève 17
+41 22 735 7760
info@exit-geneve.ch
www.exit-geneve.ch

Lifecircle
Postfach 29
4105 Biel-Benken
mail@lifecircle.ch
www.lifecircle.ch

USA
Compassion & Choices
PO Box 101810
Denver
CO 80250
+800 247 7421
www.compassionandchoices.org

Index

SOME AUTHORS WE HAVE PUBLISHED

James Agee • Bella Akhmadulina • Tariq Ali • Kenneth Allsop • Alfred Andersch
Guillaume Apollinaire • Machado de Assis • Miguel Angel Asturias • Duke of Bedford
Oliver Bernard • Thomas Blackburn • Jane Bowles • Paul Bowles • Richard Bradford
Ilse, Countess von Bredow • Lenny Bruce • Finn Carling • Blaise Cendrars • Marc Chagall
Giorgio de Chirico • Uno Chiyo • Hugo Claus • Jean Cocteau • Albert Cohen
Colette • Ithell Colquhoun • Richard Corson • Benedetto Croce • Margaret Crosland
e.e. cummings • Stig Dalager • Salvador Dalí • Osamu Dazai • Anita Desai
Charles Dickens • Bernard Diederich • Fabián Dobles • William Donaldson
Autran Dourado • Yuri Druzhnikov • Lawrence Durrell • Isabelle Eberhardt
Sergei Eisenstein • Shusaku Endo • Erté • Knut Faldbakken • Ida Fink
Wolfgang George Fischer • Nicholas Freeling • Philip Freund • Dennis Friedman
Carlo Emilio Gadda • Rhea Galanaki • Salvador Garmendia • Michel Gauquelin
André Gide • Natalia Ginzburg • Jean Giono • Geoffrey Gorer • William Goyen
Julien Gracq • Sue Grafton • Robert Graves • Angela Green • Julien Green
George Grosz • Barbara Hardy • H.D. • Rayner Heppenstall • David Herbert
Gustaw Herling • Hermann Hesse • Shere Hite • Stewart Home • Abdullah Hussein
King Hussein of Jordan • Ruth Inglis • Grace Ingoldby • Yasushi Inoue
Hans Henny Jahnn • Karl Jaspers • Takeshi Kaiko • Jaan Kaplinski • Anna Kavan
Yasunuri Kawabata • Nikos Kazantzakis • Orhan Kemal • Christer Kihlman
James Kirkup • Paul Klee • James Laughlin • Patricia Laurent • Violette Leduc
Lee Seung-U • Vernon Lee • József Lengyel • Robert Liddell • Francisco García Lorca
Moura Lympany • Dacia Maraini • Marcel Marceau • André Maurois
Henri Michaux • Henry Miller • Miranda Miller • Marga Minco • Yukio Mishima
Quim Monzó • Margaret Morris • Angus Wolfe Murray • Atle Næss • Gérard de Nerval
Anaïs Nin • Yoko Ono • Uri Orlev • Wendy Owen • Arto Paasilinna • Marco Pallis
Oscar Parland • Boris Pasternak • Cesare Pavese • Milorad Pavic • Octavio Paz
Mervyn Peake • Carlos Pedretti • Dame Margery Perham • Graciliano Ramos
Jeremy Reed • Rodrigo Rey Rosa • Joseph Roth • Ken Russell • Marquis de Sade
Cora Sandel • George Santayana • May Sarton • Jean-Paul Sartre
Ferdinand de Saussure • Gerald Scarfe • Albert Schweitzer • George Bernard Shaw
Isaac Bashevis Singer • Patwant Singh • Edith Sitwell • Suzanne St Albans • Stevie Smith
C.P. Snow • Bengt Söderbergh • Vladimir Soloukhin • Natsume Soseki • Muriel Spark
Gertrude Stein • Bram Stoker • August Strindberg • Rabindranath Tagore
Tambimuttu • Elisabeth Russell Taylor • Emma Tennant • Anne Tibble • Roland Topor
Miloš Urban • Anne Valery • Peter Vansittart • José J. Veiga • Tarjei Vesaas
Noel Virtue • Max Weber • Edith Wharton • William Carlos Williams • Phyllis Willmott
G. Peter Winnington • Monique Wittig • A.B. Yehoshua • Marguerite Young
Fakhar Zaman • Alexander Zinoviev • Emile Zola

 Peter Owen Publishers, 81 Ridge Road, London N8 9NP, UK
+ 44 (0)20 8350 1775 / F + 44 (0)20 8340 9488 / E info@peterowen.com
www.peterowen.com / @PeterOwenPubs
Independent publishers since 1951